Improving Implementation

Organisational Change and Project Management

Improving Implementation

Organisational Change and Project Management

Edited by John Wanna

ANU
THE AUSTRALIAN NATIONAL UNIVERSITY

E PRESS

ANU
E PRESS

the Australia and New Zealand
School of Government

Published by ANU E Press
The Australian National University
Canberra ACT 0200, Australia
Email: anuepress@anu.edu.au
Web: http://epress.anu.edu.au

National Library of Australia
Cataloguing-in-Publication entry

Improving implementation : organisational change and project management.

ISBN 9781921313011 (pbk).

ISBN 9781921313028 (web).

1. Organizational change - Australia - Congresses. 2.

Project management - Australia - Congresses. I. Wanna,

John. (Series : ANZSOG series).

351.94

Cover design by John Butcher

Funding for this monograph series has been provided by the Australia and New
Zealand School of Government Research Program.

John Wanna, *Series Editor*

Professor John Wanna is the Sir John Bunting Chair of Public Administration at the Research School of Social Sciences at The Australian National University. He is the director of research for the Australian and New Zealand School of Government (ANZSOG). He is also a joint appointment with the Department of Politics and Public Policy at Griffith University and a principal researcher with two research centres: the Governance and Public Policy Research Centre and the nationally-funded Key Centre in Ethics, Law, Justice and Governance at Griffith University. Professor Wanna has produced around 17 books including two national text books on policy and public management. He has produced a number of research-based studies on budgeting and financial management including: *Budgetary Management and Control* (1990); *Managing Public Expenditure* (2000), *From Accounting to Accountability* (2001) and, most recently, *Controlling Public Expenditure* (2003). He has just completed a study of state level leadership covering all the state and territory leaders — entitled *Yes Premier: Labor leadership in Australia's states and territories* — and has edited a book on Westminster Legacies in Asia and the Pacific — *Westminster Legacies: Democracy and responsible government in Asia and the Pacific*. He was a chief investigator in a major Australian Research Council funded study of the Future of Governance in Australia (1999-2001) involving Griffith and the ANU. His research interests include Australian and comparative politics, public expenditure and budgeting, and government-business relations. He also writes on Australian politics in newspapers such as *The Australian*, *Courier-Mail* and *The Canberra Times* and has been a regular state political commentator on ABC radio and TV.

Table of Contents

Acknowledgements ix

List of Contributors xi

Foreword — Ian McPhee, Auditor-General for the Commonwealth of
Australia xiii

Section I. Setting the Scene

1. Introduction — Improving Implementation: the Challenge Ahead 3
John Wanna, Sir John Bunting Chair of Public Administration, ANU

2. Driving Change to Bring About Better Implementation and Delivery 11
Peter Shergold, Secretary, Department of the Prime Minister and Cabinet

Section II. Governance, Ownership and Oversight

3. Managing Major Programs and Projects: A View From the Boardroom 23
Christina Gillies, Non Executive Director and IT Governance Consultant

4. How Boards and Senior Managers Have Governed 35
*Raymond C Young, Department of Accounting and Finance, Macquarie
University*

5. Overcoming the 'White Elephant' Syndrome in Big and Iconic Projects
in the Public and Private Sectors 47
Scott Prasser, Faculty of Business, University of Sunshine Coast

Section III. Organisational Alignment — Organisational Change

6. Organisational Alignment: How Project Management Helps 71
Abul Rizvi, Department of Immigration and Multicultural Affairs

7. 'Crazy Thought or Creative Thinking': Reform in the Real World 79
Patricia Scott, Department of Human Services

8. The Australian Taxation Office Change Program: Project and Change
Management Directions and Learnings, A Case Study 91
Bob Webb, Deputy Commissioner, Australian Taxation Office

9. Applying Three Frames to the Delivery of Public Value 107
*Jim Varghese, Director-General, Department of Primary Industries and
Fisheries, Queensland*

10. Building Capacity for Policy Implementation 113
Anne Tiernan, Centre for Governance and Public Policy, Griffith University

Section IV. Better Project and Program Delivery

11. Program Management and Organisational Change: New Directions for Implementation 123
Lynelle Briggs, Australian Public Service Commissioner

12. What is a Project Management Culture and How do we Develop it and Keep it Alive 133
Kathleen Kuryl, Manager Better Practice & Project Services, Department of Premier and Cabinet, Tasmania

13. Project Management and the Australian Bureau of Statistics: Doing What Works 147
Dennis Trewin, Australian Statistician, Australian Bureau of Statistics

14. Intervention Logic/ Program Logic: Toward Good Practice 157
Karen Baehler, School of Government, Victoria University of Wellington

Section V. Implementation Review

15. Implementing Gateway in the Australian Government 179
Department of Finance and Administration, Australian Government

16. Governments Can Deliver: Better Practice in Project and Program Delivery 189
Ian Glenday, Executive Director, Office of Government Commerce, London

17. The Gateway Review Process in Victoria 199
Wayne Sharpe, Executive Manager, Gateway Unit, Department of Treasury and Finance, Victoria

18. The Australian Government Cabinet Implementation Unit 219
Peter Hamburger, Department of the Prime Minister and Cabinet

19. Organising for Policy Implementation: The Emergence and Role of Implementation Units in Policy Design and Oversight 229
Evert Lindquist, School of Public Administration, University of Victoria, Canada

Appendix A. Annex: A Guide for Drafting Case Study Papers 257

Acknowledgements

The papers included in this collection were presented at the *Project Management and Organisational Change* conference held in Canberra in February 2006. This was the first annual research conference organised by the Australia and New Zealand School of Government in conjunction with the Department of the Prime Minister and Cabinet. The conference provided a platform for over 50 speakers and attracted over 350 attendees across the two days. Speakers included top public sector executives from the Australian jurisdictions as well as representatives from the United Kingdom, Canada and New Zealand. The ANZSOG research committee, chaired initially by Professor Ian Chubb, Vice Chancellor of ANU and then by Ken Henry from The Treasury was instrumental in framing the themes of the conference. Audio files of the full proceedings are available on the ANZSOG website (http://www.anzsog.edu.au/news/research_confer_audio.php).

In hosting such an event we incurred a number of debts. In the Department of the Prime Minister and Cabinet, Isi Unikowski led the reference group and framed the main contours of the conference. He was indefatigable in his energy, ideas and commitment. Also important in providing key support were Peter Shergold, Jim Hargreaves, Peter Hamburger, Gia Metherell and Mark Prebble. Jenny Keene managed the conference program and undertook the lion's share of the conference organisation. The Dean of ANZSOG, Professor Allan Fels, opened the conference and assisted with invitations. ANZSOG staff and postgraduates of the Political Science Program at The Australian National University helped with preparations and in administering the conference event.

Presenters at the conference who are not included in this publication include: Professor John Alford, Sandi Beatie, Lesley Bentley, Stephen Betros, Ed Blow, David Butler, David Dombkins, Tim Farland, Iain Fraser, Air Vice Marshall Norman Gray, Stacie Hall, Robert Higgins, Caroline Hogg, Elaine Ninham, Kersti Nogeste, David Paul, Kaye Remington, Ann Steward, Sabrina Walsh and Philip Weickhardt. We thank them for their impressive contributions.

The sponsors of the conference included: the Project Management Institute (PMI), the Australian Institute of Project Management (AIPM), Tanner James, PA Consulting, Palm Consulting, Compuware Corporation, Human Systems, the Australian Public Service Commission and the University of New South Wales Press.

Finally, John Butcher at the ANU was expert at pulling the publication together, chasing written papers and undertaking an initial copy edit of the manuscript. I can't thank him enough.

Professor John Wanna
Sir John Bunting Chair of Public Administration
ANZSOG/ANU

List of Contributors

Lynelle Briggs, Australian Public Service Commissioner

Karen Baehler, School of Government, Victoria University of Wellington

Department of Finance and Administration, Australian Government

Christina Gillies, Non Executive Director and IT Governance Consultant

Peter Hamburger, Department of the Prime Minister and Cabinet

Evert Lindquist, School of Public Administration, University of Victoria, Canada

Kathleen Kuryl, Manager Better Practice & Project Services, Department of Premier and Cabinet, Tasmania

Ian McPhee, Auditor-General for the Commonwealth of Australia

Ian Glenday, Executive Director, Office of Government Commerce, London

Scott Prasser, Faculty of Business, University of Sunshine Coast

Abul Rizvi, Department of Immigration and Multicultural Affairs

Patricia Scott, Secretary, Department of Human Services

Wayne Sharpe, Executive Manager, Gateway Unit, Department of Treasury and Finance, Victoria

Peter Shergold, Secretary, Department of the Prime Minister and Cabinet

Anne Tiernan, Centre for Governance and Public Policy, Griffith University

Dennis Trewin, Australian Statistician, Australian Bureau of Statistics

Jim Varghese, Director-General, Department of Primary Industries and Fisheries, Queensland

John Wanna, Sir John Bunting Chair of Public Administration, ANZSOG/ANU

Bob Webb, Deputy Commissioner, Australian Taxation Office

Raymond C Young, Department of Accounting and Finance, Macquarie University

Foreword — Ian McPhee, Auditor-General for the Commonwealth of Australia

I am pleased to provide the foreword for this collection, representing, as it does, a comprehensive drawing together of experience and insight from both practitioners and academic researchers.

The business of government is necessarily diverse, changing and of considerable scale. Against this background, policy and program implementation, organisational change and project management are recurring themes in the ongoing work of the Australian National Audit Office (ANAO). The factors for success are many and varied, and the consequences of failure can carry significant implications, not least for consumers and the public generally.

From its audit work, the ANAO has drawn important insights into what contributes to the successful implementation of government programs and initiatives. The breadth and depth of our work puts us in a unique position to compare the operations across the public sector. We've increasingly been seeking to pass on these lessons to the Australian Public Service (APS) through a range of audit products, such as our *AuditFocus* newsletters [1] and *Better Practice Guides* on specific aspects of administration, that draw lessons from relevant audits as well as international better practice. [2]

One positive development in the Australian Public Service (APS) in recent years has been an enhanced focus on the implementation of government programs and initiatives. This is important, because the community expects the Government to deliver on its policies; and so does the Government.

Delays in implementation mean that the community is not receiving the benefits of the new policy or initiative, and there is likely to be an adverse budgetary effect as well, neither of which are appreciated by Government. Parliament and its Committees are also interested in program implementation issues as evidenced by reports over many years on aspects of program administration and systems implementation.

Key factors for successful implementation

There are six themes that I feel are important factors for successful implementation. These are:

- organisational self-awareness;
- effective governance;
- the need for support from the 'top';
- an understanding of the interaction between policy development and implementation;
- engagement with other organisations; and

- continuous monitoring and evaluation.

Organisational self-awareness

Every organisation has different strengths and weaknesses that bear on successful implementation. Organisational self-awareness means being able to recognise the organisation's strengths and weaknesses. The chances of successful implementation are increased if senior management is able to recognise their own (and the organisation's) strengths and weaknesses; this in turn enables senior management to consider how to compensate for any weaknesses in a pragmatic way. This is fundamentally about risk management, taking into account the three major contributors to organisational risk:

- **strategic risk**: the concern that major strategic alternatives may be ill-advised given the organisation's internal and external circumstances;
- **environmental risk**: covering macro-environmental risks, including political, economic and market factors; and
- **operational risk**: covering compliance and process risks. [3]

There is now a recognition by most agencies that an effective risk management strategy and control environment must be in place, and refined over time to actively manage their programs in an environment of changing risk profiles — this is no longer discretionary.

The importance of risk management in today's public sector was captured by the UK Government's Strategy Unit as follows:

> Governments have always had a critical role in protecting their citizens from risks. But handling risk has become more central to the working of government in recent years. The key factors include: addressing difficulties in handling risks to the public; recognition of the importance of early risk identification in policy development; risk management in programs and projects; and complex issues of risk transfer to and from the private sector. [4]

To be most effective, managing risks should be aligned to strategic objectives, corporate governance arrangements and integrated with business planning and reporting cycles.

Effective Governance

Clear objectives and appropriate accountability, authority and reporting regimes are necessary components of effective governance. Having the right skills and methodologies is essential. Even so, do not hesitate to apply the 'blow torch' to critical judgments or assessments. Stay focused on what's important. This is particularly so with the quickening pace of public administration, including in respect to policy development and implementation. It is not uncommon for not all policy dimensions to be known before a policy is announced, nor all implementation details to be settled before an implementation commences.

Planned pilot studies can be truncated, or turned into a rolling 'implementation'. While these approaches may not always reflect best practice models of implementation, they can reflect particular priorities and/or timetables. In these circumstances, an *agile* approach to governance and risk management is required. The main message, however, is *do not lose sight of the fundamentals of good governance; they will hold you in good stead.* [5]

Support from the 'top'

Appropriate engagement by the 'top' reduces the chances of sub-optimal implementation. A recent manager's checklist argued that one of the critical things to get right is to *'have the visible support of the top of the office.'* [6] Conversely, one of the most common causes of project failure is a 'lack of clear senior management and Ministerial ownership'.

Without strong and visible top-down support, there is a risk that underlying infrastructure will be ineffective, especially if cultural change is involved. As was recently noted in the Palmer report: 'a strong government policy calls for strong executive leadership, together with careful management, to ensure that enforcement and application of the policy are justified and equitable.' [7]

To be effective, an organisation needs to be willing to give and receive 'bad news'. Successful implementation depends on having appropriate strategies for dealing promptly with 'bad news'. Key considerations include:

- do the governance arrangements within the organisation provide for adequate progress and review mechanisms. This means including escalation of significant issues to chief executive and/or ministerial level at the appropriate time; and
- does the tone and culture of the organisation enable or prevent 'bad news' to be reported and listened to?

To be effective, policy and program implementation generally requires there to be a senior responsible officer who is accountable for the success of a policy's implementation. [8] This is the person whom the relevant minister and executive can turn to for progress reports and details of emerging risks during implementation.

Policy development and implementation are not separate

Policy implementation should be an integral part of policy design – begin with the end process in mind. This means engaging those with implementation experience during the policy development stage. This is important for assessing the practicability of a policy. [9]

For example, it may enable the identification of:

- practical constraints which need to be overcome in order for the policy to deliver required results on the ground; and
- more reliable cost and uptake estimates.

There has sometimes been a tendency for those with implementation experience to be consulted fairly late in the design process, which increases the risk of encountering difficulties during implementation, with subsequent risks to the delivery of outcomes. The point is that, those with implementation experience may have far better practical knowledge of what is likely to work and what is not likely to work. [10]

It is also necessary to avoid any tendency to downplay the analysis of implementation risks. This is especially important where time constraints and complex negotiation processes create pressure to focus on the outcome to be achieved, rather than the capacity of administrative processes to deliver. The danger is of 'unwanted surprises' down the track, with mitigation usually much more difficult at that point.

The other point I would stress in this area is that lessons from ANAO audits reflect the value of systematic and structured planning for implementation. [11] Planning provides a 'map' of how an initiative will be implemented addressing matters such as:

- timeframe, including the different phases for implementation;
- roles and responsibilities of all those involved in implementation;
- resources (including funding and human resources);
- risk management, including how any potential barriers to implementation will be dealt with; and
- monitoring and reporting requirements.

Where attention is not given to these matters, problems may arise such as: overambitious timeframes; [12] resources not being available when required; [13] those implementing the initiative do not have the appropriate skills or capability; [14] and insufficient contingency planning. [15]

Engagement with other organisations

It is becoming increasingly the norm for organisations to implement initiatives with the assistance of others. This may be: other Australian Government agencies; State and Territory Government agencies; non-government organisations; or the private sector, among others. Organisational boundaries are no longer as important as they used to be: there is today a heavy emphasis on whole-of-government initiatives that bring together the essential policy and delivery skills from within the APS.

Whole-of-government implementation is often a particular challenge for agencies. Such initiatives are greatly assisted by: clear articulation of roles and responsibilities; assigning responsibility for risk and their treatment; and the ability to assess progress and outcomes from a whole of government perspective rather than in 'silos'.

Identification of a lead agency is also highly desirable for whole of government initiatives. [16] As well as working from the perspective of their agency, a lead agency is able to extol the benefits of a whole of government perspective, [17] including whether information is shared and flows between the agencies involved; performance is monitored; promotion is assessed; and the commitment by all parties is being met. [18] For the arrangement to be effective, the lead agency should be recognised and supported as acting in this capacity.

Keep monitoring!

Implementation of government and program initiatives is most commonly a staged process. Where it is not, there is value in trying to break the tasks into several manageable steps. Experience here and overseas suggests this increases the chance of success. So, do not assume that the job is done three quarters of the way through! Regular and continuous monitoring is essential to determine the extent to which the desired outcomes have been achieved. This requires structured reporting.

There is little value in agencies identifying and analysing key implementation risks, and then failing to act promptly when confronted by performance warning indicators. This is precisely when it is critical to act promptly. [19]

Good systems need to be supported by the right culture. Be willing to hear 'bad news' and react promptly. Another consideration is to keep sight of the Government's objective. During roll-out of any initiative one should continually ask whether the program's objectives are being met. This can sometimes be a challenge as the distance between the policy dimension and implementation increases during roll-out. Keep in mind the key questions: *Is the project on track, on time, and on budget?*

Evaluation at an appropriate time assists in determining the extent to which an initiative has met, or is meeting its objectives and that those intended to benefit have done so. It is evident from programs such as the reaction to the 2002–03 drought, that evaluation can help agencies learn lessons and share better practice in policy development and implementation. [20] This can lead to more informed decision-making; facilitate better use of resources and enhance accountability.

Concluding remarks

We need to recognise that a manager may be expected to deliver something very quickly with limited notice. However, a consistent message from the ANAO's experience shows that planning for, and carrying through on implementation does reduce the risk of delay to, and dilution of outcomes. This monograph offers valuable insights that, if heeded, could make the difference between a smooth implementation and hitting 'potholes' along the way.

ENDNOTES

[1] These newsletters seek to capture some of the lessons from our audit work that are likely to be of general interest and application and are intended to be easy to read for busy public sector executives The first issue of *AuditFocus* was published and distributed in November 2005. It covered: compliance with the APS Financial Framework; Audit Committees; maintaining proper records; and project and contract management. See http://www.anao.gov.au and follow the link to the *AuditFocus* newsletter.

[2] See http://www.anao.gov.au and follow the link to Better Practice Guides to see a list of the guides.

[3] Atkinson, Anthony A and Webb, Alan, *A Directors Guide to Risk and its Management*, International Federation of Accountants Articles of Merit Award Program for Distinguished Contribution to Management Accounting, August 2005, p. 26.

[4] The UK Government Strategy Unit, 2002, *Risk: Improving government's capability to handle risk and uncertainty*, p. 1.

[5] If you are looking for a useful reference there is a Better Practice Guide issued by the ANAO in 2003 on *Public Sector Governance*, and a reference published in 2004 on the same topic by CCH. You may even wish to read ANAO reports concerned with the governance of programs and projects, available from www.anao.gov.au.

[6] Office of Government Commerce, *Achieving Excellence in Construction: a Manager's Checklist*, OGC, London, 2003.

[7] MJ Palmer, Inquiry into the Circumstances of the Immigration Detention of Cornelia Rau Report, Canberra, 2005, p. ix.

[8] A recent ANAO audit highlighted that a senior responsible officer should be allocated to a project, particularly where there is more than one agency involved in implementation (see ANAO Audit Report No.40, 2004–05, *The Edge Project*). 'Senior Responsible Owner' (SRO) is a term used by the OGC with regards to the Gateway Review Process. The Gateway Review Process makes reference to the concept of a SRO as an individual who is senior and takes responsibility for the successful outcome of a program or project. See Office of Government Commerce, *The OGC Gateway Process: a Manager's checklist*, version 1.0, OGC, London, 2004.

[9] National Audit Office, *Modern Policy-Making: Ensuring Policies Deliver Value for Money*, report by the Comptroller and Auditor-General HC 289 Session 2001–2002, the Stationary Office, London, 2001, p. 42.

[10] ibid

[11] All too often ANAO audits find that agencies have not given sufficient attention to planning for implementation. Recent ANAO audits that have highlighted poor implementation/project plans include: ANAO Audit Report No.40 2004–05, *The Edge Project*; ANAO Audit Report No.36 2003–04, *The Commonwealth's Administration of the Dairy Industry Adjustment Package*; ANAO Audit Report No.15 2002–03, *The Aboriginal and Torres Straight Islander Health Program Follow-up audit*; and ANAO Audit Report No.27 2004–05, *Management of the Conversion to Digital Broadcasting*.

[12] For example see ANAO Report No. 8 2005–06 Management of the Personnel Management Key Solution (PMKeyS) Implementation Project.

[13] For example see ANAO Audit Report No.20 2003–04, *Aid to East Timor*, para. 6.16.

[14] For example see ANAO Audit Report No.36 2003–04 The Commonwealth's Administration of the Dairy Industry Adjustment Package, para. 2.44.

[15] For example see ANAO Audit Report No.50 2004–05, *Drought Assistance*, para. 2.3.

[16] See ANAO Report No.50 2004–05, *Drought Assistance*.

[17] Management Advisory Committee, *Working together: Principles and practices to guide the Australian Public Service* [internet]. Australian Government Australian Public Service Commission, Australia, 2005, available from http://www.apsc.gov.au/mac/workingtogether.htm [accessed 11 May 2005].

[18] Office of the Auditor General of Canada, *Managing Departments for Results and Managing Horizontal Issues for Results*, Report of the Auditor General of Canada-December 2000 Chapter 20, 2000, p. 29.

[19] 'In the dynamic area of immigration detention, the challenge for executive management is to recognise potential weaknesses and ensure that the arrangements for monitoring, assessment, reporting and review are sensitive to the changing environment. In particular, the arrangements should provide for adequate and early feedback to enable corrective action by management, and there should be clear triggers for involvement and oversight at executive level'. See MJ Palmer, op.cit., p. 167.

[20] See ANAO Report No.50 2004–05, *Drought Assistance.* Also see National Audit Office (NAO) *Modern Policy-Making Ensuring policies deliver value for money* report by the Comptroller and Auditor-General HC 289 Session 2001-2002; November 2001, p. 14.

Section I. Setting the Scene

1. Introduction — Improving Implementation: the Challenge Ahead

John Wanna, Sir John Bunting Chair of Public Administration, ANU

Shortly after winning the 2004 election Prime Minister John Howard reflected that 'we tend to look at service delivery as an afterthought rather than a policy priority'. He was referring to difficulties in implementing programs, especially those involved in more than one level of government or spread over several agencies. He made the statement in the context of announcing his new cabinet, including the establishment of the new Ministry of Human Services, which gave his comment added significance.

Many believe that this marked a new strategic direction for his cabinet and the policy departments. A key feature of this new direction is the insistence that project management is about transforming the culture of the public service — applying project management disciplines not only to major projects but to the harder areas of social policy and whole-of-government initiatives.

The implementation message conveyed by the Prime Minister signalled a new direction for the federal government. Entering his fourth term, Howard indicated he wanted 'can-do government' guided by expert practitioners and project managers to replace the era of 'hands-off government' of the late 1990s advocated by accountants and economists. The new focus was to be on improving implementation and delivering programs to meet higher expectations. This was an incidence of a nation-building state changing its collective mind.

But Howard was not alone in expressing such concerns. State premiers have made similar remarks over the lack of follow-through. Peter Beattie in Queensland lamented that when cabinet made decisions it often took months for action to occur. Similarly, in recent years Steve Bracks, Geoff Gallop, Jon Stanhope, Bob Carr and Morris Iemma have all emphasised service delivery and the need to focus on performance in the public sector. Implementation problems have beset all their governments, and blame-shifting has become less and less an option as a defence and no longer washes with the electorate. In their jurisdictions, when policy failures occurred critics laid the blame on predictable pitfalls, on 'learned incapacities' and 'learned helplessness', and of a malaise in management. Some have even pointed to an emerging culture of 'management deficit' where executives refused to take responsibility or washed their hands of emergent problems.

The Council of Australian Governments has also moved from a concern with national policy frameworks and new policy agendas to better co-ordination and delivery of existing services where both levels of government are invariably involved (such as in health, the environment, family services and childcare, training and education).

So, why are government leaders and their cabinets getting interested in service delivery, project management and implementation? And why now? Normally the topic would be regarded as the rightful province of line managers, with the invisible 'plumbing' taking place in the depths of departments, too miniscule and trivial to interest ministers or even their senior executives. Yet, the recent political concerns are not simply a reflection of partisan interest from one side of politics, or the preoccupations of a particular leader, or one driven by electoral cycles. The trend is too topical and widespread.

The 'take implementation seriously' movement is part of a much broader concern with governance and the effectiveness of public policy. Consider, for instance, the following trajectories and signals.

All governments report far more on their results, performance and progress towards the achievement of outcomes than ever before (financial and performance reporting, better annual reports, triple bottom line reporting, quality of services reports, outcomes reporting, state of the service reporting). How far they are believed and how far they engage in a little obfuscating is another matter, but reporting has increased visibility and in its importance to governments.

Governments are calling for greater 'passion for policy' and greater commitment in delivering outputs (see Briggs 2005). They are not satisfied with mere technical proficiency from their bureaucrats but seeking a cultural renewal in the public service and a rekindling of a sense of 'serving the public' with good policy innovations. Governments do not want their public officials to absolve themselves from responsibility but to become passionately committed to policy directions.

To date, three governments have formally established special implementation units attached to cabinet to both spur and track implementation progress according to agreed milestones (see Tiernan 2006; Wanna 2006). These units aim to help agencies 'think through' the likely implementation issues at the policy formation stage when making submissions to cabinet. Cabinet can also flag which of its decisions it wants monitoring or tracking, and call for broader reviews of implementation progress. Some of these units (as with the Delivery Unit in Britain) set targets and measure departmental performance against these standards, but so far the trend in Australian has been to establish collaborative bodies increasing the focus on implementation issues.

The Commonwealth and Victorian governments have established 'gateway review' processes to help in the management of large projects and provide project assurance. Special review teams of experienced project managers produce timely reports to executives (the so-called 'senior responsible owners') in the relevant departments. Victoria commenced in 2002 while the Commonwealth process began in 2006. Both review processes investigate risk management with projects, the necessary operational skills and knowledge of project management in administration. Importantly, while their reports remain largely confidential, their reviews function to improve the information exchange with the stakeholders (senior executives and ministers).

In similar vein, the NSW and Queensland governments have established central assessment units to investigate the cost and quality of services, and whether governments have been getting value for money in the services they provide or procure. These bodies have investigated the relative costs of provision, quality assurance and expectation management.

Most of these central agency initiatives are aimed at enabling governments to better monitor progress and review performance information. They offer practical ways of allowing risks to be assessed and managed and, if necessary, for actions to be taken so that policy initiatives that may have run into difficulty can be revived or emerging risks managed before the project or policy is seriously derailed. These initiatives are not intended to embarrass governments or to result in the release of damaging information into the public realm. They are not done for public accountability reasons, although it can be argued that they improve the oversight of executive governance.

Certainly, there were other catalysts prompting these concerns. The importance of the implementation agenda was underscored by some major policy or implementation failures where problems multiplied until they could not be hidden. Such failures were exposed in the areas of income support to families, job referrals under outsourced provisions, immigration administration and the detention of supposed illegal over-stayers or residents, child protection and health administration in public hospitals. Some major information technology and procurement projects in government agencies such as Defence or Centrelink have resulted in costly embarrassments. Other significant cost overruns have been publicly exposed.

A further problem is the issue of cultural alignment between agencies and policy intent. Is there a close alignment between organisational cultures and the policy objectives? Are traditional administrative organisations suitable for new delivery methods? Is there an appropriate synergy between policy departments and delivery agencies? Are the intentions of government clearly communicated to delivery agencies and indicated to client groups? These are some of the more difficult aspects of good implementation.

But, how then do we turn the focus on implementation and build an 'implementation culture'? What are the challenges ahead?

There are concerns among many senior advisors and executives that feedback loops have been neglected or destroyed as governments have separated policy responsibilities from delivery responsibilities. Compartmentalisition of 'policy advice' from the delivery coalface has created strains and tensions in the policy delivery chain. This is a problem that has been noted in the UK especially with executive agencies (James 2003). [1]

Policy designers may lack a detailed knowledge of implementation and delivery. Today's senior executives may not know in detail what is going on within their area of policy responsibilities. They are dependent on the provision of good and open information exchange, and in practice information asymmetries tend to occur and obfuscate close scrutiny. Whereas in the past, senior executives, who had worked their way up the organisation from the bottom up, often had extensive implementation experience in their agencies, today they are dependent on information provided by delivery agencies and contracted service suppliers in the profit and non-profit sector. Some rely on occasional audit reports to monitor performance. Often there is little implementation knowledge passed back to the policymakers and little effective monitoring of progress.

Hence, the need for governance frameworks that operate on effective project management, that provide relevant and timely information to executives with oversight responsibilities – or to put it another way 'project management is too important to be left to the nerds' (Shergold 2006). 'Senior responsible owners' who may not be personally involved in project management but who still have accountability for the results, are being directed to take a far more active interest in the governance of projects within their portfolio. They needed better information and skills to ensure projects were in line with government policy objectives, were on track with projected timelines and were achieving intended outputs. They need to employ a matrix of project management disciplines – not as a formal set of prescribed techniques, but as a range of possible tools and disciplines to apply when appropriate.

Then, there is the issue of how agencies test the reliability and veracity of feedback information? How do they ascertain that adequate tests or inspections have been undertaken and accurately reported? How do they know what issues to raise with third party deliverers, or what questions to ask if they have limited background in the area? They often do not. How should those ultimately accountable for programs and the impact of policy design, collate and interpret the information they receive from those agents responsible for their delivery?

Policy today is more interconnected and complex. It is increasingly bound up with delivery issues that cross traditional portfolio responsibilities and Commonwealth-state demarcations. Many players have legitimate involvement in policy sectors and their cooperation or involvement is crucial to success. Welfare services, for instance, now involve anything up to a dozen federal agencies as well as a host of state and third-sector agencies. Delivery issues are more a kaleidoscope of coordinating influences than a logical set of stages unilaterally declared by silo departments. Immigration, health and national security services face similar delivery issues. Effective implementation is as strong as the weakest link in the chain. When things go wrong, governments have to accept responsibility and attempt to rectify the problems often under the glare of publicity. For instance, in Immigration after the release of the Palmer report into maladministration in her department (July 2005), the Minister, Senator Vanstone, insisted that her department post its remedial implementation plan in the department's website as a discipline to her executives.

Reviews of existing implementation strategies have found agencies do not adequately identify and address barriers to good delivery. They find policy proposals conceived and devised without the benefit of implementation experience. They find that departmental cultures and administrative practices run counter to declared policy goals of the government. Departments struggle with changes of management as policy priorities change. In some cases, poor project management disciplines have been discovered, without adequate planning, risk assessment, key milestones, or with little heed paid to formal implementation plans. Government projects and investment decisions are often uncoordinated and poorly evaluated over time or between different jurisdictions.

Hence, it is clear that much of the current interest in implementation and project management is an unintended consequence of the trajectory of public sector reform followed by Australian governments since the 1980s. Governments have detached implementation 'knowledges' and are now seeking to 'rebuild the connections' in a different organisational context or changed delivery mode. They are not talking about dismantling the reforms of the past two decades but of managing the 'black holes' created, facilitating better information exchanges, and building more organic connections not just within agencies but between them also. They are attempting this within a framework of corporate governance and integrated delivery.

Those responsible for managing projects are now required to consider not just the input-output measures, but to show they understand the transaction costs, the different forms of risk, better evaluations of outcomes, the need for collaborative partnerships and synergies, and for good relationship management. They also need to be more aware of how far projects 'drift' in implementation from intentions of government.

Senior officials away from the delivery point need to become responsible owners and supplement their oversight functions with additional expertise and feedback. If the policy-delivery loop is broken it needs to be re-knitted by other means, especially with senior executives taking a closer responsibility and knowing what to ask and when. The trick is to 'manage implementation' without getting swamped in the detail of implementation or descending into micro-management.

Certainly, as this collection demonstrates, governments throughout Australia are increasingly focused on the politics and processes of implementation, and on feedback mechanisms to inform ministers and 'senior owners' on progress. Yet, it is the executives and senior managers who are the ones driving this current agenda, not the politicians. But political interest and occasional prods from the prime minister or premiers will be essential to sustain the interest of the bureaucrats. Even if politicians engage in this debate with the motivation of shifting responsibility for implementation directly to their officials, they will nevertheless be unleashing a new agenda for those delivering public policy. It may be somewhat overdue, but the new-found interest is certainly a welcome development.

The 20 contributions contained in this monograph comprise a cross-section of the best papers delivered at the ANZSOG annual conference on Project Management and Organisational Change, held at the Canberra Convention Centre in February 2006. The monograph is divided into four parts. Part 1, *Governance, Ownership and Oversight,* canvasses the range of issues affecting the basic governance and control of projects. It offers insights into the key factors for success and failure. Part 2, *Organisational Alignment–Organisational Change,* presents a range of perspectives on change management and the cultural alignment between organisations and government objectives. These papers illustrate, through real-world examples, how a well-conceived and structured project management framework can be used to secure stakeholder buy-in and achieve broad acceptance of organisational aims and means. Part 3, *Better Project and Program Delivery,* focuses on the development of appropriate project and program management cultures in organisations. It provides pertinent advice on how to improve operational management and sustain effective policy delivery. Part 4, *Implementation Reviews,* explores the factors underpinning successful implementation initiatives and sound implementation cultures. It reports on new initiatives in various jurisdictions relating to good project and program management practice.

References

Briggs, Lynelle 2005, 'A Passion for Policy?' paper presented Wednesday 29 June 2005 as part of the ANZSOG/ANU Public Lecture Series 2005.

Oliver, James 2003, *The Executive Agency Revolution in Whitehall: Public interest versus bureau-shaping perspectives*, Palgrave Macmillan.

Shergold, Peter. 2006, 'Driving Change to Bring About Better Implementation and Delivery', address to the conference, *Project Management and Organisational Change*, Wednesday 22 Februrary.

Tiernan, Anne 2006, 'Working with the Stock We Have: The eveloving role of Queensland's Implementation Unit', *Journal of Comparative Policy Analysis: Research and Practice*, Vol. 8 No. 4, December.

Wanna, J. 2006, 'From Afterthought to Afterburner: Australia's Cabinet Implementation Unit', *Journal of Comparative Policy Analysis*, Vol 8, No. 4, December, p. 34

ENDNOTES

[1] Oliver James 2003, *The Executive Agency Revolution in Whitehall: Public interest versus bureau-shaping perspectives*, Palgrave Macmillan.

2. Driving Change to Bring About Better Implementation and Delivery

Peter Shergold, Secretary, Department of the Prime Minister and Cabinet

There are three particular reasons I am glad to have the opportunity to 'set the scene' for this monograph. First, it is been two years since the last time I spoke out on issues of implementation and delivery,[1] and over two years since I established the Cabinet Implementation Unit. The conference, and this monograph, provide a good opportunity to maintain the impetus towards the better execution of government policy. My experience of bureaucratic inertia is that if one does not keep driving forward one does not stop still: one actually slides backwards down the mountain of good intentions.

Second, two years of experience of the Cabinet Implementation Unit has produced valuable lessons about the barriers to successful implementation and how they might be planned for and overcome. These issues are being explored across all the Australian jurisdictions, as well as in the UK and New Zealand. This conference provides us with an opportunity to learn from each other.

Third, I want to continue a campaign to take the issues of project and program management out of the technical context into which they are all too frequently consigned. I have a simple message: project management is too important to leave for nerds!

When I was at school, participation in the Cadet Force was voluntary. Nevertheless attendance was remarkably high – not least because the alternative activity for Tuesday afternoons was a double lesson of Latin. For me, and many others, marching around the quadrangle or crawling through muddy fields seemed far preferable to conjugating the inflected forms of Latin verbs. And, to be truthful, if the alternative had been instead a long afternoon of something called 'project management' I might still have preferred to have spent my Monday nights polishing my boots, creasing my trousers and daubing my puttees. Project management can sound dull if worthy, a matter of routine process, necessary but uninspiring.

It is not. It is about getting things done through innovative methods, organisational change and committed leadership. And its significance to public administration is even greater. The quality of the implementation of government policy is central to community support for the institutions of democratic governance, a theme to which I will return.

Although issues of implementation and delivery are attaining a higher profile in the Australian Government sector, the Cabinet Implementation Unit still gets told too often that 'the only reason we're preparing this implementation plan is because you're making us do one'. This is simply not good enough. If we are fair dinkum about accountability to our respective governments, and through them to the public, we must embed implementation planning into our routine. If planning to deliver is perceived as an additional chore, just more bureaucratic red-tape, then we will have failed.

Better project and program management cannot be left as a technical task for specialists. It is about ensuring that our organisations are able to change in order to deliver change effectively. Australian public servants face implementation challenges somewhat different from their private sector colleagues. They are marked by agency demarcations, overlapping jurisdictional responsibilities, and public accountability within an environment of fierce political contest and intense scrutiny.

And the implications of inadequate management of public policy can be worse. Poor delivery – such as inadequate service levels, lack of timeliness or burdensome regulatory processes – risks public dissatisfaction. It can reduce trust not only in public service but in the government it serves. Poor project management means that citizens are not receiving their entitlements and, in my view, that's even worse than customer dissatisfaction or a decline in shareholder value.

Implementation is necessarily a learning process. The changing circumstances and the experience of executing a policy decision have to be taken into account. Indeed they may require the policy decision to be revisited. Getting things done well in government requires more than a series of commandments (regulations, rules and guidelines) handed down to those below or transmitted from the national office to regional offices. Communication and learning have to work both ways. Policy prepared without the experience of those who deliver it across counters or from call-centres is almost certainly policy that will be poorly designed and difficult to implement.

Let me set out some of what we have learned in the two years since we established the Cabinet Implementation Unit. The Unit, as you are probably aware, lies at the centre of government. It taps into the Cabinet decision-making process, through which almost all the big decisions of the Australian government are made. It does three things:

- As policy submissions are being prepared for Cabinet consideration, the Unit works with drafters to ensure that the proposals that Ministers consider provide a summary of implementation issues, including an assessment of expected benefits, governance, milestones and risks: the goal, quite simply, is to ensure that government can decide on policy with its eyes wide open.

- For important initiatives that pose significant implication challenges, the Unit then works with agencies to develop more detailed implementation plans against which progress can be regularly reported to the Prime Minister and the Cabinet.

- On a quarterly basis, the Unit compiles short reports from agencies, in a tabular, 'traffic light' format to ensure that the government has a snapshot of how implementation is going on large or sensitive projects. The latest report covers around 150 specific initiatives of which 26 have been given 'amber' or 'red' light status.

The first thing I've learned over two years is that the successful implementation of policy is not about the adoption of any particular project management methodology, although it is essential that an appropriate methodology be employed. Increasingly it has become apparent that the pathway to better implementation is that it be consciously driven from the top down with continuing executive oversight. *Chief Executive Instructions* create a framework for due process and accountability but they do not convey the commitment and interest of leadership in implementation.

There is nothing particularly original about this insight. A recent report on IT projects around the world found that less than one third succeeded: 53 per cent did not meet expectations in terms of their timing, cost or capacity to deliver the required features and functions and 18 per cent failed completely. One of the most critical factors determining success was executive management support, in championing and resourcing projects [2] and, equally important, in making sure that there were systems in place ensuring that the right projects were selected at the right time for the organisation.

This does not mean that the heads of agencies need to go off and study the *Project Management Book of Knowledge*, or *PRINCE2*. But it does mean that they have to learn the right kind of questions to ask. In her November 2004 address to the Australian Graduate School of Management/Harvard Club of Australia, Christina Gillies [3] emphasised:

> In most boardrooms, good financial governance is understood and operates without question. Even where directors have little or no experience in financial analysis, they are aware that they must obtain a level of understanding of the financial operations of the business and have sufficient basic knowledge to interpret the books of account ... (But) for many directors, IT is a subject to be avoided. How can a director with little or no experience in IT carry out their fiduciary duties, when struggling to understand the terminology and ever-changing nature of technology?

Senior public sector managers, who find themselves charged with the oversight of major programs and projects must know what the right questions are, who might be able to answer them and how to assess the validity of the answers. With this in mind, the Cabinet Implementation Unit and the Australian National Audit Office have been working jointly on a better practice guide to implementation. The guide is not primarily about how to manage projects and programs. Rather it provides a checklist of the types of questions that need to be asked and the assurance that needs to be given to CEOs, the senior officers responsible for oversight of projects and the project managers themselves. Such a systematic approach is the key to driving the structural and behavioural changes needed in organisations if good intentions are to be turned into better practices.

The Palmer inquiry [4] into the Department of Immigration, Multicultural and Indigenous Affairs' management of detentions and deportations reveals much of what can go wrong when government policy is not effectively translated into organisational systems and processes. Palmer found that DIMIA, and by extension all public sector agencies, should have in operation 'systems that ensure integrity of application and accountability and engender public confidence … and searching processes of high-level internal review (to ensure) the organisation is achieving the outcomes expected of it. Such corporate quality assurance would (need to) be executive driven …' (p165).

Most importantly Palmer also highlighted the danger of workplace cultures preoccupied with process and rule-driven operational practice. The risk of depending upon systems alone is that implementation degenerates either into blind application of processes or into instructions which, not effectively monitored, are soon ignored. The tension between the need for systems and the need for learning can only be resolved by building into our organisations effective monitoring and communication and the will and capacity to make change in response. I think that this creative tension needs to be managed through robust, top-down project management practices mandated and championed by the agency leadership. People need to know that senior executives are serious.

I hope that the CIU may contribute to this goal. That is one reason why I have been keen to avoid the Unit becoming a centralised cudgel-wielding bureaucratic elite – what Charles F. Sable has recently called 'a commando centre' [5] or what Evert Lindquist, who is also speaking at this conference, calls 'a temporary adhocracy'. I see the Unit as a vehicle for communicating more effectively between those implementing government policy, public service leadership and government. In that role it has obvious opportunities for contributing to learning, including – formally and informally – by advising, coaching and mentoring on the basis of its accumulating experience. But to do so it has to be driven by a spirit of collegiality and cooperative partnership, not of imposed authority and blind obedience. It is about learning by doing and then spreading the learning.

Senior management has to play an increasingly important role in linking individual projects to wider organisational strategies and goals, and shaping those goals on the basis of what has been learned from individual projects. [6] They need to understand that policy development and service delivery are not in a linear chronological relationship. The making and executing of government policy is an iterative process. We can only avoid policy blunders by ensuring that policy-making is routinely and constructively informed by service delivery, in a way that transcends traditional boundaries and structures.

Learning is also prominent in the logic of the system of Gateway Reviews, developed by the UK's Office of Government Commerce, adopted by the Victorian Government and now to be introduced at the Commonwealth level. Gateway is a response to concerns about the risks of major projects going on for too long without delivering. You will shortly be hearing from other speakers on the detail of Gateway, including from Ian Glenday, who will share his experience of the OGC with us.

A central feature of Gateway which particularly attracted me was that the reports from peer review teams will be confidential to the project's senior responsible owner. This is not only to facilitate full and willing access to project data by the review teams. Crucially, it is also to facilitate learning between peers and a focus on overcoming challenges rather than denying problems, designing alibis or allocating blame.

In thinking about Gateway, for example, one might want to explore what the introduction of these independent peer reviews will mean for agencies. Are we ready for Gateway? Have we, for example, adopted consistent project management practices and methodologies across our agencies so that, if a Gateway team were to ask for the relevant documentation, or to speak to the relevant stakeholders, such information would be immediately to hand? Do we have sufficiently robust project governance practices in place to respond to the warnings and advice such reviews are designed to provide? What avenues have been established within and across our agencies to capture lessons from individual projects and disseminate them more widely?

In posing these questions I do not want to suggest that public servants are ill-prepared. My sense is that departments have responded well to the increased emphasis on project management. I now see a lot more preparatory thought on the best options for delivery, what sort of risks may emerge and how they will be handled. I discern a better articulation of the program logic and a greater understanding that effective implementation will improve the quality of the policy itself.

But we need to go further. As the outcomes of the most recent meeting of the Council of Australian Governments (COAG) powerfully demonstrated policies of national significance increasingly have to be delivered across jurisdictional boundaries. The new *National Reform Agenda* spans increased economic competition, greater investment in human capital and a less intrusive regulatory regime. When individual elements of this bold agenda are brought before governments for decision – as they must be if they are to be designed and costed – it will be crucial for governments and public servants to understand how all these pieces fit together. How does this project impact or depend on others? How can we identify appropriate pathways to deliver expensive, long-term projects, when we anticipate that the technological environment is likely to change substantially during the course of their implementation? How can we identify where the boundaries of relative certainty lie, and how we will gradually expand them in response to evolving circumstances? Can Commonwealth, State and Territory public administrations, with their inevitable bureaucratic demarcations, together develop a clear picture of the decisions that will need to be taken, when, and by whom, and the associated critical paths, risks, and interdependencies?

These are the sorts of challenges that already emerge as agencies lodge implementation plans with the CIU. Departments frequently find that they do not have the answers to all of the questions when they work up the first cut of the plan. That's quite normal. There are nearly always a swag of unknowns particularly when implementation depends legislative enactment, jurisdictional cooperation, joint funding or outsourced delivery through contracted third-parties. This is precisely where the disciplines of project and program management provide a sound basis for decision making in an environment of uncertainty. By forcing questions around the *scope* of a measure we clarify expectations and align deliverables with expectations; by forcing questions around *timing*, we clarify the critical points at which decisions about the next stage of a project will need to be made; by forcing questions around *costs and benefits*, we can disaggregate investment down into phases that help to understand what is known, and what might have to wait for legal, technological or political issues to be resolved.

Project management in the public sector is not just a matter of ensuring that government decisions are delivered to citizens efficiently, ethically and courteously while paying close attention to the appropriate and effective use of public funds. It is about more than service, timeliness and value for money. It is also about recognising that the implementation of government policy can often intrude on the lives of citizens, and impose costs on businesses, in ways that undermine self-responsibility and stifle entrepreneurship.

Bureaucratic red tape can impose regulatory costs, the scale and dimensions of which are often not sufficiently appreciated by governments who legislate and public servants who administer. There is a rising sentiment in the Commonwealth, State and Territory governments (and overseas) that it is better to regulate less and to regulate better. It is for that reason that the Banks Taskforce into Reducing Regulatory Burdens on Business was established. It will shortly deliver its findings to the public.

I am certain the report will require us to ask hard questions about the effect of regulatory policy on Australia's society and economy. Good program and project management should involve consideration of the scope of regulation and how its costs – including costs arising from uncertainty – can be reduced. Has scope creep meant businesses not originally intended to be subject to the regulation are being captured? To what extent are overlapping and inconsistent regulatory requirements across federal boundaries imposing additional burdens? Are regulations or reporting requirements justified by the original policy intent, or have they become redundant or does the policy outcome no longer justify the compliance cost. Are reporting requirements resulting in same or similar information being provided to multiple agencies? Do variations in definitional and operational reporting cause confusion in their application?

Reducing the regulatory burden on business will be a complex exercise. It will involve systemic reforms to improve regulation-making and enforcement. It will require project managers to assess the external costs of implementation on those who are subject to compliance regimes. But change – significant change – is already afoot. The Department of Industry, Tourism and Resources has developed a costing tool to better equip public servants to identify and, where possible, quantify the regulatory impact of new policy measures on businesses. It will become a requirement for this costing tool to be used in all Cabinet Submissions that propose regulation on business, to enable Ministers to make more informed policy decisions. In addition to this, the Productivity Commission will be asked, on an annual basis, to examine areas of regulatory concern to business to identify areas that could be improved.

Many of you would be aware that John Uhrig was appointed in November 2002 to conduct a review of the corporate governance of Commonwealth statutory authorities and office holders. The objective of the review was to look at the governance arrangements for statutory authorities and office holders, and come up with options for improving their performance and getting the best from their accountability frameworks. Uhrig was asked to develop a broad template of governance principles and arrangements for statutory authorities and office holders, and potentially beyond, to a wider range of public sector bodies.

Many of you would be aware that, in response to the Uhrig review more than 160 Australian Government agencies are currently being assessed against agreed governance principles. This progressive process is leading to changes in governance structures. It also involves a system of issuing *Statements of Expectation* to, and receiving *Statements of Intent* from, various authorities. Such statements will help to communicate and inform government expectations.

At the same time the Government has brought six key human services delivery agencies into the new Department of Human Services. The Department provides direct accountability to a single Minister who is responsible, in Cabinet, for ensuring that the costs and timing of administrative change are factored into consideration of health, child support or welfare policies. I can see that this discipline is already influencing for the better the policy decisions that are being taken.

– Peter Shergold

The increased interest by governments in reducing regulatory impositions illustrate the manner in which the environment of public policy changes. It will influence the character of, but not the need for project management of public policy. And there are at least three ways in which the requirements for effective execution of policy are likely to remain constant:

- first, that the disciplines of project and program management are not an end in themselves. They are the means by which the public service can best balance the increasing demand for change and adaptation by governments and the electorate with the need for administrative, technical and financial efficiency, service quality and structural innovation in program delivery;
- second, project and program management are a way of communicating from the bottom up and from the top down within and across organisations. For this to be an effective process, the senior executive must be as engaged in the development of agency capabilities in this area as the project managers themselves; and

- third, they will need support in this role. This support will not primarily be in the form of workshop training in project management techniques, but will require innovative ways of supporting senior executives in fulfilling their responsibilities, including through coaching and mentoring.

As I noted at the beginning, 'project management' would not have been a school subject that attracted me. Perhaps though if it had been called 'action' with an emphasis on 'getting things done fast and well' it might have caught my attention. Certainly that's why I am such an enthusiast now. To me project management is transformative – it turns the goals of public policy into acquisitions, investments, programs and services that are in the public interest. And that leads me, finally, to why I think project management is more than an important set of technical skills.

Public servants bear a particular responsibility, directly and indirectly, for the delivery of government policy. Every government knows that its future depends not only on how wisely it makes decisions but on how effectively its public service delivers them. In my interpretation of the Westminster tradition governments should continue or fall on how the electorate perceives the quality of their policies not on the competence of public officials to execute them. Indeed I think that public servants should exhibit bias … but the bias they display should be for delivering public policy with vigour. I want project managers who are driven by a bias for action.

ENDNOTES

[1] 'Plan and Deliver: Avoiding Bureaucratic Hold-up', Speech to the Australian Graduate School of Management/Harvard Club of Australia, Wednesday, 17 November 2004, National Press Club, http://www.dpmc.gov.au/speeches/shergold/plan_and_deliver_2004-11-17.cfm

[2] Sample research from the Standish Group, accessed at http://www.standishgroup.com/sample_research/index.php

[3] C. Gillies, 2005, *IT Governance: A Practical Guide for Company Directors and Business Executives*, CPA Australia

[4] Accessed at http://www.minister.immi.gov.au/media_releases/media05/palmer-report.pdf

[5] Sabel, C. F. 2004, 'Beyond Principal-Agent Governance: Experimentalist Organizations, Learning and Accountability', address to Netherlands Scientific Council for Government Policy (Wetenschappelijke Raad voor het Regeringsbeleid - WRR) 30 January. I thank Professor Ian Marsh for drawing this article to the attention of my Department.

[6] Jugdev, K. and Muller, R., 2005, 'A Retrospective Look At Our Evolving Understanding of Project Success' in *Project Management Journal*, 36: 4.

Section II. Governance, Ownership and Oversight

3. Managing Major Programs and Projects: A View From the Boardroom

Christina Gillies, Non Executive Director and IT Governance Consultant

I sit on a number of boards, including public, private, and not-for-profit, and I can assure you every one is different, however the debate around IT is common to all, and revolves around the question: 'How do we get a grip on this critical corporate asset that has become an integral part of most businesses and government agencies?'

The consequences of project and operational failure can bring a company to its knees, yet in the boardroom we often feel like powerless onlookers rather than informed participants.

We are spending an ever-increasing amount of money on IT and the size of the loss gets bigger every time an IT investment goes wrong. In addition, the demands of privacy legislation and compliance surrounding IT and information security are becoming more and more complex.

The incidence of IT failure continues to grow. Some incidents have had high profile, but many failures in small to medium enterprises cause equal damage with little publicity. However, as a result, we find the attention of regulatory bodies and shareholders clearly focused on what goes on behind Boardroom doors and on the accountabilities of business, audit and finance.

Most board would agree that IT should now be on the agenda, the question is once it is on the agenda, what do we do with it?

For the most part, boards get to understand that a project has problems or is completely off the rails when the damage has been done.

Why? Did the board know about the project? Did we understand the risks? Did we have sufficient information? If we had information, did we understand it?

Today I would like to talk from a boardroom perspective about:

- the relationship between the board and the project;
- IT governance and how it applies to projects; and
- how Boards can realistically get reasonable oversight of IT and know that the company is getting the planned return on investment and risk is being managed.

First, I think it is important that we start with a common view of the boardroom. A board meets formally between six and twelve times a year. Meetings are scheduled to deal with a wide range of corporate governance tasks which range through setting and monitoring strategic direction, monitoring operational performance, financial management, regulatory and compliance issues, shareholder and analyst expectation, compliance with regulatory bodies, internal and external audit, risk management, international reporting standards, *Sarbanes Oxley* [1] ... the list goes on.

The board has a lot on its plate, so projects that come to the board tend not to get a lot of *air time* once approved

The project scene from a Board perspective

Most big spend projects come to the board for approval and are normally accompanied by a well thought out presentation outlining strategic fit, costs and benefits. After long and considered debate the project will most likely be approved, with the board indicating the need for progress reports against budget and plan. Reporting at regular intervals commences and here is where the frustration starts, reports go from 'on time on budget to 'slippage with good reason'.

We have a problem

Boards are required to act in the event of either a huge failure on implementation, or a big delay in implementation causing significant business losses. The investigations commence, no doubt you have all watched or participated. The disturbing fact is the accountable parties are often difficult to identify and the reasons for failure are many and varied.

In the boardroom, the debate goes on about what to do differently and how to avoid repeat scenarios.

The key questions that need to be asked are:

- Who was accountable?
- Were post mortems conducted to identify source(s) of failure?
- Do we have consultant reviews and recommendations?
- Could the problem have been avoided?
- Did the board do its job?

What can be done differently?

Starting in the boardroom, if consultants were engaged to identify some of the problematic issues and behaviours in the boardroom around the treatment of projects, they might come up with a list that looks something like this:

- the board often make decisions in isolation due to lack of context for informed debate;
- the board treats project approval as an event – without strategic context;

- the board relies on the capability of the CIO rather than ensuring good governance is in place;
- the board holds the CIO accountable for the failure of business projects;
- the board digs into detail and misses the big picture;
- project risk monitoring can get lost in the overall risk profile of the organisation; and
- IT is not home ground for most, so the subject can get passed by very quickly.

So what is the answer? What does the board do? The simple answers include:

- implement better IT governance;
- know what questions to ask; or
- apply better project governance.

These sound good, but what do they really mean? And more importantly, will these measures address the problem?

In isolation, I suspect not: in the first place the board has to understand *what* it is governing! The answer lies in:

- implementing better IT governance in the boardroom;
- knowing what questions to ask; and
- implementing better project governance.

Before we look at the scope of IT governance, let's go back to first principles, derived from the *ASX principles of Corporate Governance*. The key phrases to note are:

- 'provide accountability and control systems commensurate with the risks involved'; and
- 'accountabilities, processes and auditable and measurable control'.

This raises questions about what we look at in the boardroom: Gantt charts or decision frameworks and accountabilities?

> **What is the Board's role?**
>
> The Board is ultimately accountable for the company's purpose and the means of delivering it ... and the Board is accountable for the Governance of the organisation:
>
> - 'Good corporate governance structures encourage companies to create value and provide accountability and control systems commensurate with the risks involved'.
> - 'Governance is a set of accountabilities, processes, and auditable and measurable controls that ensure a company is on track to achieve its objectives'.
>
> *ASX Principles of Corporate Governance* [2]

Broadbent and Weill developed a further definition which clarifies IT governance specifically. The key words here being 'IT governance is different from IT management'. Think about who makes the project decisions in your organisation and who is accountable for implementing them.

> **IT Governance**
>
> - IT governance is about who is entitled to make major decisions, who has input and who is accountable for implementing those decisions.
>
> **AND**
>
> - IT governance is different from IT management.
>
> (Broadbent and Weill, 2003; Weill and Ross 2004.)

Broadbent and Weill also recommend that we start in the Boardroom by treating IT as we would treat any other corporate asset and apply the same rigor. For IT this would mean the Board decides strategic direction, ensures accountability, makes policy and monitors and supervises. The board appoints the CEO and the CEO and the board appoints the senior executive team and they are accountable for the management of the company's key assets, including IT.

I think this is where the answer lies for boards in coming to grips with IT – it is not about project detail and Gantt charts – it about decision making, accountabilities and processes (see Fig 1).

Figure 1

Begin by treating your IT assets like any other assets...

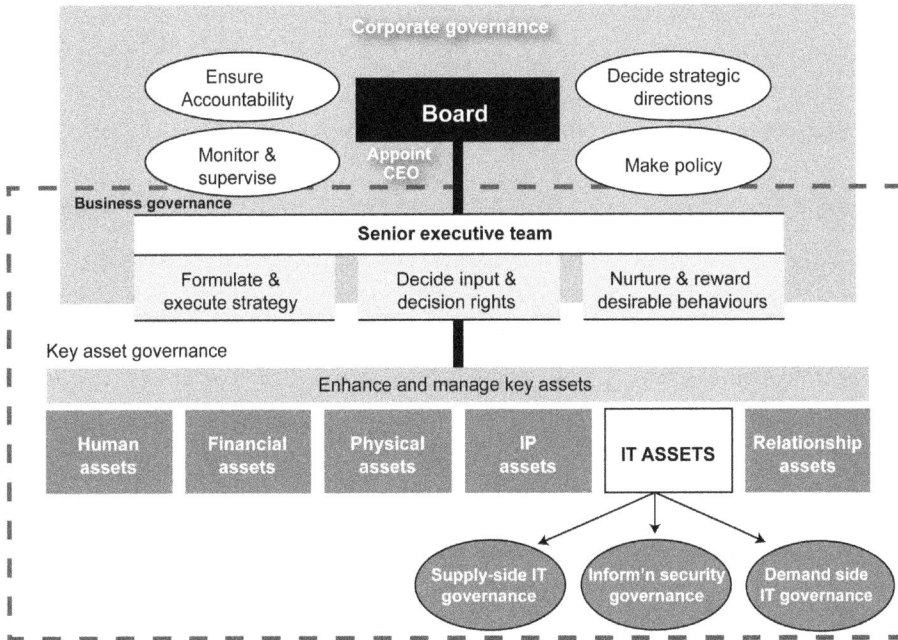

© 2004 M. Broadbent, Apapted from P. Weill & J. Ross, *Don't Just Lead, Govern!: Empowering Effective Enterprise Use of Information Technology*, Harvard Business School Press, Forthcoming and R. Tricker, International Corporate Governance , 1994.

The Finance analogy is a good one

Boards spend a lot of time on financial governance, regulation and compliance and the board along with the auditors; ensure that the accountability structures and processes are in place throughout the organisation to deliver accurate and reliable financial information to the shareholders and stakeholders.

The question is, 'why do we treat IT any differently?'. It would be reasonable to assume that we could have processes and accountabilities in place for the accurate and reliable delivery of IT projects and ongoing operations that can be are easily monitored and audited.

As an asset class, IT is new territory for boards – finance is an age old profession and we can apply many of its disciplines to establish good IT governance practices.

IT governance often gets confused with *IT management* and the CIO gets to be accountable for anything that has the word IT attached to it. As a consequence the business ends up being interested onlookers and expert critics, rather than accountable participants in any business process pertaining to IT.

IT governance includes the Board, the Business and IT

Analysis of many project failures shows that the business parties either did not understand or accept their role, and IT tried to fill in the gap. In a vacuum IT will make the decisions.

Most projects are business projects and over 60 per cent of the work is non-technical IT work, requiring business skills and knowledge such as process design, organisational change, benefits identification, product development, change management and training. As a rule of thumb, well over half of IT project costs are in the business. IT is the enabler, not the driver,

What does it mean from a governance perspective?

Let's work our way through 'who makes decisions' and 'who is accountable for what' through the lifecycle of a project from concept to outcome. It starts in the Boardroom where the Board, with the CEO and executive, sets strategic direction.

The interaction between *business* and *IT* delivers the *Business IT Strategic Plan* which outlines the key initiatives the company will implement over the next 'strategic' period. These initiatives will be converted into projects through the annual business planning process (see Fig 2).

Figure 2

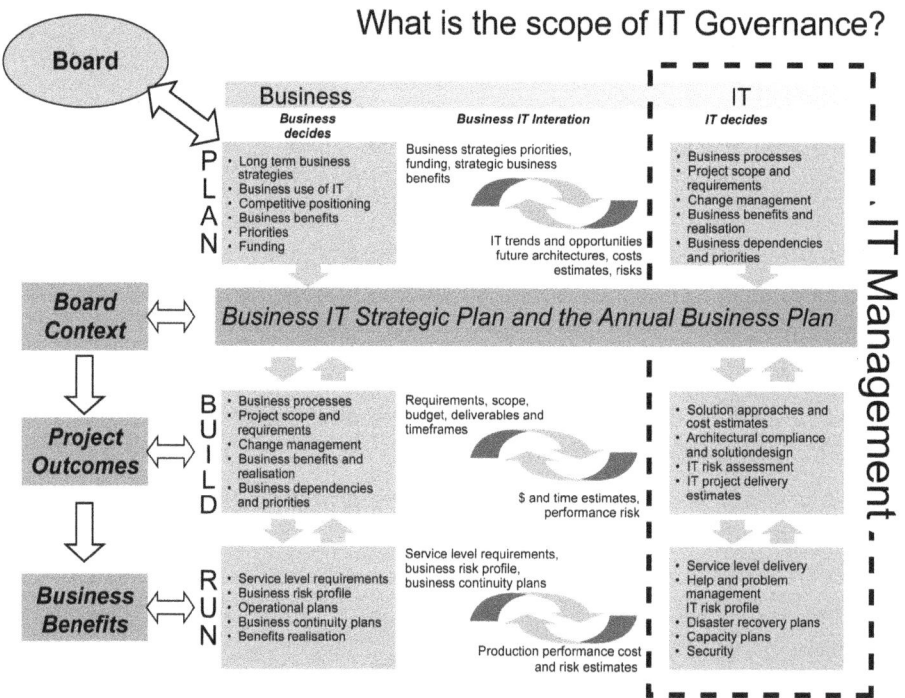

What is the scope of IT Governance?

In the boardroom, the longer term *Business IT Strategic Plan* and the *Annual Plans* are key. The plans are the roadmap for the Board. The plans set the criteria for Board decision-making and the framework for board focus, monitoring and measurement.

The board needs to be confident that governance structures (clear accountabilities and decision making frameworks) are in place throughout the life cycle and that the board focuses on the project outcomes and delivered benefits rather than specific project progress.

The bottom line is that, IT governance is *not* IT management and IT governance is *not* just inside the IT department.

IT accountabilities and processes cross all organisational boundaries and, from a Board perspective, we need to know that these processes and accountabilities are in place and are being rigorously monitored.

Nota bene!

- There is a business decision behind every IT Decision;

AND

- Business must be held accountable for these decisions.

Finally, in the context of IT governance, it is appropriate to talk about the relationship between projects and the board. We tend to put huge emphasis on getting *IT Project Management* right and *project governance* right on the IT side of the equation. Generally, IT project management reports to the CIO and, if the project has a large budget, then the CIO reports to the board. However, what about the management of and accountability for the 60 per cent of the costs and the delivery of the benefits on the business side of the equation? I agree with the statement often made that there is no such thing as an IT project – only *business* projects (see Fig 3).

Figure 3

Business Project Management and Reporting

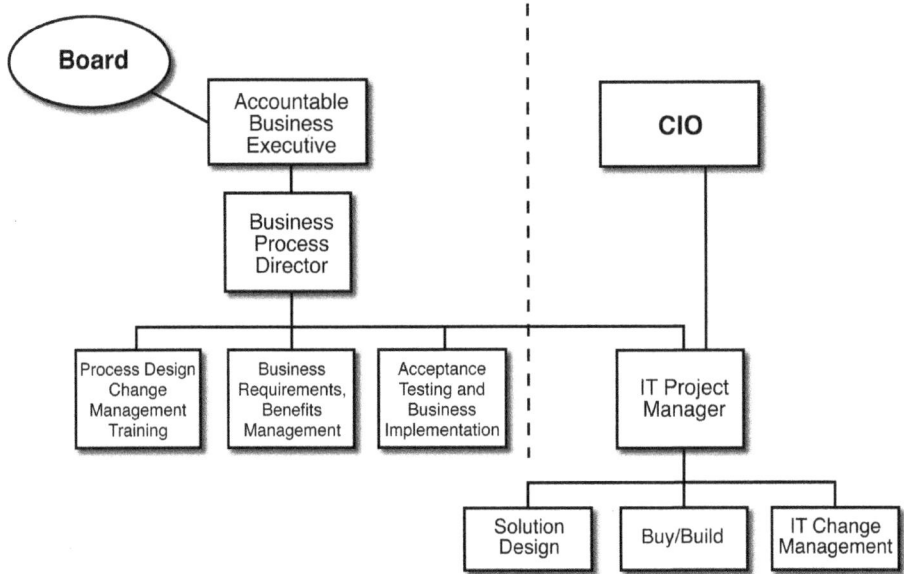

The Business is accountable for delivering the total project

The CIO is accountable for delivering the agreed IT solution to the business

Post mortems on failures tend to come up with common problems including:

* project alignment with strategic direction;
* poorly expressed business requirements;
* complete underestimation of the business effort and impact;
* untested benefits cases; and
* no plan or project to realise benefits.

All of these problems stem from one root cause: poor governance and organisation on the business side of the equation.

In too many organisations we see the IT project manager doing the job of the business project manager and making business decisions he or she is not qualified to make. As I pointed out before, IT will fill the vacuum to get the job done.

I suspect the rate of project failure would diminish significantly if IT project management disciplines were implemented on the business side of the equation and business took on the accountability for the proper business management of the overall project as described in the diagram above.

So why does not this happen? Why is not the obvious solution often implemented?

I do not have a specific answer but here are three relevant observations:

1. Running projects is foreign to most business people and for the most part they are not rewarded for implementing a large business project, they are rewarded for achieving bottom line profits. Business management is put in a conflicting situation often short term (business profit) versus long term (sustainability and growth).

2. Taking people out of line roles to populate a project is an issue. Business managers accountable for the bottom line are loath to put their best staff into projects because the business suffers.

3. Generally a lack of business transformation skills in the business including process design and change management, the people who would effectively scope the strategic business project, and help business management understand what has to be done to achieve the desired outcomes – these people tend to be in IT.

A word on the relationship between the board and IT – and IT projects

Organisations that are heavily depend on IT or which have large organisational change and IT projects to deliver, do not have the *bandwidth* in the boardroom to exercise good governance.

Many organisations establish a board subcommittee for IT, similar to the audit and risk committee and this committee deals with specific IT governance including strategic alignment, prioritisation, approval, delivery, benefits, resourcing and the balancing of supply demand equation. Implementing an IT committee to the board is one way a board can realistically govern IT. And most importantly, it is necessary to ensure that business recognition and reward structures recognise business accountability for project and benefits delivery (see Fig 4).

Figure 4

The relationship between the Board and IT ... and the Project

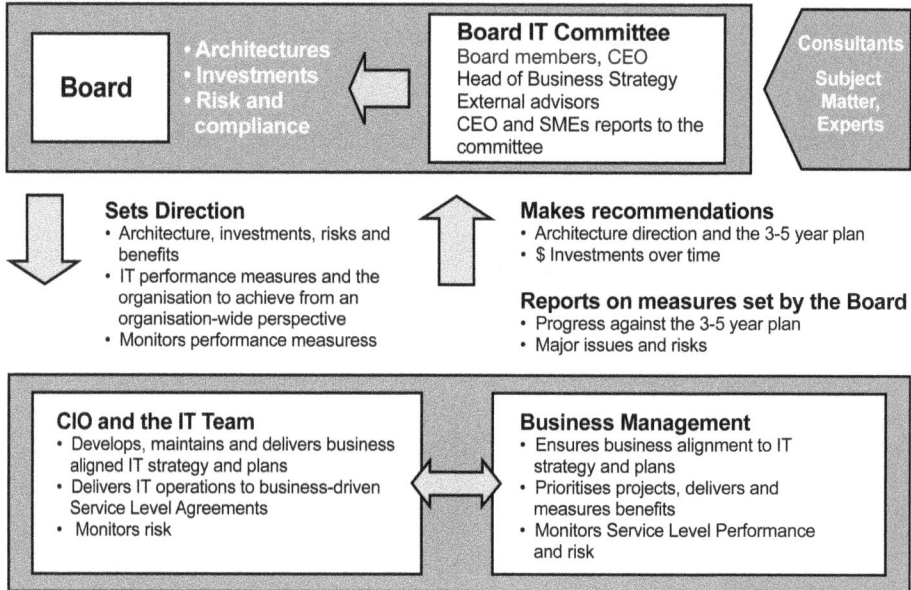

Concluding remarks

In summary the Board must:

- ensure that IT governance is understood and implemented across the organisation;
- differentiate between IT governance and IT Management;
- business management and executives own the management and outcomes of IT projects;
- insist on seeing clear and single point business accountability for strategic projects;
- monitor project risks, deliverables and outcomes rather than technical Gantt chart status reports; and
- ensure that business recognition and reward structures recognise business accountability for project and benefits delivery.

References

Weill, Peter and Jeanne Ross (2004), *IT Governance: How Top Performers Manage IT Decision Rights for Superior Results*, Harvard Business School Press.

Broadbent, Marianne and Peter Weill, 'Effective IT Governance. By Design,' *Gartner EXP Premier Report*, January 2003.

ENDNOTES

[1] The Sarbanes Oxley Act of 2002, also known as the *Public Company Accounting Reform and Investor Protection Act of 2002* is a United States federal law passed in response to a number of major corporate and accounting scandals. For a more detailed explanation, see http://en.wikipedia.org/wiki/Sarbanes-Oxley_Act.

[2] See ASX Corporate Governance Principles at http://www.asx.com.au/supervision/ governance/ principles_good_corporate_governance.htm

4. How Boards and Senior Managers Have Governed

Raymond C Young, Department of Accounting and Finance, Macquarie University

Abstract

This chapter positions IT project governance in the context of corporate governance and IT governance. It has highlighted dysfunctional behaviour and neglect of the governance perspective in project management practice and argued that the traditional measure of success 'on-time on-budget' is inappropriate for IT project governance. It presents a holistic framework of IT projects in the context of an organisation and lists six key IT project governance questions that should be asked by a board (or other approving authority), top managers and executive project sponsors. The detailed framework and questions are being published by Standards Australia as HB280 and they incorporate and extend the best of the IT project governance prescriptions that currently exist.

How Boards and Senior Managers have governed ICT projects to succeed (or fail)

Many boards are aware of the need for more guidance in the area of IT governance (Young and Jordan 2002). This is partly as a result of Sarbanes-Oxley and other international legislative responses to the spate of recent high profile corporate collapses (e.g. Enron, WorldCom, HIH, One-Tel, etc). It is also a reflection of a genuine desire of boards to improve their performance (Leblanc and Gillies 2005).

A number of good guidelines have been developed. These include a recent publication by CPA Australia (Gillies and Broadbent 2005), COBIT produced by the Information Systems Audit and Control Association COBIT 2000) and AS8015 produced by Standards Australia (AS8015 2005). However these guidelines are at focussed on IT governance as a whole and do not elaborate in any detail on how to govern IT projects. This distinction is important because 74 per cent of projects are undertaken as business improvement initiatives enabled by ICT (KPMG 2005) and belong more properly in the domain of corporate governance rather than being pure ICT projects within the domain of IT governance alone.

The objective of this chapter is to complete the picture by extending the IT Governance guidelines to describe how projects need to be governed at a board and senior management level. It summarises the findings of four years of research undertaken collaboratively with Standards Australia. This research has resulted in the award of a PhD thesis (Young 2005) and the findings are being published by Standards Australia as HB280, a handbook with the same title as this chapter.

Success from a governance perspective

A case study of an ERP implementation (Young 2005) highlights a paradox. The project is widely reported as a success because it was one of the world's fastest implementations of this particular ERP system. However, the benefits promised to the board were not realised. The business case stated that a minimum of $6 million of benefits were to be delivered over five years and that the ERP would be upgraded to underpin the organisation's long term strategy. The project ended up delivering only $3 million of benefits and the organisation lost confidence in its ability to realise benefits and deferred the upgrade indefinitely. The disappointment was compounded because management considered that they did everything right: they had formal governance structures (project sponsors, steering committee), formally documented and signed off individual responsibilities for each of the targeted benefits, followed a proper project management methodology, selected appointed a highly motivated high calibre project team, and they had the benefit of experienced consultants to guide the project.

The case study was titled 'how to fail successfully' because it was both a failure and a success depending on ones perspective. The problem it highlights is choosing which perspective to emphasise. Until now the IT vendors, IT professionals and project managers have had the loudest voices and they consciously or unconsciously dominate by abusing their so-called expertise (Thomsett 1989). By claiming to know what was wrong and assuring stakeholders the next technical solution would be the right one (Currie and Galliers 1999), for the last 20 years, the discussion of success has been confined largely to the issue of whether a project has come in on-time on-budget and whether it met specifications (Grindley 1995).

From a governance perspective this is wholly inappropriate. Governance is about both performance and risk (Standards Association of Australia 2003, Australian Stock Exchange 2003) and Hilmer captures the objectives well when he states that the objective is 'to ensure management is focussed on above average returns taking account of risk' (Hilmer 1993). Organisations do not invest in projects so that they can come in on-time on-budget or even to meet specifications! Projects are undertaken to realise benefits e.g. increased revenue, decreased costs, ability to respond faster to changing customer demands, etc. This governance perspective of whether a project is successful or not has been largely ignored. It has been overshadowed by the loud chorus of self interested vendors/professionals (wanting the next project) who claim projects were successes because technical objectives were met, users were satisfied or they came in on-time. A common practice is to choose success criteria only after a project has been implemented and to declare it to be a success based on whatever criteria of success has been met (Boddie 1987). In one perverse example a project team claimed a project was a success because they 'learned not to do that again'. Where is the governance voice asking 'where are the benefits you promised me?'

The pity of this situation is that many reputable people over the years have correctly pointed out why projects fail (Cooke-Davies 2002, Baccarini 1999, de Wit 1985, Markus et al 2000, Lucas 1975). They need to be heard because their perspective is consistent with good governance and they show quite clearly that achieving on-time on-budget or any of the lesser criteria for success (Delone and McLean 2003) does not strongly relate to the realisation of benefits. This has very important implications because the majority of IT prescriptions are focussed on how to do project management better or how to solve a technical issue. These prescriptions alone will not lead to success from a governance perspective; at best they will tend to lead to on-time on-budget. This is illustrated in Figure 1. Almost all the project advice that exists is focussed on the circled aspects of project management labelled *2–Planning, 3–Development or 4–Implementation* (Yardley 2002). This advice has value but the emphasis at a governance level needs to be on clarifying what benefits are being targeted and whether they are being realised *(i.e. 1–initiation and 5–benefit)*. There is very little guidance in this more important area, and what there is, tends to be directed at the project manager. This is wholly inappropriate because a project manager tends to leave at the end of a project, but the benefits of a project (IT projects in particular) tend to be realised some time after a project has been implemented, and is usually related to some degree of organisational change (Markus 1996). The implication is that for a guidance to be effective, it has to be directed at business managers, the owners of a project's outputs.

Figure 1: Project Management success vs. Project success

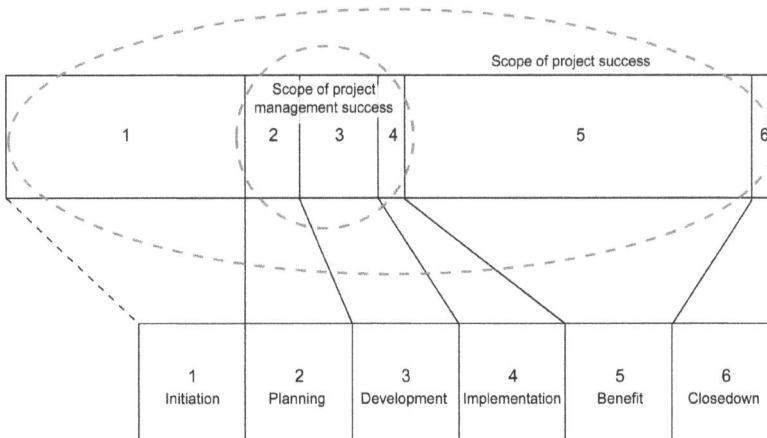

The final section will build on this discussion and present the best advice currently available for boards, top management and executive project sponsors. This audience has the largest impact on whether a project will succeed or fail (Young 2005) and is the right audience for any IT project governance guideline.

How boards and top managers should govern projects

The first half of this chapter has presented the evidence that projects can only be effectively governed when the most fundamental concepts are understood and accepted: (a) Projects are undertaken to realise some kind of organisational benefit, (b) benefits are seldom realised at the time of implementation and (c) benefits tend to be enabled by IT projects but tend only to be realised through accompanying organisational change. Project governance should therefore focus on clarifying what benefits are being targeted, what organisational changes need to be made to realise the benefits, whether the organisation has the capacity (and will) to make the necessary changes, and whether the benefits are being realised. Related to this is the issue of appointing a sponsor to be responsible for realising the benefits and choosing and implementing measure(s) to monitor on an ongoing basis whether the benefits are being realised.

This synthesis of the key aspects of project governance has been rigorously justified (Young 2005) and documented for the general public (Young, forthcoming). Considerations of length prevent a detailed explanation of the justification but it should be highlighted that it confirmed what has long been suspected Markus 1983), that top management support is the most important success factor. Project governance guidelines must therefore focus on top management responsibilities first. The existing prescriptions (e.g. project planning, project management, project staff, user involvement, etc.) do not need to be overly emphasised because they are already in widespread practice (Clegg et al 1997) and the failure statistics show quite clearly that they alone are not sufficient for success Young and Jordan 2005).

It should also be highlighted that the guidelines being presented in this chapter have taken into account all the relevant models of how IT projects deliver benefits (Yardley 2002, Akkermans and van Helden 2002, McGolpin and Ward 1997, Reich and Benbasat 1990, Soh and Markus 1995, Grover and Kettinger 2000, Markus 2000, Sharma and Yetton 2003) and well over 40 different prescriptions for top management support. What was found was that almost all the existing prescriptions focus on the 'hard' dimensions of governance (e.g. steering committees, governance processes, etc) and did not capture the essence of how top managers influenced projects to succeed. It was found that the 'soft' dimensions of governance (e.g. passion to drive change, belief in what is necessary, will to change, listening, communicating and influencing skills) were much more important and that they completely underpinned the effectiveness of whatever hard prescriptions were adopted.

HB280 & AS8016

The project governance advice to be presented therefore represents an attempt to summarise the best of what currently exists within a business/organisational framework (to overcome the deficiencies of the project-centric perspective). It is based partly on Australian Standard AS8015 on the corporate governance of ICT and it has informed the development of Australian Standard AS8016 on the corporate governance of ICT projects. It is more fully described in Standards Australia's handbook HB280.

The framework (Figure 2) shows that projects are undertaken to realise benefits by changing both ICT operations and business processes. It also shows that top management oversee or govern the change project. The framework identified six inter-related project governance activities that must be carried out by boards and top managers. These are:

1. Initiate
2. Evaluate
3. Support – motivation
4. Support – structure
5. Monitor – project
6. Monitor – benefits

Figure 2: IT Project Governance Framework

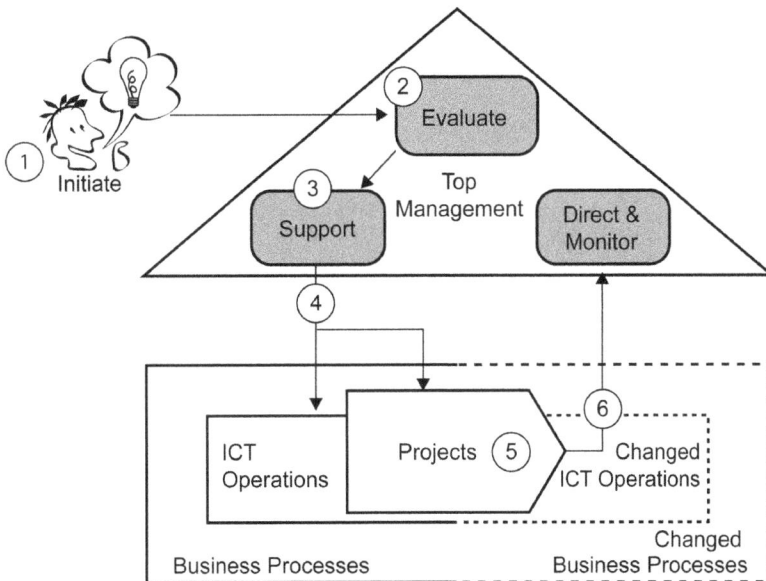

Initiate & Evaluate

The initiate and evaluate stage is traditionally understood as the hard prescription 'to prepare and approve a business case'. A board or other approving authority needs to appreciate that the current practice often treats this process as a formal hurdle to be passed and that 70 per cent of approved business cases are predisposed to fail because they do not address the right governance issues (KPMG 2005).

What needs to be asked at the time of approval is 'What are the expected business benefits?' It must be determined at the outset whether there has been a thorough consideration of how a project contributes to a strategic objective and whether it contributes directly to an objective or whether it contributes to a program of projects which collectively contribute to one or more strategic objectives for an organisation. The approving authority should be very conscious of the tendency to write into a business case whatever words it takes to get funding without any real intention of delivering against the business case. They should be making the subjective assessment of whether the project sponsor genuinely believes in the objectives of the business case and has the passion to drive through the organisational changes needed to realise the promised benefits.

Related to this first question is the evaluation of risk. The greatest risk of any project is that it will fail to deliver the promised benefits (80-90 per cent likelihood of failure) so the key question should be 'How much organisational change is required to realise the benefits?' An approving authority needs to ensure this issue has been thoroughly considered and make the subjective assessment of whether their organisation has the will to make the changes needed to realise the benefits. There are also other risk considerations that should be part of the evaluation (e.g. economic feasibility, technical/operational feasibility, resourcing feasibility, etc), but these questions are really details to help answer the overall issue of how much risk is involved.

Support

The next key governance questions are based on an understanding of how much organisation change is required. Projects that cross more organisational boundaries and require more organisational change are much more difficult because of the larger number of often very powerful stakeholders involved. The approving authority needs to assess 'Who should sponsor the project' (on their behalf and be responsible for delivering the promised benefits)? The sponsor needs not only the passion to drive through the changes, but also the ability, authority and influencing skills to make it happen. In some cases only the CEO is the right sponsor, but an alternative arrangement may need to be made because the CEO may not have enough time to govern all aspects of the project. Quite often this will relate to the reward mechanism that is adopted.

The underlying issue is how to motivate the stakeholders and in particular the sponsor to deliver the promised benefits. Historically projects have not been measured or only measured on the basis of on-time on-budget. This is not sufficient for effective project governance and an approving authority needs to specifically ask the question 'How will the benefits be measured and sponsor rewarded?' In some organisational cultures, performance bonuses are appropriate, in other cultures it may be appropriate to revise the sponsor and other stakeholder's budget to reflect the business case promises, in other cases it might be enough to focus attention by implementing a regularly reviewed board level progress report. The answer to this question should probably be proposed in the business case and it is important for the board to consider whether it is likely to influence stakeholders appropriately given the history of dysfunctional behaviour in the project space. It is almost never appropriate to monitor solely on the basis of on-time on-budget and it is incumbent on the board to insist on a more meaningful measure of success, a measure that is more directly related to the business case benefits.

Direct & Monitor

Once a project has been approved and funded, monitoring occurs at two levels. At the project level, the sponsor monitors on behalf of the board to ensure risk is being managed. At the organisational level the board monitors the sponsor to ensure (s)he is focussed on realising the promised benefits. The board must oversee some mechanism to monitor the sponsor because it would be a clear conflict of interest to have the sponsor monitor themselves. It would expose the organisation to the risk of having the sponsor change the success criteria if the project fails to deliver what was originally promised. This is the current practice and can probably only be overcome with this additional board level discipline. The advantage of having this mechanism is not that targets will cease to change, but that boards will have earlier warning and have more opportunities to cancel projects if circumstances change and make projects unviable. A board must have the discipline to intercede and cancel unviable projects because it is too much to expect a fired-up project sponsor to be objective enough to cancel his own project. The key governance question at an organisational level is 'Are the benefits on target or being realised?' This cannot be answered without some kind of monitoring mechanism (ref Q3) and related to this is the question of whether appropriate interventions are being directed if the benefits are not on target.

Monitoring at a project level is generally not the direct responsibility of the board. This activity can be performed on their behalf by the project sponsor and can be thought of as risk management. The main mechanism for risk management is the preparation of a project plan to manage all the expected risks. Project plans are usually well done by following existing project management guidelines. However, project plans do not plan for unanticipated risks and the majority of projects need to be changed as these unanticipated risks arise (Dvir and Lechler 2004). There is almost always a warning signal (Nikander and Eloranta 2001) and the key from a governance perspective is to ensure the project culture encourages stakeholders at any level to raise issues that may compromise the targeted benefits. This requires at one level a clear understanding by all the stakeholders of what the targeted benefits are, and at another level the willingness to listen and explore the business impact of issues as they are raised. It is particularly difficult with IT projects because the connection between technical issues and business outcomes is often not immediately apparent when they are first raised. The right culture seems to require a sensitivity and humility (willingness to learn) on the part of all stakeholders and in particular on the part of the executive project sponsor, because they set the tone for what will be addressed and what will not. This has many parallels with what is referred to as establishing a whistle-blowing culture within the corporate governance literature (Near and Miceli 1995, Smith and Keil 2003). Once a project has been commenced by following the traditional project management guidelines, the key governance question is "Is the culture right for unexpected issues to be raised?"

Conclusion

This chapter has positioned IT project governance in the context of corporate governance and IT governance. It has highlighted dysfunctional behaviour and neglect of the governance perspective in project management practice over the last 40 years. It has shown that a fundamental part of the solution is to recognise that projects are undertaken to realise some organisational benefit and recognise that these benefits are usually delivered some time after a project has been implemented. This insight was extended to show that benefits are delivered mainly by operational management rather than project management and that the proper audience for IT project governance includes operational managers, board members and top managers in particular.

The chapter argues that the traditional measure of success 'on-time on-budget' is inappropriate for IT project governance. It presents a holistic framework of IT projects in the context of an organisation and lists six key IT project governance questions that should be asked by a board (or other approving authority), top managers and executive project sponsors. The framework and questions are being published by Standards Australia as HB280 and they incorporate and extend the best of the IT project governance prescriptions that currently exist.

Six key IT project governance questions are presented, corresponding to different parts of a project lifecycle.

1. What are the expected benefits?
2. How much change is required to realise the benefits?
3. How will the benefits be measured and the sponsor rewarded?
4. Who should sponsor the project?
5. Are the benefits being realised?
6. Is the culture right for unexpected issues to be raised?

References

Akkermans, H and K van Helden 2002, 'Vicious and virtuous cycles in ERP implementation: A case study of interrelations between critical success factors', *European Journal of Information Systems*, 11(1), p. 35-46.

Australian Stock Exchange 2003, *ASX, Principles of Good Corporate Governance and Best Practice Recommendations*, Sydney.

Baccarini, D 1999, 'The Logical Framework for Defining Project Success', *Project Management Journal*, 30(4), p. 25-32.

Boddie, J 1987, 'The Project Post-Mortem', *Computerworld*, 21(49), p. 77-82.

Clegg, C et al 1997, 'Information Technology: A study of performance and the role of human and organizational factors', *Ergonomics*, 40(9), p. 851-871.

COBIT, *Framework 2000*, IT Governance Institute, Rolling Meadows.

Cooke-Davies, T 2002, 'The "Real" Success Factors on Projects', *International Journal of Project Management*, 2002, 20, p. 185-190.

Currie, W. and B. Galliers eds. 1999, *Rethinking Management Information Systems*, Oxford University Press, New York.

de Wit, A 1985, 'Measurement of Project Success', *International Journal of Project Management*, 6(3), p. 164-170.

Delone, W.H. and E.R. McLean, 2003, 'The Delone and McLean Model of Information Systems Success: A ten-year update', *Journal of Management Information Systems*, 19(4), p. 9-30.

Dvir, D. and T. Lechler, 2004, 'Plans are Nothing, Changing Plans is Everything: The impact of changes on project success', *Research Policy*, 33: p. 1-15.

Gillies, C and M Broadbent eds. 2005, *IT Governance: A Practical Guide for Company Directors and Corporate Executives*, CPA Australia.

Grindley, K 1995, *Managing IT at Board Level: The hidden agenda exposed*, 2nd edition, London, Pitman.

Grover, V and WJ Kettinger 2000, 'Business Process Change: A reflective view of theory, practice, and implications', in *Framing the Domains of IT Management: Projecting the Future Through the Past*, RW Zmud (ed.), Pinnaflex Educational Resources, Cincinnati, Ohio,. pp 147-172, 433-435.

Hilmer, FG 1993, *Strictly Boardroom: Improving governance to enhance company performance*, The Business Library, Melbourne.

KPMG 2005, *Global IT Project Management Survey: How committed are you?*, KPMG.

Leblanc, R and J Gillies 2005, *Inside the Boardroom: The coming revolution in corporate governance*, John Wiley and Sons, Toronto.

Lucas, HC 1975, *Why Information Systems Fail*, Columbia University Press, New York.

Markus, LM 2000, 'Toward an integrated theory of IT related risk control in IFIP TC8 WG8.2', *International Working Conference on the Social and Organizational Perspective on Research and Practice in Information Technology*, Kluwer Aalborg, Denmark.

Markus, LM 1996, 'Change Agentry - The next IS frontier', *MIS Quarterly*, Dec., p. 385-407.

Markus, LM 1983, 'Power, Politics, and MIS Implementation', *Communications of the ACM*, 28(6), p 430-444.

Markus, ML et al 2000, 'Learning from Adopters' Experience with ERP: Problems encountered and success achieved', *Journal of Information Technology*, 15, p. 245-265.

McGolpin, P and J Ward 1997, 'Factors Influencing the Success of Strategic Information Systems', in *Information Systems: an emerging discipline?*, J Mingers and F Stowell (Eds.), McGraw-Hill: London. p. 287-327.

Near, JP and MP Miceli 1995, 'Effective Whistle-Blowing', *Academy of Management Review*, 20(3), p. 679-707.

Nikander, IO and E Eloranta 2001, 'Project Management by Early Warnings', *International Journal of Project Management*, 19, p. 385-399.

Reich, BH and I Benbasat 1990, 'An Empirical Investigation of Factors Influencing the Success of Customer-Oriented Strategic Systems', *Information Systems Research*, 1(3), p 325-347.

Sharma, R and P Yetton 2003, 'The Contingent Effects of Management Support and Task Interdependence on Successful Information Systems Implementation', *MIS Quarterly*, 27(4), p 533-555.

Smith, HJ and M Keil 2003, 'The Reluctance to Report Bad News on Troubled Software Projects: A theoretical model', *Information Systems Journal*, 13(1), p. 69-95.

Soh, C and ML Markus 1995, 'How IT Creates Business Value: A Process Theory Synthesis', in the *Sixteenth International Conference on Information Systems. Amsterdam*, The Netherlands.

Standards Association of Australia 2005, *AS8015, Corporate Governance of Information and Communication Technology*, Sydney.

Standards Association of Australia (forthcoming), *HB 280, Case Studies - How boards and senior management have governed ICT projects to succeed (or fail)*, R Young, (ed.), Sydney.

Standards Association of Australia 2003, *AS8000, Corporate Governance - Good Governance Principles*, Sydney.

Thomsett, R 1989, *Third Wave Project Management*, Prentice-Hall, Englewood Cliffs.

Yardley, D 2002, *Successful IT Project Delivery: Learning the lessons of project failure*, Addison-Wesley, London.

Young, R and E Jordan 2005, 'The Implications of Australian ICT Governance Standards for COBIT', in *2005 IT Governance International Conference*, Auckland, New Zealand.

Young, R 2005, 'Case 2005-2: How Projects Fail "Successfully"', *Macquarie Graduate School of Management*, Macquarie University, Sydney, Australia.

Young, R 2005, 'Explaining Senior Management Support Through IT Project Governance', in *MGSM*, Macquarie University, Sydney.

Young, RC and E Jordan 2002, 'Lifting the Game: Board views on e-commerce risk', in *IFIP TG8.6 the Adoption and Diffusion of IT in an Environment of Critical Change*, Sydney, Pearson Publishing Service.

5. Overcoming the 'White Elephant' Syndrome in Big and Iconic Projects in the Public and Private Sectors

Scott Prasser, Faculty of Business, University of Sunshine Coast

Introduction

This chapter[1] analyses 'big,' 'iconic' or 'mega' projects and their impact on effective project management and also on the effective allocation of funds for priority infrastructure. It is argued that part of the problem of Australia's perceived present infrastructure shortfall is not just the lack of spending on infrastructure as many suggest. Rather, it is as much about the misallocation of spending on 'big' and so called 'iconic' or prestige projects that too often become expensive 'white elephants' requiring considerable post-completion maintenance and support and further wasting valuable resources that could be used elsewhere. Such projects, because of their status, size, and complexity too often disrupt effective project management practices in their original scoping, assessment and implementation and fail to have clear purposes or functions.

This is not a project management or even an infrastructure problem confined to Australia. Concerns about misallocation of funding of big, mega or iconic infrastructure type projects have been observed elsewhere. Flyvbjerg (2003: 3, 9) in his overview of 'megaprojects' around the world noted:

> At the same time as many more and much larger infrastructure projects are being proposed and built around the world, it is becoming clear that many such projects have strikingly poor performance records in terms of economy, environment and public support. Cost overruns and lower than predicted revenues frequently place project viability at risk and redefine projects that were initially promoted as effective vehicles to economic growth as possible obstacles to such growth ... Megaprojects are becoming highly public and intensely politicised ventures ...

Indeed, despite all the techniques now available in project management what is striking, as the *Economist* (2005) recently lamented, was the large proportion of major projects across both the public and private sectors that failed to deliver on time and within budget. The problems that the Australian based firm, Multiplex is having with the Wembley Stadium project in the United Kingdom is a further recent example of poor project management (Australian Broadcasting Corporation 2006a).

Australian Infrastructure Spending and Misallocation: So What's the Problem?

In Australia, many commentators and interest groups argue that there is an infrastructure-spending shortfall. Declining infrastructure spending give some credence to this view. In 1969, 8 per cent of Australian GDP went on infrastructure. By 1975 this had fallen marginally to 7.2 per cent. In 1989 it was 5.5 per cent and down to only 3.6 per cent of GDP five years later (2004). While some blame the Whitlam Labor Government's (1972-75) changed expenditure priorities from infrastructure to welfare services it has been a pattern that was not reversed by subsequent federal governments (EPAC 1985; EPAC 1990). Others contend that the problem has been exacerbated by the drive for governments to run 'balanced' budgets, to accrue surpluses and meet the demands of external credit rating agencies than the real needs of their respective communities (Anderson 2006; Allen Consulting 2003).

A similar decline in infrastructure spending is evident across the states. In New South Wales the public transport crisis has been blamed on low state infrastructure spending. Queensland has seen infrastructure spending as a proportion of Gross State Product fall from 5.4 per cent in 2000 to 4.2 pr cent in 2003 (see also Allen Consulting 2003). Given that Queensland is responsible for key Australian exports like coal that rely on the provision of extensive infrastructure then any shortfall in this area has the potential to adversely affect Australia's overall economic growth. Reports recently commissioned by the Queensland Government have also highlighted inadequate spending on refurbishing energy infrastructure.

Concerns about infrastructure spending have prompted calls from the federal Opposition (Australian Broadcasting Corporation 2005), the business sector and other interest groups for an infrastructure summit (Taylor 2005), special infrastructure councils between business and government and increased spending. Partly in response to these demands the Howard Government in March 2005 appointed the *Taskforce on Export Infrastructure*, headed by Henry Ergas, to assess the issue.

While much of the debate has been about the amount being spent on infrastructure, some have suggested that the problem, especially for the public sector, is more about the need for better targeting and priority setting. Reluctance to accept this view is understandable. It is easier to increase spending than to make choices. It is easier to satisfy everyone by spending more than to disappoint some and set priorities. It is also easier to take broad strategies than to try to set long term goals and stick to them. Such strategic activities are inimical to government and interest groups. As commentator Alan Wood (2004) summed up the issue thus:

> The lack of cost-benefit analysis means a significant amount of the money spent on infrastructure has been wasted ... But establishing whether there is in fact a critical shortage of national infrastructure is impossible to achieve with any degree of accuracy.

Obsession with 'Big', 'Iconic,' and 'White Elephant' Projects

One of the underlying problems of why funds are misallocated is that governments, and, sometimes even the private sector, have sought to develop, 'big', 'iconic,' 'landmark' or 'signature' projects. These projects are characterised by their large physical size (buildings), extent (e.g. events like Olympic or Commonwealth games), costs, and alleged 'iconic,' prestige and symbolic value. Such projects are often linked to the use of technology in their construction, appearance or operations, that too often becomes an end in itself (Scott 1992). The issue, concluded Flyvbjerg (2003: 6) is that 'more and more megaprojects are built despite the poor performance record of many projects'. There is a long record of these project management failures (see Hall 1968 for some earlier examples).

The most notable example of an 'iconic' project is the $400 million Guggenheim Art Gallery in Bilbao in northern Spain. Its aim was to help revive a depressed area by being an 'attraction' in its own right because of its size and stunning building design rather than because of the quality of the art gallery it was built ostensibly to house. Form dominated function. Although its wider regional economic benefits have been less than expected (tourists fly in and fly out rather than stay), many have sought to emulate the 'Bilbao' effect with each new construction more expensive than the one before, but often having only limited success. In Australia the Geelong City Council tried vainly to attract the Guggenheim to duplicate the Bilbao project, while in 2000 the Queensland Government established a taskforce to examine the possibility of developing a 'Landmark Building' in Brisbane. One architect described this obsession with 'big' projects by governments as 'monumental madness' (Hall 2001).

Enthusiasm for 'big' iconic projects also pervades the event attraction industry with nations, states and regions often competing for major events like the Olympic or Commonwealth games, and Formula One car racing to surf life saving carnivals. However, the stated economic benefits of events have often been contested.

At a regional level this is most explicitly seen in tourism based projects that ostensibly act as destination attractions to boost economic growth (e.g. South Australian Wine Centre, Queensland's Stockman's Hall of Fame), have been built.

The problem with many of these 'big' or 'iconic' projects is that they are frequently undertaken more for reasons of prestige (personal, governmental, organisational) than for reasons of function. Broad, ill defined 'public' benefits are usually stressed in relation to these projects rather than any quantifiable economic positives. Recent comments by the organisers of the 2006 Melbourne Commonwealth Games in the light of its less than expected economic impacts (Australian Broadcasting Corporation 2006b) highlights this sort of justification. The emphasis was on the 'profile' the Commonwealth Games gave to Victoria and, Australia, than its tangible economic benefits. Similar justifications have been offered for numerous projects across Australia ranging from Queensland's Suncorp Football Stadium (a world class sporting facility), and the Adelaide-Alice Springs train-link (a symbolic linking across Australia, see Brockman 2005). Even scientific projects like the synchrotron project that Victoria snatched (thankfully) from Queensland in 2000 (Baker 2003) have stressed the broader scientific capacities of such a facility than its direct economic benefits.

'White Elephant' Projects

Many of these 'big,' 'iconic' projects too frequently degenerate into what has been described as 'white elephant' projects (Scott 1992). 'White elephant' projects are not only often large and expensive to build and take longer than originally estimated, but also form and 'prestige' so dominate over function that the project never performs satisfactorily either in terms of stated role, unclear as it is often is, or financially. Moreover, what really make these projects 'white elephants' is that they become expensive to maintain because of poor design, confused role and lack of what may be best described as a 'business case' for their very initiation. These problems are most explicitly seen in those projects in the arts such as art galleries and museums where even in the best of circumstances purpose is often ill-defined and clear criteria for success, difficult to articulate. Such buildings are characterised by a failure to meet anticipated attendance levels and frequently need repeated and expensive refurbishments that often cost more than their original construction. Scott (1992) reminds us of 'white elephant' projects covering many other areas ranging from technology parks, very fast train proposals, spaceports, to the famed multifunction polis.

Of course, 'white elephant' projects are not limited to the public sector. Examples in the tourism industry include the construction by various entrepreneurs during the late 1980s and early 1990s of numerous 'prestige' and 'iconic' resorts up and down the Queensland coast. Most ran at a huge losses and were usually on-sold several times at a fraction of their original development costs. Indeed, many of these resorts today, although apparently viable, are only profitable in terms of their operating, rather than full capital costs (Syvret and Syvret 1996) and have become viable by considerable changes in their scope and range of activities. Development of strata title units for on-selling has been one strategy used for these tourism developments. So numerous are 'white elephant' projects that one commentator suggested they were not limited to one off examples, but had become a 'herd' that pervaded the Australian landscape too frequently (Scott 1992).

Problems of 'Big,' 'White Elephant' Projects and Project Management

The important feature of these 'big' of 'iconic' projects is that many of the key elements of good project management are downgraded, distorted or ignored. These problems include:

- Goals both at the beginning, during and after the project remain unclear and are dominated by post-project justification;
- Overt and covert political goals and political interference in setting the project goals;
- Limited initial or independent evaluation of the project's viability so that expectations are exaggerated, over optimistic, or unspecified;
- Often supply rather than demand driven – the we can build it rather than we need it, often expressed in the 'build it and they will come syndrome,';
- Poor risk analysis;
- Suffer from the 'sunk costs' mentality whereby even if project value is correctly challenged, the project is continued because of previous investments (financial, personal and political);
- Changing specifications during the project implementation phase;
- Budgets are poorly developed and expansive;
- Timeframes are compressed, uncertain, or established to meet election cycles, with little accompanying consultation with relevant stakeholders;
- Poor project governance with little separation between project management and project client resulting in excessive interference in both design, budgets, and management;
- Long lead times so that their full impacts (and costs) are not appreciated till project is nearly or fully completed and frequent changing goals;

Examples of Australian 'White Elephants'

A number of projects undertaken in Australia have highlighted the problems of 'big', 'white elephant', and 'iconic' projects.

The Port Adelaide (SA) Flower farm

The Port Adelaide Flower Farm (PAFF) project illustrates very clearly deficiencies in project conception and definition.

On August 1988, the South Australian Minister of Local Government approved the development by the Port Adelaide Council of a farm on the LeFevre Peninsula for the growing of native plants. The project became known as the 'Port Adelaide Flower Farm'. Work started in September 1988 but, after continual financial losses in operation, the farm closed on 3 August 1995.

PAFF would have created much needed employment in the Port Adelaide area at a time of significant economic recession. The aim was to successfully grow, harvest and export Kangaroo Paw and Geraldton Wax flowers to Japan and Europe with prospects of extending to the North American market (South Australia 1997). The demise of the project after such a short time was a waste of public money and resources.

PAFF provides important lessons, particularly for local government, including:

- PAFF was not only a new venture, but it was a new venture in a fledgling industry. At the time, 'no one had any long experience' in the growing of Australian native plants for the international cut flower trade (South Australia 1997). More importantly, this was not made clear in the project Business Plan. The lesson is that government is not the appropriate vehicle for taking such economic and technical risks, particularly with totally inadequate research and planning;
- The Business Plan as presented to the Port Adelaide Council was deficient in a number of areas. Financial projections were overly optimistic, significant technical issues relating to the varieties of plants to be grown were not addressed, the marketing plan was extremely ambitious and based on dubious information and the risks associated with the flood-prone location for the farm were not identified;
- The Business Plan set out a number of 'wider social, economic and environmental objectives for the project,' but did not relate these to the critical success factor – that the flower farm had to be commercially viable for the project to achieve its objectives;
- Key project sponsors, that is councillors who were in office at the time, were advised by consultants and council officers that the project would be profitable and provide benefits to ratepayers and other key stakeholders. They were not adequately briefed as to the significant risks associated with the PAFF project. Failure to adequately assess project risks is a common theme in the audit reports on public projects.

A key lesson from PAFF concerns the identification of a clear business need to underpin public projects. In the mid to late-1980s councils were being encouraged to be more entrepreneurial and to become less reliant on revenue from ratepayers and government funding. While this may explain to some degree the willingness of the Port Adelaide Council to embark on PAFF it does not justify undertaking such a high-risk venture with totally inadequate research and planning.

Magnesium 'Light Metals' Project (Queensland)

For some time a light metals industry was mooted based in Rockhampton.[2] It was to produce magnesium for use in the car industry. However, no commercial backer came forth. Nevertheless, the Queensland Department of State Development pursued the project, despite advice from a major industry partner of the project's lack of long term viability, and even internal departmental assessment that questioned many of the basis of many of the project's underlying assumptions. This critical view was echoed even more strongly by Treasury assessment. In addition to these economic issues, there were technical concerns. For instance, the technology for the production processes was not satisfactorily resolved even as government funds started to be allocated to the project.

Nevertheless, both the Queensland and federal governments provided over $300m worth of funding, though this was still not enough to attract major commercial interest. The Queensland Government subsequently developed a scheme to attract small investor support. Sadly, the project then collapsed with reputed losses of $450m that has been borne by the two governments and small investors (Cunningham 2006). Ultimately, it appears the project has cost taxpayers alone $240m (Fraser 2004).

The magnesium project reflected all the aforementioned problems of poor project management. It also highlighted what happens when projects are hijacked for 'political' purposes to meet electoral timeframes and how the lack of transparency concerning advice, clothed as it was in the cloak of 'commercial in confidence' arrangements (de Maria 2002) in a public service, in this case the industry department, lacking independence and too eager to please the government rather than analyse.

National Wine Centre, Adelaide

The National Wine Centre in Adelaide was conceived and built for the purpose of focusing national and international attention on the Australian wine industry and South Australia as a principal wine-growing and wine-making state (DiGirolamo and Plane, 2002). The business need as set out in the *National Wine Centre Act 1997* (SA), stated that the purpose of the centre was to conduct a range of functions, 'including the promotion and development of the Australian wine industry and the management of a wine exhibition (South Australia 2002). Under the Act a board of directors was established to control and direct the centre with the board responsible to the appropriate Minister.

Construction of the National Wine Centre in Adelaide was problematical enough with cost overruns and time delays, but those difficulties were overshadowed by the crippling losses that the Centre made on operations subsequent to its opening for business in early October 2001. Reports suggested that the centre was costing South Australian taxpayers $50,000 per week, despite major cost cutting measures (*The Australian*, 2 October 2002). The South Australian Treasurer, Kevin Foley described it as the 'cash-burning' National Wine Centre.

The original business need for the National Wine Centre could be questioned. Less than two years after its opening under State government ownership, operation of the debt-ridden facility was handed over to the Winemakers' Federation of Australia. Eventually, on 1 July 2003, it was taken over by the University of Adelaide for $1 million on a 40 year lease.

This project highlights the issue that public 'icon' projects are frequently launched without an adequately identified business need. In fact, unlike private-sector projects, taxpayer funded projects are frequently conceived and defined to meet a political need or justification while the business need is cobbled together to 'legitimise' the expenditure of significant public funds. This is not to say that a political need is not legitimate, but the 'what?' and 'why?' questions must be clearly stated and agreed by all stakeholders if large, complex projects are to have any chance of proceeding successfully.

Hindmarsh Soccer Stadium Redevelopment Project (South Australia)

The Hindmarsh Soccer Stadium Redevelopment Project (HSSR) provides another important example of the dangers of inadequately defining the business need of a large public project. In February 1994, the South Australian Soccer Federation proposed to the South Australian Government that Hindmarsh Soccer Stadium be upgraded to a 22,000 seat facility at an estimated cost of $22.5 million. The redevelopment received bi-partisan support (SA Auditor-General 2001).

From December 1995, under the sponsorship of the new Minister for Recreation, Sport and Racing, the scope of the project was increased. In the opinion of the South Australian Auditor-General (SA Auditor-General 2001: 3) 'that increase was pursued without proper or adequate due diligence'. In June 2001, the total cost of the redevelopment of the stadium was $41 million.

The business need identified for the redevelopment of the Hindmarsh Stadium was to secure the staging of preliminary matches in the 2000 Sydney Olympic Games. No alternative to the upgrading proposal 'was given serious consideration'.

The subsequent controversy over this project damaged the already embattled Liberal government of South Australia. The difficulty for the government was in providing sufficient justification for the escalation in the scope of the project. True, South Australia acquired a soccer stadium of international standard (with seating capacity for 15,000 spectators) and seven Olympic soccer matches were played there in September 2000. From then on, however, Hindmarsh Stadium was used for a limited number of National Soccer League (NSL) and other soccer matches and trials with an average attendance of less than 3,700 spectators (SA

Auditor-General 2001: 10). Premier and State League finals attracted over 1,000 spectators with other events not achieving this level. Attendance has not exceeded 5,500 and income generated by ticket sales has been far less than required.

The South Australian Auditor-General (2001: 10) concluded that, 'In economic and financial terms, there is a very strong basis for concluding that the Hindmarsh Soccer Stadium Redevelopment Project was not cost-effective'. The political damage that was caused to the government and the relevant ministers was severe. The apparent waste of taxpayers' funds was also significant and increasingly apparent to the general public. So what went wrong?

First, the government committed to the expenditure of substantial sums of public funds without adequate justification (business need). In fact, the Auditor-General could not find that either the Sydney Olympics organisers (SOCOG), or South Australian soccer officials had insisted on the redevelopment of the stadium in the first place. The business need was never clear and the decision to proceed was taken entirely by Cabinet on the recommendations of the relevant ministers.

Second, project management controls existed but were repeatedly ignored (SA Auditor-General 2001: 11). The controls ignored included:

- inadequate feasibility study or cost/benefit analysis was undertaken;
- cabinet submissions recommending major contract and financial commitments were 'inaccurate and incomplete in material aspects';
- an alternative to redeveloping Hindmarsh Stadium was not adequately considered;
- Treasury instructions on project management were disregarded;
- FIFA and SOCOG requirements were inadequately defined. As a result, the required minimum pitch size was compromised to provide for corporate boxes and other non-essentials; and
- ownership and management issues were not resolved before the project commenced.

The main lesson from this case was that proven project management practices should have been followed to avoid fundamental mistakes. There was ample evidence of previous bungled projects, but that experience was ignored. There appears to have been a strong element of groupthink in the South Australian government's management of the Hindmarsh Stadium project. Once work started, error piled on error, despite the then government being in considerable political difficulty. Unacceptable risk was built into the project from the start, but the government apparently failed to identify and analyse the risks and to manage them effectively.

The Millennium Train Project (New South Wales)

The Millennium Train project was initiated on 8 October 1998 when the New South Wales State Rail Authority signed a contract for the design, construction and in-service management of 81 new suburban double-deck electric passenger trains. These became known as the Millennium Train.

While the New South Wales Auditor-General (2003) found that the train represented value for money, the project came in well beyond schedule and considerably over budget. As at June 2003:

- capital costs had increased by $114 million or 24 per cent to $588 million; and
- total project costs had increased by $98.4 million or 17per cent to $658 million.

The Millennium Train project highlights issues concerned with technically complex and innovative public projects. Risk management is an essential element of such projects, particularly where the number of suitable suppliers or contractors is limited. This inevitably places the client (government) in a relatively weaker bargaining position and the supplier in an almost monopolistic position (New South Wales Auditor-General 2003).

The risks of achieving contract delivery requirements in the Millennium Train project were significant but the New South Wales State Rail Authority and the Minister for Transport were not provided with a risk management plan for the Millennium Train. With an aggressive delivery schedule (prompted by government election commitments to meet public transport service goals) the risk was borne disproportionately by the client. As the New South Wales Auditor-General (2003: 5) rightly pointed out:

> ... because governments cannot readily walk away from such projects, even if difficulties arise, they necessarily carry significant risk for such projects. Contract provisions designed to share risk with private sector providers thus need to be robust and enforceable should the need arise.

An essential requirement in this type of project is that government contracting authorities must be both competent and experienced. Private sector suppliers in this type of project are commonly blessed with long-serving project managers and contract administrators. Government managers and staff, on the other hand, frequently occupy their positions for a relatively short period of time and may lack the longevity and experience of their private-sector counterparts with whom they must conduct complex project negotiations involving very significant sums. The New South Wales Auditor-General (2003: 5) stated that:

... the restructure of the New South Wales rail authorities in 1996 and a disruptive purchase environment at State Rail had some effect on the Millennium Train project.

The lesson is that risk management plans must be adequate to protect the public interest. Considerable information on public project management exists in a variety of sources and governments should share expertise and experiences to offset the disadvantage of public-sector employment policies and practices.

Melbourne's Federation Square Project

Federation Square is situated at the corner of Flinders and Swanston Streets, Melbourne. A major 'icon' project, the objective was to redevelop the site of the old Gas and Fuel Corporation building to provide a range of recreational, commercial, cultural and communication facilities. Project performance was anything but satisfactory. The Square was opened in October 2002, two years behind schedule but with all construction still not complete (Vic Auditor-General 2003). From an original estimate of $110 million when the Square was conceived in 1996, the estimated cost rose to approximately $395 million by June 2002 and by May 2003 had risen to $473 million, with work still required for completion.

The Federation Square project had major 'icon' implications and was high profile, located as it is at a major inner-city intersection. Accordingly, any difficulties with the project were bound to become very public and reflect on the project sponsors, the Victorian State Government. The project had its fair share of difficulties including the other original joint venture partner, the City of Melbourne, withdrawing and a requirement to change the status of a function centre from privately to publicly-funded.

In his *Report on Public Sector Agencies* for June 2002, the Victorian Auditor-General (2002: 4.21) reported that:

> Two of the key drivers of cost increases included the adoption of a 'fast track' approach to construction, whereby construction moved ahead of the detailed design work, and the adoption of a complex and unique architectural design.

These issues echo the experiences in the Sydney Opera House project almost 40 years before and yet they still bedevil public projects today. Significant risk was obvious from the start of the Federation Square project, but risk management still appears to have fallen far short of the standard required.

The Auditor-General reported in May 2003 (Vic 2003: 2.236) that the Federation Square Management Pty Ltd's 'quantity surveyors' have progressively identified a number of major risks that could impact adversely on the latest estimated completion cost of the Square. These risks, which represent ongoing project management challenges for the company, involve the potential for higher costs arising from:

- cost variations associated with incomplete documentation;
- trade contract disruption and delay claims;
- managing contractor cost increases (due to further project delays);
- tenancy fit-out costs borne by the project;
- consultants' fees and management delivery expenses;
- unplanned prolongation to completion of outstanding works leading to additional costs for the project;
- latent design defects;
- operator initiated changes (post-completion);
- poor or uncoordinated workmanship; and
- failure to secure full reimbursement for costs of works undertaken on behalf of major tenants.

The main lesson from Federation Square is that project definition and planning processes must be improved, particularly for large-scale, complex 'icon' projects. Prestige projects such as Federation Square have the capacity to create lingering major controversy and to become a sinkhole for taxpayers' funds and maybe the government of the day.

Parallels with Overseas Experience: The Holyrood Building Project, Scotland

There are certain similarities between the Federation Square project and the construction of the new Scottish Parliament House (the Holyrood Project). Holyrood was an extremely difficult and complex project. The Auditor-General of Scotland (2004: 8) commented that, 'in the recent history of Scotland there has not been a public building project as complex or as difficult to deliver as the Holyrood project'.

In 1998, the client (the Scottish Parliament Corporate Body) required the new parliament house to be built by mid-2001. In fact it was not completed until 20 months after that date while cost more than doubled from £195 million in September 2000 to £431 million in February 2004. There is no doubt that the resulting building is an outstanding facility and an 'icon' for the Scotland's new found independence, but the excessive cost could have been reduced by better project management practices.

The Holyrood project was faced with a very tight and far too ambitious construction program. The use of the 'construction management' method of procurement and contracting was identified as the main reason for the significant cost increases. In construction management the design is incomplete and uncertain when construction starts, whereas in normal construction contracting most of the costs are determined at the time when the contract is awarded. In the Holyrood project, the Auditor-General (2004: 6) identified that, 'design development became a process of costing a developing design rather than developing the design within a cost limit'. Given the high degree of uncertainty and complexity associated with the various work packages, there was significant risk. The method of contracting placed most of the burden for risk on the client and not the contractors, and also left open the opportunity for contractors to claim additional payment for time-related cost increases.

One of the main criticisms made by the Auditor-General of Scotland was in regards to project management and control of the Holyrood Project. Leadership and control of the project was apparently not clearly established (2004: 7). The Project Manager (or project director) was the Chief Executive of Parliament who should have been assigned clear responsibility for making decisions about balancing time, quality (performance) and cost. The Auditor-General stated that the client (in effect the Parliament) did not give the project director the responsibility for managing the project. The report states, 'in the Holyrood project there was no single point of leadership and control' (2004: 7). As a result, the parties to the project could not agree on a cost plan and, when a draft plan was prepared in late 2000, 'it was an indicator of the costs rather than a reliable estimate of the costs'.

The Scottish Auditor-General's report identified a number of important lessons for management of public-sector projects.

First, the form of contracting adopted should place the risk on those best able to manage it. Using construction management methods the risks stay with the client and not the contractors. In public 'icon' projects, the temptation exists to err on the side of performance (including prestige and appearance) rather than on cost and time. Consequently, public project sponsors should ensure that appropriate measures including adequate safeguards are put in place to ensure that construction costs do not 'run away' on technically complex projects.

Second, there is a need to 'scrutinise the business need for a project at key stages in its life-cycle, before key contracts are awarded, to provide assurance that it can progress successfully to the next stage' (2004: 8). In project management this can be achieved by establishing key milestones or decision review points where 'go/no go' decisions can be assessed and made.

Third, the Auditor-General of Scotland (2004: 9) recommended that, 'In all projects, care should be taken to put in place a payment regime that provides incentives to contractors to perform against clear targets for quality, time and cost'. In 'icon' projects this is especially relevant, as the practice has often been to chase quality, prestige and performance, by committing funds well over initial cost estimates.

Fourth, there should be a clear distinction between the project sponsor and the project director. This is particularly important where governments are concerned as the political need is so inextricably linked with the business need. If big projects are to be effectively and efficiently managed, there must be a clear separation between project sponsorship and project direction or management. There should be a single point of leadership and control for a project.

Fifth, to ensure that time, cost and performance targets are met, there should be agreed project budgets, timetables and specifications. Key performance indicators that can be used throughout the project to measure performance should support these.

Last, the Auditor-General (2004: 9) emphasised the importance of adequate project planning, particularly in projects where there is significant complexity or technical risk, or when there is a tight schedule for completion. There may be some political cost in establishing more realistic time frames for big projects, but these costs are preferable to the death of a thousand cuts situation experienced by governments as scandal-ridden projects struggle to completion.

The Project Performance Paradox

These cases highlight the very real problems of effective project management in relation to particular types of projects. The paradox is that, despite long experience in public projects, governments (and many private sector firms) repeatedly make the same mistakes.

Why are the lessons of the past apparently not learned and applied in big projects? One a New South Wales may be the 'phenomenon of institutional amnesia' (Pollitt 2000: 5). Seeking to explain 'the declining ability – and willingness – of public sector institutions in many countries to access and make use of possibly relevant past experiences,' Pollitt offers the following causes:

- Constant restructuring of departments and institutions. As governments and/or chief executives change, each one seeks to put their signature on the administration (the 'new broom'), frequently through the vehicle of organisational change. One of the adverse effects of this is that organisations and key people lose touch with experience and/or records that contain important lessons.
- Changes in the form of record keeping, from one media to another, or to a new and different operating system or software, may mean that important information on lessons learned is lost or the location of the information is forgotten;
- The decline of the concept of public service as a permanent career (to which could be added the increasing politicisation of the public service). Thus important project decisions may be made by managers with little or no experience of past debacles and little interest in longer-term perspectives.

- The embrace of 'unceasing, radical change', with its attendant dismissal of the past and primary focus on the future.

Lessons for Project Management: Let's Not Do it!

There are some important lessons in the history of big projects in Australia and overseas.

First, in the conceptual phase of the project it is essential to establish and agree the business need among all stakeholders. Failure to agree and accept the business need is at the root of many poorly performed public projects. The business need should be clearly distinguished from the political need (where appropriate) and offered to stakeholders to obtain consensus *before any planning is commenced*. Where a strong business need cannot be established and agreed, decision-makers would be well advised to resist the temptation to proceed, but to seek alternatives. A valid alternative is always to do nothing. If only the Queensland Government had not persisted with the magnesium project despite the lack of commercial partnerships, then the taxpayer would not have seen several hundred million dollars wasted and small investors would not have lost considerable funds they had so hopefully invested in a project seemingly guaranteed by government.

Second, in setting up a project management structure, there should be a clear separation between the project sponsor (often individual politicians or the government of the day) and the project director/manager. The project sponsor's role is to provide political and other support to the project management organisation, not to manage the project. The project sponsor should prepare a project charter or directive and, in it, assign specific responsibility to the project director for decisions on cost, time and performance. The Hindmarsh Soccer Stadium Redevelopment Project provides clear evidence of the problems when this distinction between project sponsorship and management is blurred.

Third, there should be increased emphasis on project definition and planning to ensure that adequate consideration is given to how the project objectives can best be achieved. The temptation to plan on the basis of 'ready, fire, aim' should be avoided. Additional time spent in planning may not satisfy the need to appear to be doing something, but it can provide an opportunity to consider how best to award contracts, how to deal with complex, technically demanding projects and how to identify, assess and manage risk. The Federation Square project could have benefited from these basic guidelines.

Last, there should be an improvement in the procedures for identifying, assessing and managing risk in big projects. A common thread of numerous adverse reports by the respective auditors-general is inadequate risk management. Measures for avoiding political embarrassment, an area where the public sector frequently outperforms the private sector, are an inadequate replacement for disciplined project risk management techniques. There needs to be more realistic assessment of the risks involved in big projects, not least because the costs of doing otherwise are so great. The Adelaide Port Flower Farm highlights the need for this risk analysis.

Some Reforms

All these issues highlights the need for some fresh thinking about the way new major project proposals are assessed so that they do not turn into 'white elephants'. Flyvbjerg *et al* (2003: 7) concluded in their international survey of poor megaproject management that:

> ... good decisions making is a question not only of better and more rational information and communication, but also of institutional arrangements that promote accountability ... We see accountability as being a question not just about periodic elections, but also about a continuing dialogue between civil society and policy makers and about institutions holding each other accountable through appropriate checks and balances.

It seems that existing processes and institutions and now accepted norms in public sector management are no longer adequate in ensuring effective project management of major public infrastructure. Auditor general reports, as highlighted in this chapter, do provide useful insights into what went wrong. However, these evaluations are necessarily after the event. Nor can exhorting elected officials to act in the public interest be effective. Such exhortations are like asking children put in charge of a sweet shop not to eat the merchandise! Treasuries certainly have the capacity to do the analysis, but treasuries are part of the bureaucracy and face all the limitations that this imposes as has been discussed above. As Ian Lowe (1992:142) suggested:

> The crucial lesson to be learned (from white elephant projects) ... is that we ought to be able to do a better job of foreseeing problems. The need is for improved foresight: an enhanced ability to analyse the future impacts of our decisions and actions.

Others too, have stressed the need for improved long term policy development processes in Australia, but these suggestions have focussed on the broader policy framework (Marsh and Yencken 2004). The need, it seems, is to provide some brake of the 'Let's do it' approach in project initiation which while possibly acceptable for entrepreneurs like Richard Branson of Virgin Airlines fame, are so patently unsuitable for major long term public sector projects, and one suspects most private sector ones.

While Lowe stresses the need to challenge some of the underlying rationale of many projects such as the obsession with growth and faith in technology, what is also needed is some institutional renovation to better manage infrastructure issues in general. This is especially needed at the state level where many infrastructure decisions are made. Also, at the state level there are fewer and less transparent processes of decision making, accountability and advice giving than nationally.

Indeed, in many ways the problems in effective project management now so evident in the public sector are similar to those that surrounded industry assistance at the beginning of the 1970s. In those times there was a lack of any real independent and public evaluation process of what industry assistance was really costing the Australian public both directly in the form of subsidies and indirectly in terms of extra costs to consume certain products. The solution was the establishment in 1973 by the Whitlam Labor Government of the expert based, independent Industries Assistance Commission (IAC), which has now become the Productivity Commission Notwithstanding the potential narrowness of IAC's economic analysis, it gave the Australian public some insight into the real costs of assistance across both the manufacturing and agricultural sectors through a very public and consultative process (Rattigan 1986; Warhurst 1982). John Howard (1976:12), when Minister for Business and Consumer Affairs in the Fraser Government summed up the rationale for the IAC:

> Most economic issues involve some kind of dilemma, some kind of striking a balance and that is one of the reasons why it is important as part of the process of arriving at decisions on industries, that you have an independent advisory body such as the IAC to give government advice.

While different state business groups have proposed an infrastructure council composed of representatives of government and business, this smacks of decisions behind closed doors between consenting interest groups. Such an infrastructure council would lack any sense of independence or have any real research and analytical capacities.

Another suggestion to tackle both the infrastructure selection issue, to improve choice, ensure public involvement, enhance accountability and potentially improve subsequent project management is for an expert, statutory base state priorities commission.

Such a body would audit a state's present infrastructure needs, identify gaps, and make public recommendations for improvement. Done annually, this would provide a report card on a state's infrastructure needs and their overall performance. In addition, such a commission could evaluate openly any new proposals for new infrastructure or events and to provide a means for effective consultation with both the business and wider community. It could provide government with a convenient post box to which complex proposals could be despatched and so give everyone time to think, before acting. The government could lay down priority areas and criteria that the commission would use to determine priorities and make assessments.

Of course, a priorities commission could only provide advice to governments – elected officials would have to make the final decisions. Nevertheless, such a process would give governments a better means of making choices from a range of projects that maximise benefits. It would also provide greater public participation in decision-making, improve accountability and assist in more efficient allocation of taxpayers' funds on big projects.

Conclusion

'Iconic', or 'big' projects are an important component in infrastructure. They can provide significant benefits and focus, but not if they are mismanaged and do not meet clear performance criteria. Public cynicism towards politicians and public organisations is reinforced when taxpayers see examples of where more and more of their funds are seemingly squandered on projects that run seriously over cost estimates and well exceed scheduled completion dates.

More importantly, the failure of 'big' projects to meet performance criteria through poor project management can mean that an otherwise important 'icon' can present an ongoing reminder of the failure and inefficiency of public administration. Successful projects on the other hand, while often not attracting the same degree of spectacular media reporting as problematic projects, can deliver the lasting economic and social benefits that were intended and build a positive image for a government.

'Good' government is not just about having grand visions and building 'big' projects. These have their place, but ultimately, 'good' government is about allocating funds in a timely manner to maximise benefits and meet real needs. Project management is tools to assist governments achieve these goals, nothing more and nothing less. Project management cannot make up for poor policy choices and craven political behaviour. However, adherence to project management principles and processes can help improve public policy outcomes if it accompanied by the same features that improve all aspects of accountability – transparency and integrity of process. Too often in the past the 'Let's do it' approach, the obsession with project prestige and the electoral cycle driven timeframe has so overwhelmed project management as to render it useless. The result has been poor project conception, design and execution, resulting all too often in 'white elephant projects. This is bad policy and ultimately bad politics when the money runs out, the roads become clogged and taxes have to be increased to pay for urgent and overdue infrastructure repair.

References

Auditor-General of Victoria 2002, Report on Public Sector Agencies, June 2002, Part 4 - Infrastructure, including Local Government, http://www.audit.vic.gov.au/reports_mp_psa/psa0204.html#P22_480

Australian Broadcasting Corporation 2005, 'Beazley Says Govt has Missed Building Up Nation's Infrastructure,' *AM*, Wednesday 2 March, http://www.abc.net.au/am/content/2005/s1313908.htm

Australian Broadcasting Corporation 2006a, 'Wembley Stadium Delays Fuel Controversy', *AM*, Saturday 1 April, http://www.abc.net.au/am /content/2006/s1605511.htm

Australian Broadcasting Corporation 2006b, 'Games Business Upturn Disappoints Some', *AM*, Saturday 25 March, http://www.abc.net.au/am/content/2006/s1600095.htm

Allen Consulting Group 2003, *Financing Public Infrastructure in Queensland*, December, Melbourne.

Anderson, G. 2006, 'The Loan Council, International Credit Rating and the Australian States – The Implications of State Borrowing for Fiscal Federalism', paper presented to the *Public Policy Network Conference*, Curtin University of Technology, February, Perth, http://www.ssn.flinders.edu.au/spis/ research/2006papers/GeoffAnderson-ConferencePaper.pdf

Armitage, C. 2005, 'Beware White Elephants', *The Australian*, 23 March.

Audit Scotland 2004, 'Management of the Holyrood building project', http://www.audit-scotland.gov.uk/publications/index.htm

Bachelard, M. 2004, 'Capital Projects Hit a Brick Wall', *The Australian*, 10 July.

Baker, R. 2003, 'Labor "lying" over Synchrotron Plan', *The Age*, 26 August.

Brockman, M., 2005, 'Train Link Fails Trade Test', *The Australian*, 26 February.

Cunningham, M 2006, 'Achieving Sustained Economic Growth', in D. Moore, *The Role of Government in Queensland, Report to Commerce Queensland, May 2006*, Brisbane, pp. 42-56.

DiGirolamo, Rebecca and Plane, Terry 2002, 'Wine centre 'burns cash'', *The Australian,* 15 March 2002, p. 4.

Economic Planning Advisory Committee (EPAC) 1985, *Public Sector Expenditure in Australia*, AGPS, Canberra.

EPAC 1990, *The Size and Efficiency of the Public Sector*, AGPS, Canberra.

Flyvbjerg, B., Bruzelius, N., & Rothengatter, W. 2003, *Megaprojects and Risk: An Anatomy of Ambition*, Cambridge University Press, Cambridge.

Fraser, A. 2004, 'Mag Deal Costs the Taxpayers $240m', *The Australian*, 26 March.

Hall, P. 1968, *Great Planning Disasters*, Methuen, London.

Hall, R. 2001, 'Monumental Mess', *Courier-Mail*, 1 June.

Harris, T. 1999, 'The Auditor-General's Last Stand', *Canberra Bulletin of Public Administration*, No 93, October, pp. 1-3.

Johnston, J. 1999, 'Serving the Public Interest: The Future of Independent Advice', *Canberra Bulletin of Public Administration*, No 91, March, pp. 9-18.

Lowe, I. 1992, 'Learning from the Elephants: Toward a Rational Future,' in P. Scott (ed.), *A Herd of White Elephants: Some Big Technology Projects in Australia*, Hale and Iremonger, Sydney, pp.142-153.

de Maria, W. 2002, 'Commercial-in-Confidence: An Obituary to Transparency,' *Australian Journal of Public Administration*, Vol 60, No 4, pp. 92-109

Marsh, I., and Yencken, D. 2004, *Into the Future: The Neglect of the Long Term in Australian Politics*, Australian Collaboration and Black Ink, Melbourne.

Moore, D. 2006, *The Role of Government in Queensland: Report to Commerce Queensland, May 2006*, Brisbane, <http://www.ipe.net.au/ipeframeset.htm>

New South Wales 2003, *Auditor-General Audit Report*, Performance Audit, 2003, *State Rail Authority, Millennium Train Project*.

Pollitt, C. 2000, *Institutional Amnesia: A Paradox of the Information Age?*, in *Prometheus*, Vol. 18, No. 1, 2000, pp. 5-16.

Rattigan, A. 1986, *Industry Assistance: The Inside Story*, Melbourne University Press, Melbourne.

Scott, P. (ed.), 1992, *A Herd of White Elephants: Some Big Technology Projects in Australia*, Hale and Iremonger, Sydney.

South Australia 1997, *Report of the Auditor General, Special Audit Report - Port Adelaide Flower Farm*.

South Australia 2002, *Report of the Auditor-General for the Year ended 30 June 2002*, Part B, Vol III.

South Australia 2001, *Final Report of the Auditor-General on the Hindmarsh Soccer Stadium Redevelopment Project*, Part 1, Adelaide, Government Printer.

Syvret, P., and S. 1996, 'Williams Dives into Troubled Waters,' *Australian Financial Review*, 22 July.

Taylor, L. 2005, 'Push for Infrastructure Summit,' *Australian Financial Review*, 7 March.

The Economist 2005, 'Overdue and Over Budget, Over and Over Again', 9 June.

Warhurst, J.,1982, *Jobs or Dogma? The Industries Assistance Commission and Australian Politics*, University of Queensland Press, St Lucia.

Wood, A. 2004, 'It is Worth Spending Time to Find Facts,' *The Australian*, 13 November.

ENDNOTES

[1] This chapter originally began with a focus on regional issues. Special thanks is given to John Wilson who co-authored the original draft.

[2] This case study is based on a report Mike Cunningham, a former Queensland State Treasury official, in D. Moore, *The Role of Government in Queensland: Report to Commerce Queensland, May 2006*, Brisbane.

Section III. Organisational Alignment
— Organisational Change

6. Organisational Alignment: How Project Management Helps

Abul Rizvi, Department of Immigration and Multicultural Affairs

As many of you will know, in February 2005 the Minister for Immigration and Multicultural Affairs, Senator Amanda Vanstone commissioned Mr Mick Palmer to investigate the circumstances of the immigration detention of Ms Cornelia Rau.

During the process of this investigation, another report, by Mr Neil Comrie, into the Circumstances of the Vivian Alvarez Matter, was also commissioned.

Mr Palmer delivered his report in July 2005 and Mr Comrie in October. These reports were highly critical of the Department and made a number of recommendations – most of which addressed shortcomings they saw in DIMA's culture and organisational practices.

Both reports found DIMA wanting on a number of fronts and have lessons perhaps for many government agencies about:

* communication;
* structure & governance;
* accountability;
* contract management;
* case management;
* IT Systems;
* identity issues;
* quality decision making;
* leadership; and
* training.

Late last year the Government accepted the broad thrust of the findings and recommendations in the Palmer Report and the Comrie Report. This kick-started a major organisational change process.

The change agenda we are undertaking is substantial. It is across the whole department, and has to be carried out against a background of keeping the business going – and what a business it is.

In last 12 months DIMIA has

* responded to more than 1.6 million telephone inquires;
* facilitated the arrival of more than 5.7 million temporary entrants;

- granted visas to over 12,000 migrants. Granted humanitarian visas and then settled more than 11,500 refugees and people in humanitarian need;
- heard around 4,800 applications for AAT or judicial review of Departmental or tribunal decisions; and
- been mentioned at least 31,750 times on the TV or radio and over 37,800 in newspapers.

Everyday, DIMA staff have to make decisions which can dramatically affect peoples' lives. We recognise that this is a big workload on which to place such a substantial change agenda. We are doing this in the glare of public scrutiny and in the face of competing (and often conflicting) expectations about what it is that DIMA should do.

DIMA business is complex and diverse. We range from working across government on counter-terrorism and border security, playing our part in the international response to humanitarian crises (in the short and medium term), promoting the benefits of cultural diversity in the Australian community, helping new migrants become active and productive members of that community and contributing to economic growth by facilitating the entry of people to fill skilled positions or who come as tourists or as students.

We deliver services on behalf of a number of other agencies – health, education, industry, security and community services. These other agencies require different approaches and have different objectives and we have to balance each one against the other.

The Australian community also has different expectations of our work. Business wants easy and seamless access to skills and a competitive environment for attracting tourists and students. Families want to be able to bring their loved ones to Australia. Some sectors of the community think we should do more on the humanitarian front, while other sectors want to feel assured that we administer a strong immigration policy with inbuilt safeguards against introduced disease, abuse and possible criminal activity.

Measuring the success of the changes in the light of these competing objectives will not be easy.

So, how do we go about doing this?

To respond properly to the Palmer and Comrie reports, and to meet the expectations of the Government, the Parliament and the wider community, we have identified that we must do three things:

- become a more open and accountable organisation;
- deal more fairly and reasonably (and lawfully) with clients; and
- have staff that are well trained and supported.

Being more open and accountable

Since the Palmer and Comrie reports, the Minister has twice directly and personally addressed all DIMA staff on the Government's expectations of the reform agenda. She continues to encourage staff to share ideas for change and improvement. The Secretary has continued his practice of communicating twice weekly with all staff in the Department and delivering keynote addresses, updating staff on current issues and achievements and seeking their input and ideas.

The Senior Executive has travelled to all of our capital city offices in Australia and a number of our overseas posts to discuss the reform agenda and hear first hand the impact it is having on our state and territory and overseas operations. We have continued to engage with our clients, critics and other organisations, particularly those who have a role in scrutinising the activities of the Department.

We have very constructive relationships with the Commonwealth Ombudsman's Office and the Office of the Federal Privacy Commissioner and their feedback is highly valued. A privacy training strategy has been developed and training has commenced. The restructure of our National Office is complete and new and stronger governance arrangements are in place.

A whole range of appointments have been made to Senior Executive Service and State Director positions. The new Values and Standards Committee is up and running. With its three external members (from the Ombudsman's Office. The Australian Public Service Commission and the community), it is well placed to ensure that the Department is meeting community expectations. An expanded Audit and Evaluation Committee, with an external chair, is providing rigorous oversight of the enhanced internal audit program.

For the first time in many years, there has been a comprehensive staff survey to assess the views of staff and to provide a benchmark for monitoring change. The report will be available shortly and the Department's executive will be taking a strong personal interest in developing the responses to staff ideas and concerns.

Being more fair and reasonable with clients

Improving client service must be a key focus of our efforts. Client Satisfaction surveys and Values Creation Workshops, where DIMA staff must actively listen to the views and concerns of clients, will be conducted in the early part of this year. This will allow us to better understand the differences between client groups and their needs and will allow us to respond to systemic concerns that clients raise.

DIMA's National Office in Canberra is a long way from the service counters where we interact with our clients. We have therefore also asked all of the senior executives in DIMA to spend some time in operational or service delivery parts of the Department in the first half of this year to get first-hand experience in client service.

The draft Client Service Charter released last year for public comment is being finalised at the moment to take account of the largely positive feedback. It will set out clearly the expectations for both clients and DIMA staff. Better arrangements are being put in place for handling client feedback and providing clients with choice about how they connect with the Department.

Every month the Secretary recognises a member of staff or team through the Secretary's Award for Service Excellence (ASCE) on the basis of positive client feedback.

We have further built on improvements made last year to health service delivery for immigration detainees, in particular at Baxter with other centres to progressively follow over coming months.

All detainees are screened for mental health problems using two internationally recognised screening tools on admission and they are routinely and regularly screened after that. Mental health plans are developed for any detainee who screens positive. We are currently finalising the membership of the Detention Health Advisory Group, which will provide expert professional health advice on health service standards and research projects to improve health outcomes for people detained.

Physical improvements at Baxter and other immigration detention centres have been made, well beyond the recommendations made in the Palmer Report. *The Baxter Plan*, launched by the Minister in September 2005, included development of the Interim Visitor Processing Centre, which opened in December, and sporting facilities. Self-catering options have improved and further design options to open up the closed compounds, develop a new primary health care facility and a new central cafeteria have been developed.

Considerable progress has been made in developing a new, holistic, case management framework for the case management of clients with exceptional circumstances. In conjunction with case management, DIMA is developing a 'community care' pilot in Sydney and Melbourne to trial and evaluate a model where case management is supported by access to additional community services to vulnerable clients.

Appropriately skilled and qualified case management staff have been recruited, trained and are now working in our Sydney and Melbourne Offices. Our compliance activities have been properly criticised and will continue to be criticised in those cases which come to light where people have been improperly determined to be unlawful and detained.

Clearly, DIMA officers exercise extraordinary powers and we have to be extraordinarily careful in our decision-making where the outcome can be the deprivation of liberty. We are making committed efforts to ensure decisions to detain are only made where there is no realistic alternative, and that they are subject to ongoing review. We will continue to place a strong focus on training for staff in these operational roles, and in ensuring there are strong accountability mechanisms in place.

This is especially the case where we are faced with people who are not easily identified, either because they do not wish to cooperate, have mental health issues or for other reasons. These difficulties do not release us from our obligation to make each decision on the basis of law and the facts and to review those decisions regularly.

Having well trained and supported staff

Enhanced training for staff is the centrepiece of the reform agenda for DIMA. Plans for the new College of Immigration, Border Security and Compliance are on track to commence training in mid-2006.

In the meantime, specialist technical training is being provided, addressing areas such as making decisions on the basis of 'reasonable suspicion', using all available methods to identify people, issuing search warrants and case management. These courses will ultimately become part of the College curriculum.

Enhanced training in ICSE, DIMA's main processing system, was rolled-out in November and December last year and further modules in this e-learning program are being delivered in 2006.

Leadership, values, standards and management skills were also areas of concern identified by both Palmer and Comrie and a new National Training Manager was appointed in early December to develop and lead the new department-wide training programs in these areas.

The Executive Leadership program commenced delivery in September last year. All DIMA executive level staff will undertake this course. A development program for lower-level managers, a *Fundamentals of Leaderships Program* and enhanced induction training are all being delivered to staff.

The significant systems issues identified by Palmer and Comrie are being addressed. Independent reviews of DIMA's business information needs, systems governance, the IT platform and records management arrangements have been finalised and their recommendations are currently being considered. Pilot projects to better support DIMA staff in the field have also been completed, including using Blackberry technology to connect remotely to the ICSE system and trialling a field office. These pilots have shown acceptable results and will be considered for further development.

If implementation is to be driven hard it, is important that there be clarity of purpose, powers and relationships and transparency of authority, accountability and disclosure. Project and program management techniques help do this. At one level project management is a discipline, but at another level it is just common sense. It is about setting objectives and planning how to meet them

We have recognised this and have incorporated in our new structure a *Program Services Office* (in the Strategic Policy Group) to help business owners develop plans and to monitor progress on the implementation of the Palmer Projects and other key initiatives.

To ensure that DIMA staff, including those in the *Senior Executive Service* understand the principles of project management, a series of information sessions and one and two day workshops are underway. Response to project training has exceeded our expectations and regular project management training will be part of the long term training strategy.

Regular reports are fed up to the Executive Management Committee and to the Cabinet Implementation Unit (CIU) of the Department of the Prime Minister and Cabinet.

We are also required to report to the Minister on progress on a regular basis and we are required to report progress to Parliament in September 2006.

We could not do this successfully and honestly without a program management approach.

Our success in achieving change will be measured by improvements in the confidence the Department is able to inspire in the broader community, including recognition of the benefits delivered by a well managed and administered immigration program.

Success will be reflected in the fact that our decisions are fair and reasonable, that implementation of policy is open and there are clear lines of accountability through the DIMA executive, to the Minister and Government and to the Parliament and the broader community.

Measuring our success must take place on a couple of different planes. Our overall success will be measured through things such as:

- the community's acceptance of the level and nature of our immigration program;
- the recognition of the net economic benefits delivered by a well managed immigration program, including how it assists in Australia's economic growth through improved productivity and export performance;
- the settlement success of migrants; and
- our contribution to border security by preventing people with major health or criminal issues from entering Australia.

The success of the Palmer Plus program of work can be measured by:

- positive feedback from our clients (even if they do not like the decision, do they feel that they have been treated fairly and reasonably throughout the process?);
- easier and faster access to information by the staff and the public;
- faster resolution of identity issues;
- reduction in visa *overstayers* through improved education of both visa holders and employers;
- improved processing times for complex cases;
- positive audit and Ombudsman reports; and
- feedback from staff on whether the changes are making it easier for them to do their jobs in a fair and reasonable way.

Change does not come easily to large organisations – it takes time and commitment. And while under no illusions about the scale of the task, we are confident that we have the capacity to deliver on the change agenda. We shall be judged on what we have achieved.

7. 'Crazy Thought or Creative Thinking': Reform in the Real World

Patricia Scott, Department of Human Services

Introduction

In this chapter, I intend to focus on the following;

- practical ways to drive reform;
- ensuring alignment to government objectives;
- exerting influence when you cannot simply use control; and
- how to use cultural differences between agencies to speed reforms.

Backgrounder to the Department of Human Services

The Department of Human Services (DHS) occupies a unique space. It is chiefly concerned with issues affecting service delivery and improving the connection between policy and service delivery so that we get better outcomes. The core department is tiny – around 75 permanent staff. But *small* does not mean *insignificant*, as we are working with six agencies that employ 37,400 staff in 850 locations around Australia delivering over $90billion of government services and transfer payments. We are also working on some significant proposals including a Health and Social Services *Smartcard*, and on the implementation of key elements of the government's agenda, including *Welfare to Work*.

Human Service agencies have to deliver on two key programs:

- Welfare to Work; and
- changes to the Child Support formula currently under consideration by the Government

The six agencies are:

- Centrelink with 6.5m customers;
- Medicare Australia has all Australians as customers with 20.5 million customers;
- Child Support Agency with 1.3 million separated parents;
- Health Services Australia;
- CRS Australia, with 43,000 customers; and
- Australian Hearing with 200,000 customers.

It would be a mistake to imagine that Human Services is a monolith – a mega department. Decisions are not taken by one individual or one board or one executive. DHS seeks to *influence* the agencies and the policy departments. A unique feature of DHS is that it does not have financial responsibility for the great bulk of the operating or program expenditure of the agencies under its umbrella.

The Minister sets the directions for each organisation and, in my case he has set out a series of objectives for 2006 against which he will assess both my and the department's performance.

In relation to Centrelink and Medicare Australia, which are separate entities under the Financial Management Act, the Minister has exchanged letters with the CEO of Medicare Australia and the CEO of Centrelink that set out the Minister's expectations and, in return, how the CEOs propose to meet those expectations. This exchange of letters is in accordance with the Uhrig reforms which are now moving through the Australian Government.

Health Services Australia and Australian Hearing are bodies under the Commonwealth Authorities and Companies Act where the two separate Boards have financial responsibility.

DHS as a legal entity does include two divisions which are separately and publicly identified given their strong and separate stakeholder interests: CRS Australia and the Child Support Agency. Those two agencies do not have a great deal in common and it would be a mistake to treat them as homogenous parts of a department like any other.

Figure 1

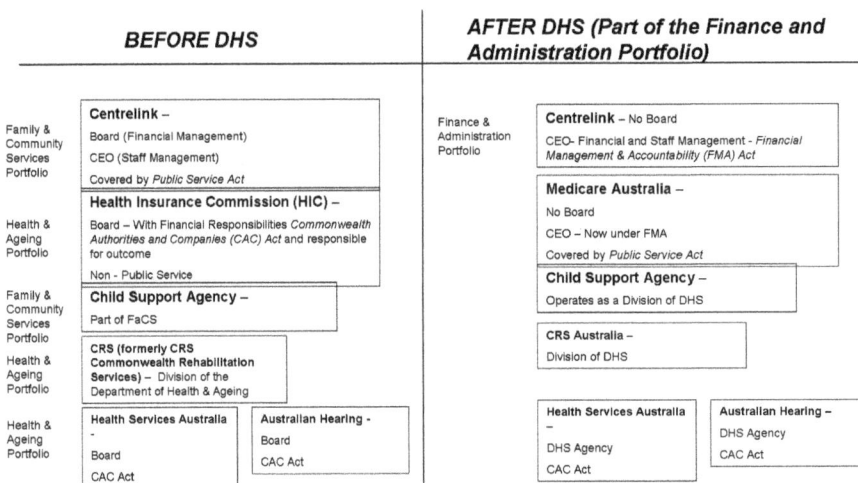

The lines of reporting from the CEOs to the Minister are through the CEO of DHS, consistent with the Prime Minister's statement that:

> The new department will ensure that the development and delivery of government services is placed under strong ministerial control with clear lines of responsibility through the Secretary.

This gives me considerable responsibility, although not control, in that four CEOs and two Boards have financial responsibility in their own right.

Our citizens and customers have distinct and diverse needs across the 6 agencies. It would be a mistake to imagine that the service offer has to be the same or should be the same. The legislation and policies, set by the policy departments, that drives our agencies and the programs they deliver, are not the same.

The idea of a mega department has been rejected. As an economist I know that mega organisations with diverse client bases can be plagued with poor service and poor management because size doesn't mean quality. There is nothing in the Prime Minister's announcement which is about watering down the purpose for which each of the agencies were created.

Knowing that project managers, team leaders and even executives do not control all elements necessary to successfully achieve their agendas, I will use examples to illustrate how DHS has driven reforms in ways that are more about influence and outcomes and less about *dictates* and control.

Practical Ways to Drive Reform

One of our most successful and very low cost initiatives is the Local Liaison Officer (LLO) Program.

LLO Program

Establishing the Local Liaison Officer network was one of the Minister's first priorities for the new Department. This program was established to improve the level of support and advice provided to customers who take their service delivery query or complaint to their local MP.

Every Member of the House of Representatives and Senator has been allocated an LLO from one of the six agencies in their local area. This provides an additional mechanism to Members and Senators for the resolution of any bottlenecks with regard to constituent inquiries.

With just one person initially working on this full time and, later, one person working on it part time, we have been able to draw on the network of the agencies to provide a fast and very personalised service to every Member of Parliament.

The LLO Program has been highly successful. In its first 12 months around 4,600 queries have been referred to the LLO network by Members of Parliament. With the exception of only 14, all queries have been responded to within two working days.

As at the end of January 2006, 97 per cent (145) of the Members of the House of Representatives and 62 per cent (47) of current Senators have utilised the LLO program.

The first task for DHS was to build a network of contacts in the agencies. These agency contacts were required to undertake any internal consultation required within their own agencies and present a coherent and agreed agency perspective to DHS (Centrelink had a good foundation already in place).

Development of the LLO program involved both one-on-one discussions between DHS and individual agencies, as well as combined forums when all agency representatives met to discuss the project. At all times DHS' leadership role and responsibility for delivering the LLO program was clear with the LLO Project Manager as a virtual team leader.

The Project Manager in DHS sought to give agency contacts as much autonomy as possible in tailoring the requirements of the program to their own agency's operations. In practical terms this meant that while there were certain non-negotiable elements of the program, agencies were given leeway to develop agency specific responses to some aspects of the program where this flexibility did not threaten to compromise the consistency and quality of the LLO network.

Not only has the LLO program been a way to improve services to MPs and their constituents, it has provided a network for DHS to use in obtaining information and feedback from staff at the front line.

Better Alignment to Government Objectives

UHRIG

The Uhrig Review identified options for Government to improve the performance and get the best from statutory authorities.

The Review found that generally Boards do not work unless the Board can appoint and sack the Chief Executive Officer and determine strategy. This usually applies in a commercial enterprise, or where there are multiple owners, but it does not apply in regulatory agencies or where an agency is expected to efficiently deliver a service specified by the Government.

Uhrig also found that good governance requires owners or their representatives to be clear about they want to be achieved, establishing an unambiguous purpose for the entity and developing clear expectations of the meaning of success. Uhrig was not supportive of Boards where Ministers exercised control. It was the case of too many cooks spoil the broth.

The Centrelink Board and the Health Insurance Commission were replaced on 1 October 2005 by two agencies, each headed by a Chief Executive Officer appointed by the Minister, accountable to the Minister and reporting through me. This is consistent with the Uhrig report.

The Health Insurance Commission was renamed *Medicare Australia* and brought under the *Financial Management and Accountability Act*, rather than the *Commonwealth Authorities and Companies Act*, and the staff, who were employed under conditions determined by the Commission, were brought under the *Public Service Act*. To provide clarity of purpose for the agencies, the Minister issued Statements of Expectations on 27 October 2005, setting out his requirements for the agencies for the next twelve months. These are publicly available.

Exerting Influence When You Cannot Simply Use Control

From the outset the Prime Minister wanted us to increase participation for those people who are on benefits, are able to work and are currently not working.

Our role was to increase referrals to the Job Network for those who do not have a mandatory requirement to look for work, such as parents. Our objective was clear. We gave clear and unambiguous guidance to Centrelink on what was required and, in consultation with the Department of Education and Workplace relations (DEWR) and DHS, Centrelink set about delivering.

This is an example of influencing behaviour rather than controlling it as legislation up to 1 July 2006 does not compel these people to work. Centrelink embarked on an active strategy of contacting voluntary customers, when they visited Centrelink to see if they were interested in working, and later extend the contacts to calls from call centres. As a result of this strategy over 141,000 voluntary job seekers have been referred to the Job Network for the period November 2004 – January 2006.

The average number of referrals to the Job Network increased from 4,100 per month (July 2004 – November 2004) to over 9,400 per month (November 2004 – January 2006).

As you can see in Figure 2, referrals directly and dramatically change with the effort Centrelink puts into this strategy. Referrals dropped over the period of January, as a result of cessation of strategy over the Christmas/New Year period.

Not only have referrals gone up, there has been a marked increase in job placements for voluntary customers: job placements increased from around 2,400 per month (July 2004 – November 2004) to over 4,000 per month (December 2004 – January 2006).

Figure 2

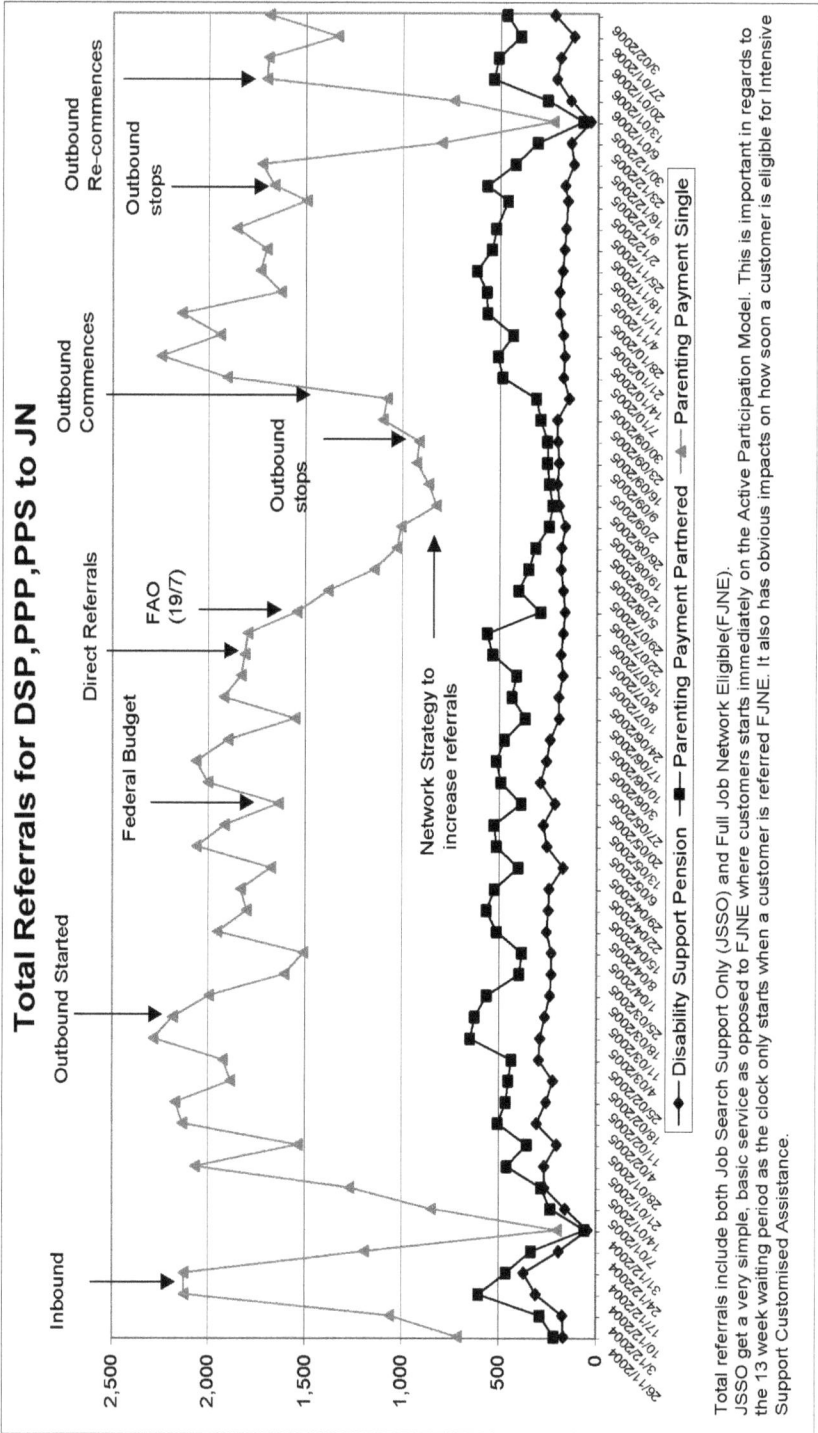

Total Referrals for DSP,PPP,PPS to JN

Total referrals include both Job Search Support Only (JSSO) and Full Job Network Eligible(FJNE). JSSO get a very simple, basic service as opposed to FJNE where customers starts immediately on the Active Participation Model. This is important in regards to the 13 week waiting period as the clock only starts when a customer is referred FJNE. It also has obvious impacts on how soon a customer is eligible for Intensive Support Customised Assistance.

Figure 3

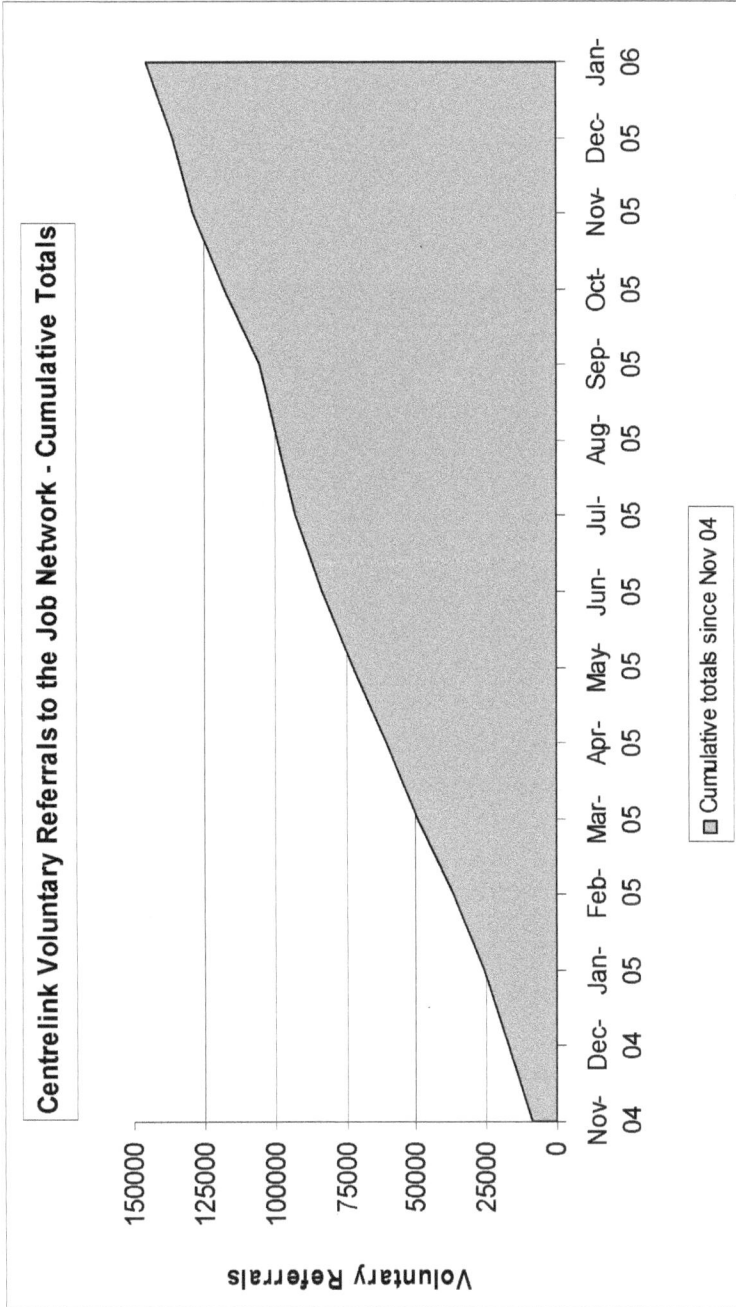

Centrelink Voluntary Referrals to the Job Network - Cumulative Totals

Communications

Partnership and influence has been a feature of our communications activity. Last year, we secured funding of $4 million to pilot a new way of informing people about the benefits and payments available from the Australian Government. And as we were developing the pilot, we were invited by the Ministerial Committee on Government Communication to play an active role in other major Government campaigns.

Why is it that DHS with a short term budget allocation of only $4 million has been asked to be involved in some very significant campaigns worth many tens of millions? It is because government campaigns usually direct people to a service, and the service is usually provided by a Human Services agency.

What we bring to the communication is a customer perspective, through the everyday experience of our agencies. And because our agencies, in particular Centrelink, have strong media teams, they can also play a valuable role in securing unpaid media coverage that informs the customer and supports the larger campaign.

The DHS pilot I mentioned earlier is now concluding, with excellent results. We invested the $4million across a *Drought Assistance Campaign*, a component of DEWR's *Support the System that Supports You* campaign and a *Student On-line* campaign.

The common thread for all three was the use of spokespeople who could engage and inform the target audience. In the case of drought assistance, our two-week campaign lifted awareness and understanding by over 30 per cent and generated triple the number of calls from farmers to the *Drought Assistance Hotline*. For *Support the System*, insertion of an infomercial featuring Centrelink spokespeople into the campaign caused a noticeable spike in calls registered via the call centre. The latest campaign, encouraging students to apply for Student Youth Allowance and Austudy on-line is generating an excellent response.

In our communication activity, DHS never acts alone. In the Drought Assistance Campaign we worked closely with the policy owners, Department of Agriculture Fisheries and Forestry, and with Centrelink, our Human Services agency charged with delivering the services.

In the *Support the System that Supports You* campaign we were partners with DEWR. Because the call to action – that is, updating your details at Centrelink, is entirely handled by that agency, we produced an infomercial that had Centrelink staff talking to people about their responsibilities.

Currently we are working with DEWR and our delivery agencies in developing the communication support and call to action for *Welfare to Work*. DHS, policy and delivery colleagues together present a whole of government communication approach to MCGC (Ministerial Committee on Government Communication). We are influencing both the Policy Departments and our Agencies to ensure that the customer is at the centre of all our strategies and approaches. Through our 'spokesperson' strategy we provide a human face for what has traditionally viewed as a faceless bureaucracy.

How to Use Cultural Differences Between Agencies to Speed Reforms

Absenteeism is a problem in three of our agencies but thankfully not all. Some are already making progress on reducing absenteeism and some of our agencies are specialists in getting people back to work so we are collectively working on ways to reduce absenteeism. The problem is significant and a blight on our service delivery.

On an annualised basis the Child Support Agency (CSA) experiences *unplanned leave* at the rate of almost 18 days on average. This is an extraordinarily high figure and makes CSA a leader in the pack across the Australian Government in terms of unplanned leave. One way of looking at this is to say that the average person in CSA would be entitled to 4 weeks annual leave, 12 public holidays and on average takes a further 18 working days which in accumulative sense would mean that they would start work mid March. As a Secretary charged with improving service delivery to customers and as a taxpayer, this is entirely unacceptable.

Here are six months figures for organisations to the moment.

Figure 4

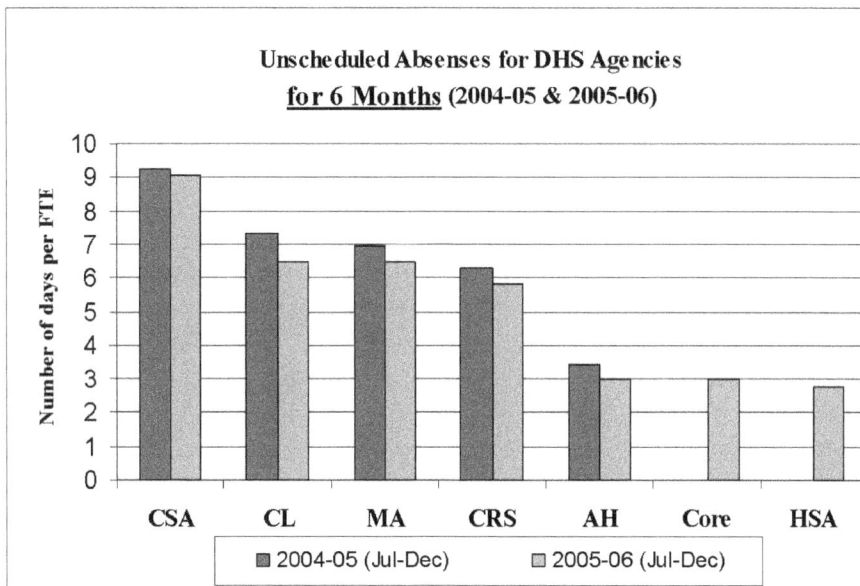

Unscheduled Absenses for DHS Agencies
for 6 Months (2004-05 & 2005-06)

Number of days per FTE

CSA   CL   MA   CRS   AH   Core   HSA

■ 2004-05 (Jul-Dec)   ▨ 2005-06 (Jul-Dec)

Medicare Australia and Centrelink figures are nothing to write home about and clearly all three organisations need to improve their outcomes. On the other hand, Health Services Australia is well below the median for the APS at 8.94 days per FTE employee (in 2001-02) and in the 6 months to December has had an unplanned leave of less than 3 days – the same as the core Department. So for this graph anything above 41/2 puts the agency on the wrong side of the APS median.

I appreciate why CSA may have a higher level of unplanned leave than other places: CSA staff face a particularly challenging role in dealing with parents that have complex issues often in an environment where there is ongoing conflict in their relationships. The average CSA officer dealing with clients spends 4.6 hours on the phone every day. Those calls go from simple transactions (such as changing addresses) to high level interpretation of legislation. Officers at the APS 3 and 4 levels are dealing with people who are in difficult emotional states or in financial crisis and they are the go-between for separated parents.

That said, having a level of absenteeism that is 99 per cent over the APS median of 8.9 means that those staff that are at work on any given day face greater pressure, customers have to wait longer for service, productivity is diminished, management is more difficult and costs to taxpayers are increased. CSA managers should not feel overwhelmed. Clearly managers and team leaders can make a substantial difference.

Let me illustrate using an example from Centrelink. A new Centrelink manager in Parramatta achieved a remarkable breakthrough working with his staff to address the ongoing issue of the increasing size of office queues. After having observed the office for a few days he summarised the following:

- some staff had a preference to start work at 7am and leave at 3pm;
- queues were generally longer in the afternoons;
- staff were often dealing with aggressive clients and reacted accordingly; and
- prisoners (from a nearby prison) were generally released in the afternoon (when there were longer queues and fewer staff).

The manager held a staff meeting and offered them an extra two experienced officers to carry the workload. The workers were excited by this prospect. He then went on to explain that the two extra staff would come from them working hours that were the same as office opening hours. He also spoke to the prison authorities and formed a new arrangement whereby Centrelink officers would see prisoners *before* they were released (in the prison) and he asked the line managers sit near the front of the office to watch and actively manage the queues.

The results were outstanding – shorter queues and happy staff, lower absenteeism. As it turned out, queues were a manifestation of other problems.

That is just one story in an organisation with over 25,000 staff working across Australia. Can drawing attention to this problem make a difference? Absence rates at December 2005 have dropped by an average of one full day per employee when compared to a similar period in 2004. This improved attendance has allowed Centrelink to provide additional service to the Australian community. Over the six-month period to December 2005 the improved attendance is estimated to have allowed an additional 142,000 face-to-face contacts and an additional 168,000 phone contacts with Centrelink customers.

Centrelink commenced in January 2005 with a three prong attack on unplanned leave:

- Communication and Awareness Raising;
- Leadership Accountability and Support; and,
- Performance Monitoring and Reporting.

Communication and Awareness Raising

Unplanned leave was raised as a key area of focus for all levels within Centrelink with managers being asked to review their existing attendance plans. Messages from the CEO and Executive emphasised the impact of absenteeism on productivity and Centrelink's reputation, and encouraged team leaders to improve attendance rates.

Leadership Accountability and Support

A project manager was assigned to develop and support the strategies for reducing absenteeism and provide advice to Centrelink managers. Training programs were developed to assist managers in the task of dealing with staff absences earlier and more consistently. A resource kit was developed and distributed regarding better practice in attendance management.

Performance Monitoring and Reporting

A visual tool was developed to provide a quick snapshot of absence rates within Centrelink. A simple traffic light approach was used to quickly identify sites that were performing well and those sites that required additional assistance. The culture in Centrelink is changing in response to managers adopting a more consistent approach towards absence cases while at the same time dealing with individuals more flexibly. Employees are being encouraged to be more honest about their needs and commitments, and told they have an opportunity to negotiate with their manager rather than calling in for a day off as they may have done in the past.

Figure 5

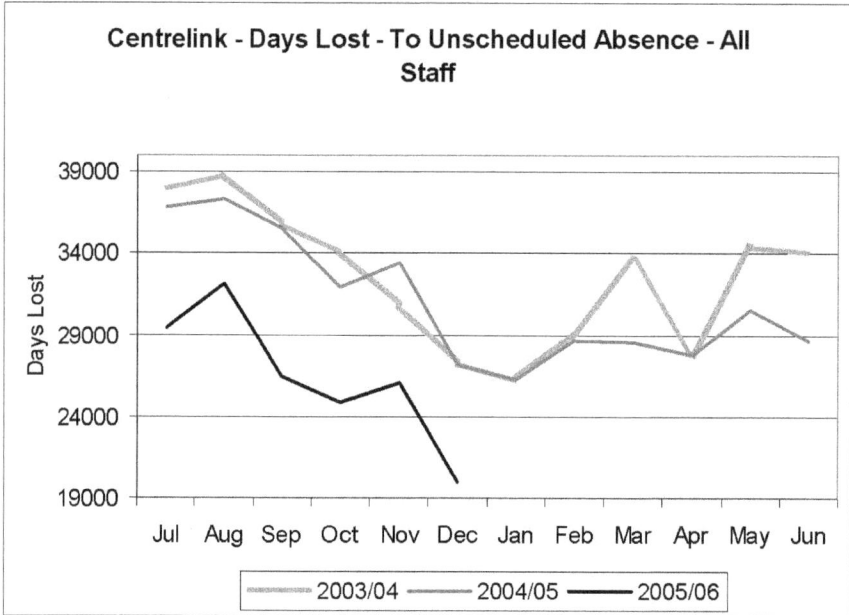

Centrelink - Days Lost - To Unscheduled Absence - All Staff

In Conclusion

There is still much work to be done to entrench a positive attendance culture; experience has shown that the relationship between employees and their immediate managers is a critical factor in assisting this change. In summary, influence is not as good as control but it is good enough when you can harness the talents of others. That is the role of the project manager – that is the role of all managers.

8. The Australian Taxation Office Change Program: Project and Change Management Directions and Learnings, A Case Study

Bob Webb, Deputy Commissioner, Australian Taxation Office

Introduction

Corporate policies, the literature and any number of very capable consultants provide frameworks to successfully tackle project and change management.

Nobody doubts the increasing significance of project management in a world where change and flexibility at speed have become a part of life, and an expectation on all organisations. So if the literature and experience are to be believed, why is it so hard to succeed?

This chapter uses the sometimes successful, sometimes painful, but never dull experience of the Tax Office as a case study.

In particular, it tells the story of lessons from the introduction of major tax reform, and how we have drawn on that experience in the current fairly ambitious enterprise-wide *Change Program*.

Figure 1

The Tax Office's continuing project management journey

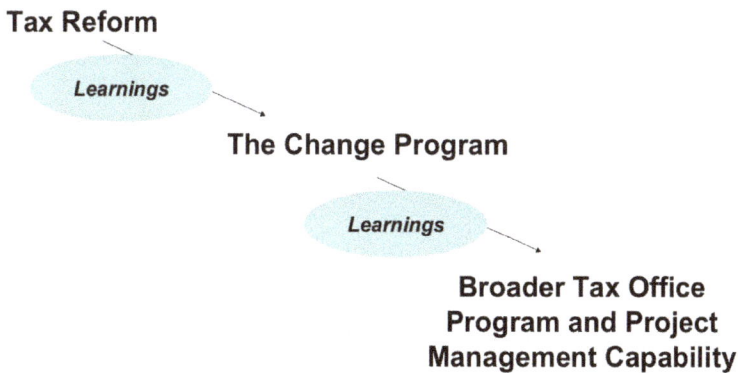

Tax Reform

Learnings

The Change Program

Learnings

Broader Tax Office Program and Project Management Capability

It also briefly covers how our organisational learning is continuing, as we attempt to build a practical and flexible approach to project and change management as an ongoing capability for the Tax Office. This is increasingly important to manage a growing portfolio of program and project activities.

Context and Drivers for Change

The Tax Office administers a range of revenue legislation including income tax, GST, excise and superannuation, which generates 89 per cent of Commonwealth Government revenue and about $35 billion for the States and Territories. Less publicised is that we also provide benefits of about $4 billion to the community.

The Office has about 22,000 staff at around 60 locations around Australia. We interact with just about every segment of the community. There are fairly high annual volumes of phone enquires (11 million), returns for processing (14 million income tax returns and a similar number of activity statements), and debt collections (1.4 million for $52 billion).

Major tax reform was announced by the Government in 1997. It was introduced primarily in 2000/2001 with the GST, the Australian Business Number (ABN) and a series of business and personal tax reforms. Three years might sound like a reasonable period to plan and deliver, but for more than half that period the Government was defining and negotiating what the actual reform was going to look like, so the period for implementation telescoped down fairly dramatically.

In hindsight we can see that, partly because of the 'telescoping', but also because of some things we just did not anticipate, our consultation processes were not fully up to the job. Our systems were outdated and fragmented, and we implemented the program internally in a quite devolved style. We had, perhaps, not appreciated how difficult it was going to be to bring about a major reform or change with that sort of fragmentation.

At one level we succeeded – all policies were delivered on time and the revenue came in – but some of adverse consequences started to manifest themselves in 2001 and 2002, particularly amongst the tax agents and business community. This is evident from some media reports of the time.

Basically tax agents said 'if things do not improve in terms of our experience of the administration, we will stop dealing electronically with the Tax Office'. They knew this would cripple our activities. Suffice to say we were building up a pretty significant set of issues around 2002 which we had to respond to.

So we took a step back and commenced the 'Listening to the Community' initiative. This took about nine months during 2002. We listened not only to our client segments – individuals, business, large business, small business – all of whom had some very different perspectives and priorities – but also to our staff. This involved surveys, user clinics and focus groups, and testing prototype products at creative retreats with Tax Officers and the community.

Figure 2

Listening to the Community - 2002

- **We learned how we were not meeting taxpayer expectations**

- How did the process work?
  - quantitative surveys to find out how well we listened and responded to the community's concerns
  - user clinics to understand administrative issues from a user perspective
  - prototype products developed and tested at creative retreats involving the Tax Office and the community
  - all client segments and staff

A question often asked is whether the sort of change we subsequently embarked on is best managed from the top down or the bottom up. There is no doubt that establishing the strategy and implementation I will describe later has been driven from the top down, otherwise it would not have worked at all. However if we had not had the bottom up 'listening' step first, so that we could distil an agenda to address both client and staff concerns, we could easily have missed the mark.

We distilled many messages and priorities from the listening initiative. I will use an example from the tax agents' feedback. One of the things they wanted was more detailed and on-line access to the information we hold on their clients. It became obvious that we had to do something about that issue. I will mention later how the tax agent portal, which allows tax agents to access their clients' information directly from our systems, has been the single biggest benefit to that segment of the community.

Suffice to say we got real benefit out of the listening exercise, and the findings are still a major driver of the current program.

There have been other drivers for change as follows:

- *Government expectations for policy change* – At any one time we have about 100 policy projects on the go, not quite as big as the tax reform period, but nevertheless quite significant;

- *Technology* – The fact that technology is moving so fast which in turn is changing community expectations quite significantly; and
- *Community confidence* – If we do not maintain community confidence in the taxation system then we really have a problem, as the revenue base to a significant extent depends on voluntary compliance.

The Easier Cheaper and More Personalised Change Program

The *Easier, Cheaper and more Personalised Change Program* is the program developed to address these issues, including the priorities from listening to the community and the staff.

What is this program? It is primarily about improving the client and staff experience. However it is also about improving productivity and flexibility, to respond to both government and community needs in an ongoing way. It is a five-year program, started in 2003 after listening to the community. It covers new products and services for all segments and channels of interaction with the community.

It has had quick wins such as the *tax agent portal*. We realised that while some things will take until 2008 to achieve, if we were waiting until then to start the real improvements for the community, we would have long ago lost the confidence that we needed to gain and regain.

The program replaces essentially all existing Tax Office business processes and systems, front and back end. One way of typifying the change is that a call centre representative currently responding to a tax payer or tax agent enquiry may have to access anything up to 16 systems. Following the introduction of the Change Program it will be just two systems, a quite radical improvement for staff.

The program is based on enterprise-wide approaches. Often in the past we have had different approaches and systems according to which revenue product or which client segment was being served. In the new approach we only customise where necessary.

The program will affect most of our staff over the period. We have just introduced the new Client Relationship Management system to our call centres (about 3,000 staff). In further releases during this year we will add case and correspondence management, content management, reporting and record keeping to about 12,000 staff. In our final releases during 2007/08 we will replace all our processing systems, and nearly all staff will be involved. The total cost is about $450 million.

A key learning from previous attempts at large scale change was that we needed to address the program and manage risks at three levels – *Strategic Positioning and Intent, Program Design and Development, and Program Implementation.*

Figure 3

A strategic approach

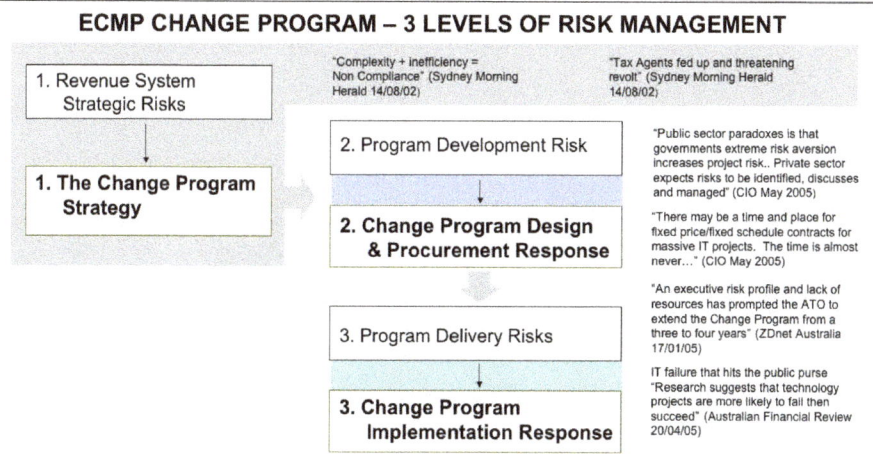

ECMP CHANGE PROGRAM – 3 LEVELS OF RISK MANAGEMENT

We also decided to separate our approach into very deliberate phases.

Figure 4

Change Program timeframe and phases

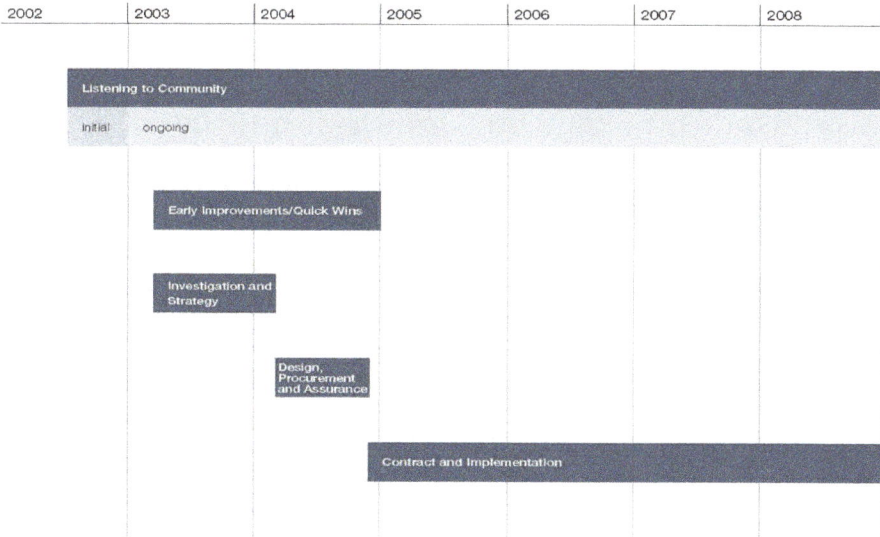

Strategic Positioning and Intent

A key part of strategic positioning is that the Change Program is explicitly linked to, and supports delivery of, the ATO Business Model.

Figure 5

Relationship of the *Easier, Cheaper and More Personalised Change Program* to the Tax Office Business Model

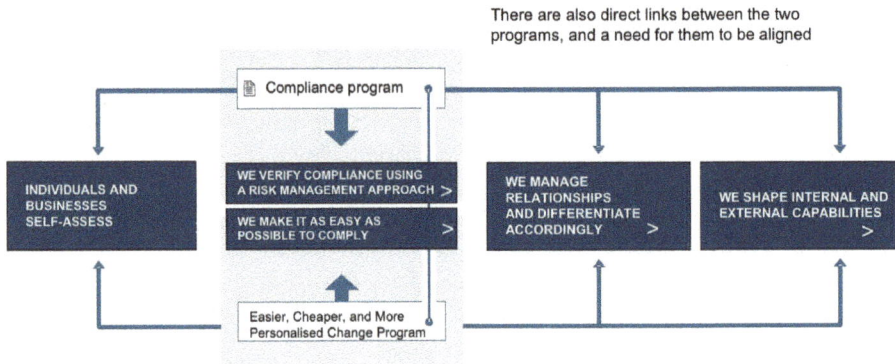

There are also direct links between the two programs, and a need for them to be aligned

Compliance program

WE VERIFY COMPLIANCE USING A RISK MANAGEMENT APPROACH >

WE MAKE IT AS EASY AS POSSIBLE TO COMPLY >

INDIVIDUALS AND BUSINESSES SELF-ASSESS

WE MANAGE RELATIONSHIPS AND DIFFERENTIATE ACCORDINGLY >

WE SHAPE INTERNAL AND EXTERNAL CAPABILITIES >

Easier, Cheaper, and More Personalised Change Program

While we were developing the Change Program, we realised that something we were in want of was a clearly articulated business model – what is our business philosophy, what is the way we thing about the business, starting from the self-assessment system which itself conditions a lot of our approaches? There are two main strategic planks in the model. One is the compliance strategy and program. Under a self assessment system you need risk based compliance approaches. The second is the *Making it Easy to Comply* strategy, of which the main component is the *Change Program*.

Some additional aspects of the strategic positioning were as follows.

- *A contract with the community.* Having listened to the community we fed back to the community what we had heard through a booklet (also provided electronically on our web site) entitled *'Making it Easier to Comply'.* We first published this in 2003. We put it out every year to say 'these are the commitments we are making in terms of some really specific future products and services we are going to introduce; and this is how we delivered against the commitments made in the previous year'. Making such an external commitment is also useful internally in keeping us focussed on the main strategic intent.
- *Both external and internal transformation.* Whilst the program started from the external stakeholders' needs we realised early on that we would not be able to sustain and deliver many improvements unless we also transformed our internal capabilities (people, process and technology).
- *Emerging community based systems and whole of government.* The changes we make are also intended to provide the foundation for a whole range of community based approaches (for example the ability for small businesses

to lodge and finalise their returns directly from their accounting software), and improved whole of government approaches, for both businesses and individuals.

- *Leverage off capabilities and experience of other organisations.* When we think hard about our business, most of what the Tax Office does, broken into its component parts, is actually very similar to what a lot of other organisations do. We have taken a strategic position to learn and take product from others, rather than (our traditional approach) do everything ourselves and build our own unique systems and processes.
- *Phase the program over the minimum reasonable timeframe.* We talked to a number of our colleague revenue agencies and other big organisations around Australia and the world about their experience. A common finding was that many tried to transform too quickly and found there was too much happening in parallel. But an even greater number saw failure as a result of the change taking too long. They were living in two worlds, the new world and the old world for too long. Investment in both worlds was costly and complicated, and people also lost focus. So we chose an ambitious, but feasible, implementation timing as a deliberate trade-off between these two tensions.
- *Quick wins.* As I mentioned earlier we committed to a significant number of improved products and services across all segments and channels. This bought some critical time to allow us to deliver the underlying changes, and also provided external and internal credibility to the program.
- *Top level leadership.* The Commissioner led the effort right from the outset, and frankly, in an organisation as complex as the Tax Office, you would not want to try such a large scale change unless this was the case. This was complemented by a number of joint strategy and design activities including the senior management from across the organisation, as well as external expertise at key stages.

Program Design and Development

Once we had the strategic positioning settled we moved to the second phase of program design and development.

The following were key features of this phase:

- *Ongoing engagement with stakeholders.* We had completed the initial listening to the community, but the fact is you have to keep at it: reviewing directions and co-design of products, as well as monitoring perceptions and feedback. We found that even as we designed the various products, some of the things we thought we understood out of the *listening to the community* phase, had to be modified.
- *Formal blueprint and transition plan developed throughout 2004.* The Solution Blueprint covered the people, process and technology aspects of the future

design. An integrated Transition Plan set out the sequence and timing of packages of change (or releases) through to 2008.

- *A whole-of-program business case.* In previous change initiatives we had attempted a separate business case for each component of the change and it never quite stacked up, it never quite justified the investment. It wasn't until we lifted the business case up to the level of the integrated outcomes and benefits that it became *viable*.

- *Selecting off the shelf and transfer technology.* Although this particular change initiative is not a *technology* program, the technology component is critical. Through a number of market tenders we selected a small number of suppliers – one for *Client Relationship Management*; one for *Case and Correspondence Management*; one for *Content, Document and Records Management*; and one for our core processing systems.

- *Obtaining the required program management and integration expertise.* We are a revenue agency not a program management agency. For a program like this we decided to buy in the expertise of people who do this as their daily living. We also decided we wanted a single program partner with clear overall accountability for delivery across the program. Through an open market exercise we selected Accenture as the Program Implementation Partner. They can and do sub-contract others in, but we deal only with them.

- An outcomes-based fixed-price contract.

Outcomes-based means that the contract deliverables are specified as higher level business outcomes within eight categories.

Figure 6

Change Program – Measures of Success

The Change Program will deliver the following outcomes and our success will be measured by KPIs in 5 categories

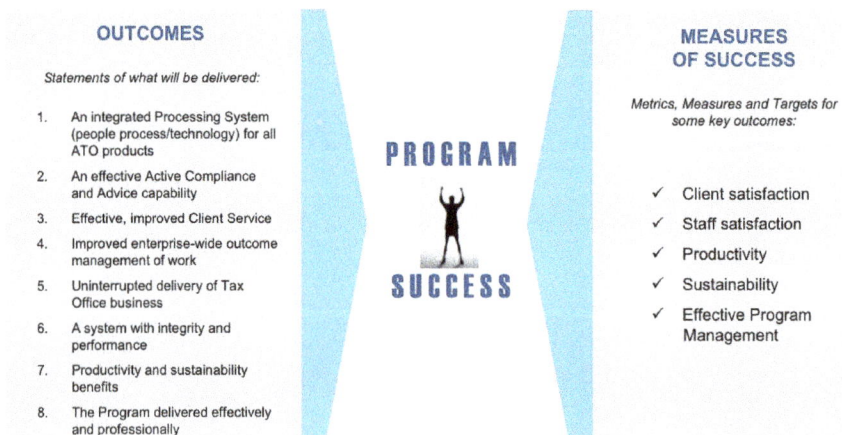

OUTCOMES

Statements of what will be delivered:

1. An integrated Processing System (people process/technology) for all ATO products
2. An effective Active Compliance and Advice capability
3. Effective, improved Client Service
4. Improved enterprise-wide outcome management of work
5. Uninterrupted delivery of Tax Office business
6. A system with integrity and performance
7. Productivity and sustainability benefits
8. The Program delivered effectively and professionally

PROGRAM

SUCCESS

MEASURES OF SUCCESS

Metrics, Measures and Targets for some key outcomes:

✓ Client satisfaction
✓ Staff satisfaction
✓ Productivity
✓ Sustainability
✓ Effective Program Management

Something we had found out through experience was that if you try to contract to detailed specifications of what you think you need for the next three or four years, your imagination fails you, and sure enough down the track you have countless scope variations and increases. However if you pitch expectations at the outcomes level, they are much more likely to remain valid over the period.

Fixed-price in this case means not only for the partner's consulting fees, but also for our own costs which are about half of the total program costs. If there is a greater use of Tax Office staff than anticipated in the fixed price, the extra cost is underwritten by the program partner. This is possible because they manage the project, and they manage the Tax Office staff who work with them on the project. For us this was fairly innovative.

- *Expert independent advice.* We selected *Capgemini* as Independent Assurer to look over both our and *Accenture's* shoulders. Whilst we may get enmeshed in the daily run of things they are able to step back and point out if we are overlooking key issues. They have been involved in design, planning and implementation phases.
- *Procurement practices.* We followed Australian National Audit Office best practices, particularly around probity and risk management aspects of the procurement.
- *Leadership.* There has been a Change Program Steering Committee throughout, comprised of the four Commissioners. We report twice a month as to how we are going and to seek guidance or direction on any major strategic or design issues. This has been going for two and a half years and will continue through the life of the program.

Program Implementation

Having established the strategic positioning, program design and development, and with key procurement complete, we moved to the major phase of implementation.

It has been mentioned elsewhere that 66 per cent of programs and projects fail and 33 per cent succeed. Of those that fail most are classified as failures of implementation. I have to say, though, unless we had done the work in the prior phases as described above, the task and risks of implementing would be much greater.

Having said that, there are still 'bucket loads' of implementation risks, so we need overt strategies to address these:

- *Continuing strong governance and accountability arrangements.* I already mentioned the Change Program Steering Committee. Below this, the program design and delivery has been the responsibility of a single integrated Change Program team. When we delivered tax reform we did it in a very devolved way. The different revenue product areas had the major responsibilities for introducing the change, including business processes and systems, and, whilst we had an overall Reform Program Office for planning and monitoring, the approach was very decentralised. We have taken a very different approach this time. We have brought the *Accenture*, business area and IT people into the one team, quite a large team of around 500 people, to form a new Tax Office division for the duration of the program.

- *Formal program and project management methodology.* Obvious in a sense, but not always easy to make work in an organisation where very large scale program management is not a way of life. We decided to essentially use the methodologies of our program partner and our independent assurer.
- *Formal stage gates.* The Government has recently introduced the requirement for formal stage gate type approaches in significant projects. This project is not subject to these Government arrangements because it was committed before they came into effect. However we have in any event incorporated a total of ten key stage gates throughout the program. We effectively have a go/no go decision at each of these, and get an independent assessment of how we are going, as well as a self assessment.
- *Staying outcomes-focussed and realising benefits.* The Tax Office has found this a difficult area in the past. With continuing intensive policy and community agendas, the tendency is to get one project almost finished when another comes rolling over the top. So we have been very intentional this time with a 'formal benefits realisation measurement process' built in, and an ongoing assessment of how we are going against the initial intent and outcomes.
- *Supporting existing business operations.* Implementation of major change causes a lot of transition issues, so the engagement with the other Tax Office divisions or sub-plans, particularly the compliance and the operations areas of the office, is very intense indeed, to help manage the impact of the changes.
- *Growing emphasis on people and change management.* Some people have said 'you will need a culture change program to complement the other activities'. We thought about that pretty hard, and concluded people are not going to change their attitudes or approaches until there is something tangibly different in their work life. So we have tailored the approach to people and change management to be much more closely aligned to the period just before they are about to experience something that is significantly different. In a 4-5 year program this is not immediate.

However I mentioned that we directly impacted 3000 staff last year, and will impact 12,000 staff this year. So people and change management is about half of our focus and concentration at this time.

We have adopted a model to frame our approach. At one end of the spectrum there are some very hard or concrete process and systems elements – for example, of course you have to train people on the new systems and help them with ongoing performance support. There are organisational job design issues to be addressed. That's all very concrete. At the other end there are many softer but equally critical elements such as sponsorship and communications, and behavioural change and expectations.

Figure 7

People Change Management Approach

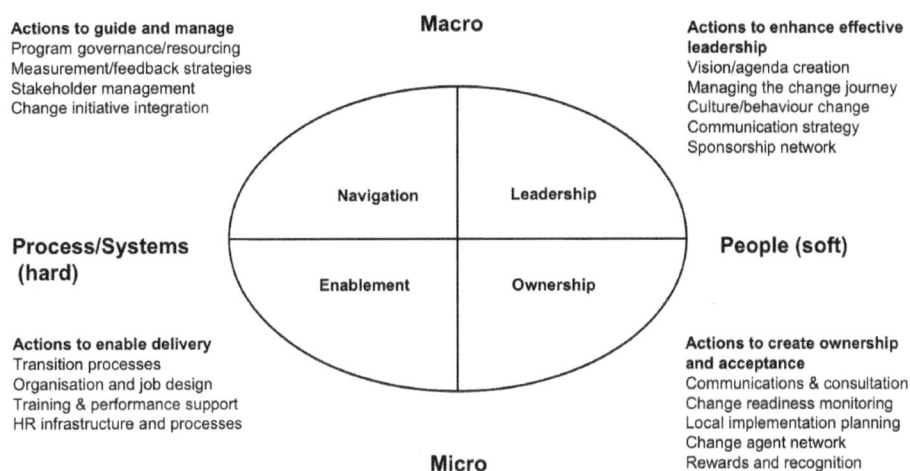

Actions to guide and manage
Program governance/resourcing
Measurement/feedback strategies
Stakeholder management
Change initiative integration

Macro

Actions to enhance effective leadership
Vision/agenda creation
Managing the change journey
Culture/behaviour change
Communication strategy
Sponsorship network

Navigation   Leadership

Process/Systems (hard)

People (soft)

Enablement   Ownership

Actions to enable delivery
Transition processes
Organisation and job design
Training & performance support
HR infrastructure and processes

Actions to create ownership and acceptance
Communications & consultation
Change readiness monitoring
Local implementation planning
Change agent network
Rewards and recognition

Micro

Results and learnings to date.

With implementation of the major changes well under way we are about half way through the Program. How are we tracking against the original intent?

Most client product and service commitments have been delivered on schedule with some, however, being several months late. Surveys and product uptake indicate we have been particularly successful with tax agents. Individual taxpayers' uptake of enhanced products like e-tax has been very strong. Our biggest challenge remains with business and especially small business where satisfaction levels and uptake are increasing slowly, and from a low base.

As for internal systems and business process releases, we are still on track for the original plan to be completed by 2008. We have had some delays of around six months overall on the first and second of the three main releases, but the first was completed last year and the second is well progressed for completion during 2006. The fixed price means that there has been no material cost increase as a result of these delays. The evidence to date is that we can still achieve all of the expected outcomes by 2008, although we have often had to revisit the exact way we do this. Basing the contract on *what* we want to achieve rather than the detail of *how* we achieve it, is already paying dividends.

We have some additional learnings from the implementation phase so far:

- *Technology*. Introducing a new platform entails risk. So far, in the Change Program, where we are introducing several new platforms and systems, most have now settled in, but only after a range of problems – unexpected issues, integration issues – which have been the prime cause of the temporary delays noted above;
- *Rapid decision making versus wide engagement*. One of the continuing struggles is to find the right balance between the need for well informed but quick decision making, and wide consultation with the rest of the business. Engagement has been intensive but we have also had to recognise when we need to go forward on an 80-90 per cent confidence level rather than 100 per cent;
- *The call on other Tax Office business areas*. We attempted to factor the costs of this fully into the Business Case but clearly underestimated the level of resource demand on the rest of the Office, to play their critical part in both design and deployment;
- *Value of the stage gate reviews*. These have been invaluable in forcing us to step back and assess how we are going and making any necessary adjustments; and
- *Staying focused*. There is a lot of pressure from both inside and outside the organisation to add scope. In a program of this size one of the main tasks is to stay focused. One of the key roles for the leadership team has been to keep the program in line with the original outcomes, and recognise that we cannot deliver everything in the first wave.

Project Management in the broader ATO

Finally let me reflect on some of the approaches we are taking to program and project management across the Tax Office.

We categorise our projects into *policy*, *compliance* and *administrative* projects – and we have literally hundreds of them.

A part of the challenge is the sheer number and variety of projects that exist at any one time. At any one time, we have 100 or so policy projects at various stage of maturity. We also have a large number of compliance projects, not all of which are managed formally as projects at the moment, and we have a number of administrative projects. The Change Program is easily the biggest of these and, in fact, through the Change Program we have closed down a number of other projects to keep the focus on the main game.

Apart from the Change Program, the main corporate project management focus to date has been on policy and on IT projects. There has been hesitancy in some other areas to apply project management approaches. This might be because of behaviour, attitude or cultural issues or just unfamiliarity. But there are also some more direct barriers. These include:

- poor understanding of how to differentiate between project and business as usual work;
- a perception, often justified, that full project management methods are too complicated for many situations, so that 'one size fits all' is not appropriate; and/or
- limited integration with other governance and management processes e.g. business planning in the annual planning cycle and regular governance reporting.

To address these and other issues, and with the Commissioners' endorsement, we commenced a *Project Management Improvement* project about 18 months ago.

Some initiatives at the governance level include:

- integration of project management into existing business processes such as business planning, to achieve an equivalent standard of governance and reduce duplication;
- clearer project sponsor and manager accountabilities;
- introduction of formal review points (stage gates) for major programs and projects; and
- review of the relevant corporate policies, including a new Practice Statement for project management and a formal assurance process – particularly important in the complex and decentralised environment in which most of our projects necessarily live.

At the methodology level we are developing:

- clearer 'program' as opposed to individual 'project' approaches, recognising that it is very common for projects to be part of a larger program;
- uniform approaches to project identification and profiling;
- methodologies that can be more readily tailored to suit project characteristics, including a *3 Tiered Approach*, with more rigour required for larger high impact projects (Tier 1) and less for smaller low impact projects (Tier 3);
- alignment of related methodologies and disciplines (e.g. change management, design, systems development) within the overarching project management approaches; and
- appropriate technology support to assist managers and staff in project governance and management.

Figure 8

How are we using the learnings to improve the Tax Office's Project Management approach?

3 Tiered approach to profiling projects

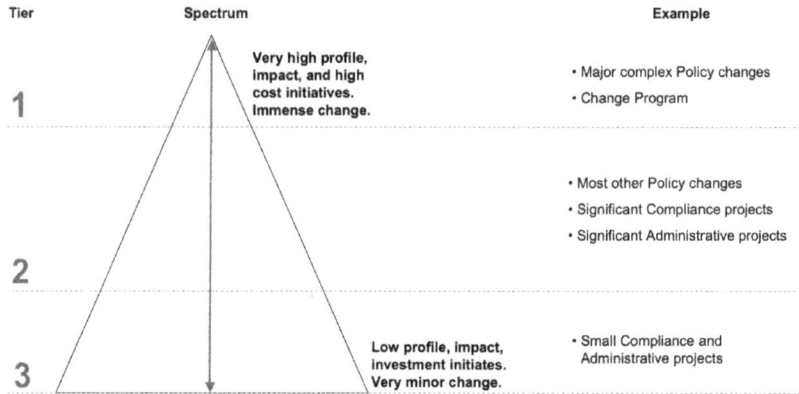

These initiatives are, in some cases, building on the learnings from the Change Program. However, they also recognise that such approaches would be 'overkill' for many of our projects. The work is showing promising signs of bringing a practical approach to achieving the undoubted benefits of project management approaches, without burdening managers out of all proportion to the value.

Conclusion

This chapter has focussed primarily on the Tax Office Change Program as a case study. When you hear that sobering statistic that 66 per cent of projects fail you could be forgiven for believing that embarking on such a program is either foolhardy or courageous.

In our case we concluded there was no option *but* to change, and to do so in an ambitious way, in order to fundamentally address the growing range of issues and expectations. What we have tried to do, is to mitigate the undoubted risks, by learning from our own and others' experience, and so improve the odds in our favour. So far we have negotiated a range of issues and obstacles, and remain essentially on track.

We can expect that many more issues will need to be navigated throughout the remainder of the program. The decisions that have positioned the program at each of the strategy, design, and implementation phases have undoubtedly helped. But from here it will be continuing attention to rigorous program and change management approaches, anticipation of those issues that might be predicted, and responsiveness to the unexpected, that will be the prerequisites of success.

9. Applying Three Frames to the Delivery of Public Value

Jim Varghese, Director-General, Department of Primary Industries and Fisheries, Queensland

I recently attended an ANZSOG CEO workshop where I was particularly encouraged and interested in the work of Harvard University academic Mark Moore on public value. Moore (1995) offers the notion of public managers creating public value for society (for the short and long term) for strategic management in Government. Drawing on Moore's definition, public value is understood to be the achievement of favoured outcomes by the use of public resources in the most effective manner available (Moore 1995).

In this presentation, I would like explore the idea of using a management process called the 'Three Frames' to deliver innovative public value. During my public service career, I have had the opportunity to work in a number of different agencies. I have served as Director-General of four Queensland Government Departments – Main Roads, Education, Employment and Training, and Primary Industries and Fisheries. I am also the Government champion for Lockhart River – a remote community in Cape York.

Each department and the community presents its own set of challenges, diversity and opportunities for creating public value. Some significant results for public value ranged from completing roads projects such as the Pacific Motorway in Main Roads to shaping the Learning, Skilling and Work agenda for Employment and Training and the creation of the Lockhart River fishing company.

In a case study by Dr Kerry Brown and Christine Flynn on the Queensland Department of Main Roads, they concluded that:

> The integration of relationship-building with high quality technical service delivery (at Main Roads) gives new insight into public sector management strategies, as traditional internal strengths were built on at the same time as efforts to broaden and enhance organisational capabilities in different ways.

In all of these cases, my focus has been on creating the purpose and mission of these organisations to shape their identity.

I developed the *Three Frames* management process and successfully implemented this in the Government agencies where I have served as Director-General—most recently, the Department of Primary Industries and Fisheries (DPI&F).

While it can be described as a management tool, the *Three Frames* process is not limited to management in a purely business sense. It is a methodology, or a philosophy, that can be equally well applied to personnel management or to the way in which agencies such as my own can deliver on government priorities and meet the many challenges we face daily.

One such challenge was the response to the recent oil spill in Gladstone Harbour where a fuel tanker on a bulk carrier from Korea was ruptured when it was hit by a tugboat in Gladstone Harbour on 24 January 2006. For around 40 minutes, the ship's fuel spilled 25,000 litres of heavy fuel into Gladstone Harbour, creating a slick.

Apart from the immediate environmental impact, this oil spill had the potential to have a long-term economic impact on the local fishing industry – contaminating prawns, crabs and fin fish, making them unsuitable for sale, and destroying local breeding grounds. The immediate environmental and economic impact would also have significant social implications for the local community.

The Department of Primary Industries and Fisheries was charged with ensuring that the impact on the fishing industry was minimal and that the local community supported the actions the department would take to remedy this situation. Our response was based on the *Three Frames* approach with the aim of creating public value. This involved having a clear understanding of the desired outcome, connecting the people and organisations involved and identifying problems and responses together.

This approach can be applied on our general business operations. Each day, the operations of public sector operations consume public resources and produce real consequences for society. Moore provides the idea of a strategic triangle with the intersection of legitimacy and support, public value and organisational capabilities as essential elements in this outcome. He challenges public managers to imagine and articulate a vision of public value that can command legitimacy and support and is operationally 'doable' in the domain for which they have responsibility.

This framework helps us, as public managers, to connect what we believe is valuable, and requires public resources, with improved ways of understanding our public value. I believe that there is a strong congruence between Moore's premise and the *Three Frames* methodology – of performance, relationships and alignment to create innovative public value and leadership of strategic management in Government.

The *Three Frames*

The *Three Frames* approach consists of three interacting, learning frames, being:

- the Relationship Frame;

- the Performance Frame; and
- the Alignment Frame.

The Relationship Frame

The aim of the relationship frame is to build and sustain a safe, non-threatening environment in which people feel able to share information including their thoughts, feelings and values honestly with others.

This frame of reference acknowledges the individuals and relationships within the system and also recognises these within social capital theories. Robert Putman put it this way:

> Stocks of social capital, such as trust, group norms, and self help networks, tend to be self reinforcing and cumulative. Successful collaboration in one endeavour builds connections which makes further collaboration possible.

The Relationship Frame helps individuals and groups develop a rapport with others, providing the best environment to solve problems, support each other and to achieve desired outcomes.

The Performance Frame

The Performance Frame looks at what we want to achieve and provides a clear and measurable picture of what we want, and need, to achieve to meet our goals. In a business management context a balanced scorecard approach can be used to set goals and accurately monitor performance. In the macro sense 'government' expectations are the benchmark. In this frame we need to determine what we as a department want to achieve and the way we want to achieve it.

The Alignment Frame

The Alignment Frame looks at the relationship between or within organisations and their members, and identifies any blockages that are stopping them from achieving their goals as set in the performance frame. The alignment frame accepts as its basic premise that poor alignment of relationships creates barriers to the achievement of an organisation's goals.

The Alignment Frame acknowledges the importance of both the organisation and the individual, and in so doing, highlights the importance of each to attaining of the goals of the other.

The *Three Frames* approach has been, in my view, the critical success factor in delivering what the Government requires from my agency. Effective relationships breed productive connections, both for the individual and for the organisation. Through relationships, information is created, transformed and passed on, and confidence and empowerment are built. This spirit of connectedness (relationships), coupled with a supportive environment that brings commonality of purpose (alignment) for all parties, will ensure that departmental delivery is aligned to government expectations (performance).

The *Three Frames* supports Moore's idea that public managers are seen as explorers (through the alignment frame) who with others (in the relationship frame) seek to discover, define and produce public value (the performance frame). I see the strategic triangle as an 'organic' system. Our reliance on mechanistic and controlling approaches to leadership and management stand in the way of innovation and effective leadership over participatory and self-organising processes. There is an intrinsic value in participation.

Moore's strategic triangle neatly overlays with this and the *Three Frames*. As Moore suggests: 'Managers should interact with the political system not simply through the medium of their mandated purposes but instead through more continuous and interactive dialogue'.

The *Three Frames* supports participation and engagement through dialogue, in a committed and consistent manner, to respond effectively to issues.

The features of dialogue are:

- welcoming multiple viewpoints and maximum interaction;
- behaviours that encourage co-operation with and acceptance of others;
- talking and learning about shared issues which effect public value; and
- inquiry, exploration and participation with the authorising and un-authorising environment.

Dialogue creates and recognises the humanised social systems of internal and external relationships which exist in all authorising environments. I believe the government's response to the Gladstone oil spill is one example where *Three Frames* has been successfully applied to support a dialogue-based process to enhance public value.

Legitimacy and Support

As mentioned previously, the Gladstone oil spill had economic, social and environmental consequences for public value. It had the potential to generate public and political controversy. A wide range of interests were affected, including local and State government, industry, environmental groups and the local community, among others.

Commercial fishermen, seafood processors and local seafood retailers were worried that their industry would be devastated, with potential long-term impacts on fishing stocks. Environmentalists worried about the impact on sensitive seagrasses and mangroves, as well as local dolphin and dugong populations. The wider Queensland community was concerned about health and safety issues in consuming seafood from the Gladstone area.

The Gladstone community was concerned about the impact on its seafood industry. The Queensland Seafood Industry Association was worried about the impact on consumer's perceptions of wild caught product.

The public value lay outside the scope of one public organisation. It involved Queensland Transport who were responsible for cleaning up the oil spill; the Environmental Protection Agency who were responsible for managing the impact on wildlife and water quality; Queensland Health who administer 'The Food Act' and is responsible for ensuring the seafood is safe to eat; Primary Industries and Fisheries who is responsible for the local fishing industry; The Premier and Cabinet who is responsible for the government's response to this incident and the local council.

DPI&F facilitated the co-ordination of these diverse interests and perspectives.

Organisational Capabilities

I facilitated a learning circle dialogue in Gladstone with key players in the authorising environment to respond to the issue. The objective of the dialogue was to commit to a course of action with specified outcomes, responsibilities and timeframes. The result of the dialogue-based learning circle was a commitment to a course of action by a range of groups with multiple public value dimensions. We convened the learning circle in the place where the event occurred in order to empower local groups with a perceived stake in the decision-making affecting their community. While we used the learning circle in this particular instance, I have developed a range of techniques to support the *Three Frames* in delivering innovative public value.

These include:

- *Achievement Planning*—a system for creating individual staff achievement plans to link staff outcomes, results and behaviours to priorities and directions that maximise public value (DPI&F is also introducing the *Leadership Impact* tool by Human Synergistics to measure leadership impact of our Executive and senior leaders);
- *Dialogues for Action Forums*—engagement and dialogue with external stakeholders;
- *Three Frame Audits*—engagement and dialogue with internal stakeholders;
- *Strategic Conversations*—face-to-face dialogues between the Director-General and groups of staff to discuss a current business issue;
- *Management Learnings*—a dialogue to reflect, learn and improve from an activity or event; and
- *Director-General Chat-line*—an on-line communication system for staff to engage with the DG by posting direct messages/questions and answers to business issues and issues of public value.

There have been over 60 *Three Frame*-based engagement sessions used in DPI&F to interact in a meaningful way with our internal and external stakeholders. This is also being recognised internationally with DPI&F currently being short listed as a semi-finalist in the Commonwealth Awards for Public Administration and Management for its citizen engagement work.

Conclusion

In the case of the Gladstone oil spill, in February 2005 we were able to inform the commercial seafood operators that their catches were cleared for market. As promised during the Learning Circle, the department collected more than 100 seafood samples from commercial operators. All of the samples were tested by Queensland Health and showed that the seafood was suitable for sale. Also as promised, the affected area will continue to be monitored over the next five years to ensure there are no long-term effects.

DPI&F is working in concert with stakeholders, the Gladstone City Council, the Central Queensland Ports Authority and others to rebuild the reputation of the city's seafood. This is just one example of where the *Three Frames* gives a simple heuristic tool for public managers to address performance, relationships and alignment to enable and deliver corporate strategy and create public value.

References

Moore, M H (1995), *Creating public value: Strategic Management in Government*, Harvard University Press, Cambridge Massachusetts.

Wheatley, M (2005), *Finding our way: Leadership for an uncertain time*, Berrett-Koehler Publishers, San Francisco.

10. Building Capacity for Policy Implementation

Anne Tiernan, Centre for Governance and Public Policy, Griffith University

Introduction

In Australia and internationally, the discourse of 'declining policy capacity' is pervasive. Politicians, practitioners and scholars have expressed concern about the ability of the public service to support policy processes through its analysis, advisory and service delivery functions. There is particular concern about policy implementation – about the ability and willingness of the public service to promptly deliver on government commitments and priorities, and about the extent to which policy and program design is informed by operational realities. Anxieties about the potential for 'disconnect' between policy and service delivery have been heightened by recent high-profile failures in sensitive areas of government policy. This chapter examines recent efforts by the Commonwealth and Queensland governments to build capacity for policy implementation, notably through the establishment of implementation units. It offers an assessment of their potential to address the dilemmas of implementation exposed by recent policy failures.

Declining policy capacity

Both in Australia and internationally, there is concern that governments have lost policy capacity (Parsons 2004; Peters 1996; Savoie 2003). The concept of policy capacity is complex and ambiguous, but is typically concerned with policy advising – specifically the availability of high quality information, analysis and advice to support decision-making.

Perceptions that policy capacity has declined are widespread, including in Australia (Edwards, Ayers and Howard 2003). Under a variety of labels including 'capacity', 'competency' and 'capability', concerns have been expressed about the ability of governments to make intelligent choices (Painter and Pierre 2005), to scan the environment and set strategic directions (Howlett and Lindquist 2004; Savoie 2003), to weigh and assess the implications of policy alternatives (Bakvis 2000), and to make appropriate use of knowledge in policy-making (Parsons 2004; Peters 1996). Others question the ability of existing processes and structures to ensure an appropriate flow of information, analysis and advice to decision-makers (Painter and Pierre 2005; Walter 2006), particularly around issues of policy implementation and delivery, and whether after two decades of almost continuous public sector reform, the public service has the requisite expertise, knowledge, skills and resources to support decision-making through its policy advising functions (Bakvis and Aucoin 2005).

Concerns about declining policy capacity have been expressed by ministers, senior public servants and scholars. Prime ministers from Australia's John Howard, to New Zealand's Helen Clark to Britain's Tony Blair have stated publicly that they have been *underwhelmed*, and at times let down, by advice from their bureaucratic advisers. The Australian Wheat Board (AWB), Iraq weapons intelligence and 'children overboard' controversies are recent cases in point. In Queensland, Premier Peter Beattie, has complained bitterly about the quality of advice provided to him by public service departments and agencies. Public service leaders have also expressed concern about declining policy advising skills and competencies (Briggs 2005; Podger 2002; Wintringham 2003), particularly in moments of crisis (Shergold 2004b).

Though expressed in similar terms, the discourse of declining policy capacity means different things to different people. It has become an umbrella term encompassing a variety of concerns about:

- the research, analytical and advisory skills and abilities of the public service;
- the ability of the public service to recruit and retain people with requisite knowledge, skills and experience;
- the nature of relationships between officials and political executives; and
- the policy advising role of the public service in an increasingly dynamic, pluralised and contestable environment.

Within the discourse of declining policy capacity, concerns have also been expressed about implementation and delivery, specifically:

- the ability and willingness of the public service to promptly deliver government commitments and priorities;
- the potential for policy intent to become distorted or diffused during implementation. That is, for the 'line of sight' between policy formulation and implementation to be obscured;
- the public service's ability to mobilise and coordinate around whole-of-government issues and priorities; and
- the potential for unanticipated or unintended consequences to flow from government policy interventions.

Such concerns have sparked a more general renewal of interest in policy implementation – a much neglected topic in policy studies (Barrett 2004). The Blair government in Britain is frequently credited with spearheading this agenda, mostly tangibly through its creation of the Prime Minister's Delivery Unit (PMDU) in 2001. The PMDU is dedicated to ensuring that the government delivers on its priorities in key areas of public service provision (Smith and Richards 2006).

A major reform effort is currently focused on enhancing the British government's capacity for policy delivery, including the requirement for regular departmental 'capability reviews' to be conducted by the PMDU. [1] Implementation Units have emerged within the core executives of other jurisdictions including the Australian Commonwealth (Wanna 2006) and Queensland (Tiernan 2006). The Victorian and South Australian governments have also established implementation units recently. This suggests that there is broad interest in strengthening capacity for implementation and that significant policy transfer and learning is occurring between jurisdictions – a finding endorsed by comparative research. Lindquist (2006) notes that first ministers in each of these locations have instigated the development of new central capacities to 'advise, monitor and ensure better implementation of policy initiatives'.

The renewed focus on policy implementation has been primarily driven from the political centre. In the Commonwealth and elsewhere, implementation units are co-located with Cabinet support functions in Prime Minister's and Premiers' departments. As with much of the infrastructure supporting first ministers, they are instruments of central control, principally concerned with advancing the political interests of the incumbent leader (Peters, Rhodes and Wright 2000, p. 266).

Since their establishment in late 2003 and early 2004 respectively, the Commonwealth and Queensland implementation units have established strong central monitoring and reporting of commitments and priorities. Procedural changes to focus agency attention on implementation planning during policy development have been introduced and the units are engaged in a variety of awareness and consciousness raising initiatives – the Commonwealth much more so than its Queensland counterpart. [2] Secretary of the Department of the Prime Minister and Cabinet, Dr Peter Shergold, has been an energetic champion of the Cabinet Implementation Unit, and of the utility of project management techniques in implementation planning and monitoring (see, for example, Shergold 2004; 2006b).

Concerns justified: delivery failures

Concerns about implementation capacity have been reinforced by high profile implementation and delivery failures. In Canberra, the treatment of two mentally ill Australian citizens wrongly deported by the Immigration Department became a major scandal, precipitating wide-ranging reforms to the structure and culture of the agency (Palmer 2005). The botched repatriation of the body of Australian soldier, Jake Kovco, accidentally killed in Iraq, exposed coordination difficulties in the interface between the Department of Defence and private contractors, at the cost of great hurt to the bereaved family, and major embarrassment to the Defence Minister and the government. In Queensland, a litany of delivery problems has plagued the Beattie Labor government during its third term, most seriously the 'crisis' in the State's public hospital system (Tiernan 2006). These cases have served as ominous reminders to politicians and public administrators alike of the serious political costs and consequences of implementation failure. As Peter Shergold noted recently:

> Poor delivery – such as inadequate service levels, lack of timeliness or burdensome regulatory processes – risks public dissatisfaction. It can reduce trust not only in public service but in the government it serves. The quality of the implementation of government policy is central to community support for the institutions of democratic governance (Shergold 2006b, p. 1).

Much of the focus of the Australian implementation units has been on ensuring delivery issues are planned and addressed in new policy areas. The problems and failures afflicting the two governments have occurred in established service delivery systems. In the Immigration and Queensland hospitals cases, governments responded by establishing independent inquiries, including in the Queensland case, a royal commission. As well as providing forums for investigating the factors that led to the events in question, the reports of these inquiries have generated useful blueprints for reform and change. They have highlighted a serious disconnect between policy and service delivery – the classic implementation deficit identified by Pressman and Wildavsky (1973) in their seminal study of implementation failure.

In Queensland, consultant Peter Forster (2005) who led the independent review of public hospitals, was particularly critical of central agency and head office officials for failing to appreciate and address systemic problems of under-funding, workload issues, and the difficulties of recruiting and retaining appropriately qualified staff to work in the state's public hospital system. Forster (2005) describes a major 'expectation gap' between what politicians and the public expect can be delivered and what service systems are actually capable of. Managing public expectations is an invidious and likely insoluble implementation dilemma for politicians, as recent criticism of the Commonwealth and Queensland government responses to the Cyclone Larry disaster have again demonstrated. Despite a swift and focused emergency response to widespread damage wreaked by the cyclone, and the difficulties of establishing services in the absence of electricity and transport access, governments were criticised by some locals, frustrated by delays in gaining access to relief supplies and funds. Their complaints were amplified through the broadcast media – a young woman's anger at perceived inaction of 'bureaucrats', broadcast to an attentive national audience.

The Immigration and Queensland hospitals cases also highlight the difficulties of ensuring that operational realities are reflected in policy advice and decision-making, though it is interesting to note that both have been identified primarily as public service failures – as failures of analysis and persuasion (see Briggs 2005; Shergold 2006b), rather than failures on the part of policy-makers to understand systemic problems and direct energy, attention and resources towards addressing them before they escalated.

In the wake of these controversies, the Australian and Queensland governments have initiated wholesale changes to affected departments. In Immigration and in Queensland Health, the entire senior leadership teams were replaced, and the organisations were radically restructured. There have been major funding injections, and agency-based implementation units are bolstering the commitment to 'fix' the identified problems. Strong central monitoring and reporting arrangements have been established, including requirements to provide regular reports to Parliament. [3]

But rather than building local capacity, the appointment of significant numbers of central agency staff to leadership positions in agencies like Immigration and Queensland Health raises questions about the value placed on content knowledge and service delivery expertise. Though perhaps understandable in an increasingly personalised governance context, there are tensions between building capacity for implementation and parachuting it in. It may further undermine confidence in agencies already regarded as having failed in their duties to government and the community. In both cases, delivery problems have persisted after some initial blood-letting; agencies and their responsible ministers remain in the media spotlight, as new leaders try to bed down hastily devised political 'fixes' and confront the very genuine complexities of large-scale system reform.

These developments reflect the inherent tensions between 'the normative expectations of managerial control of policy implementation processes' (Barrett 2004, p. 260) and the realities of implementation in a networked and highly politicised service delivery context. Tiernan (2006) notes the predominance of a 'top-down' view of implementation in the development of implementation units and their monitoring strategies, especially in areas that have caused political embarrassment. Barrett (2004) and Hudson (2006) observe a similarly *top-down* orientation to implementation in the British context, noting 'there is a lack of recognition of the time and resources involved in achieving the organisational capacity to achieve effective change' (Barrett 2004, p. 260).

Political pressure to quickly address problems and failures in sensitive areas of public policy may have perverse unintended consequences, potentially embedding new and different implementation challenges down the track. For example, Barrett (2004, p. 260) describes how 'top down coercive pressure to meet prescribed targets' has 'led to the skewing of service priorities' (in this case hospital waiting lists), and 'even the manipulation of figures for the fear of the consequences of failure'. Shergold, however, is unapologetic about the need for the focus on implementation and delivery to be driven centrally. He argues that 'better implementation must consciously be driven from the top down', while simultaneously acknowledging that policy prepared without the experience of those who deliver it 'is almost certainly policy that will be poorly designed and difficult to implement' (Shergold 2006b, p. 3). Reconciling these competing imperatives would seem to be the key challenge facing governments in building capacity for policy implementation.

What role will implementation units play in this agenda, and how and in what ways will their establishment help to address the problem of implementation capacity in contemporary government? What are the prospects of addressing the capacity problem through the establishment of implementation units? The papers contributed to the special issue of the *Journal of Comparative Policy Analysis* (JCPA) on the emergence of implementation units demonstrate clearly that some progress has been made. Central units are playing leadership roles in promoting and raising awareness of implementation at the 'front end' – during policy development and design, though there are issues about their capacity to do so. As fairly small units, whose work is closely linked to the strictures of the Cabinet timetable, and driven by the priorities of the first minister, central implementation units have limited capacity to undertake the kind of outreach activities that would help to build capacity for implementation across government. Peter Shergold (2006b, p. 3) describes these functions as being about 'learning by doing and then spreading the learning'.

The Immigration and Queensland hospitals controversies suggest that if the goal of the new focus on implementation is capacity building, a more constructive role for central units may be in helping promote better understandings of implementation issues and challenges, particularly among decision-makers. There is also an important role to be played in assisting agencies to more effectively communicate the complex realities of translating decisions into actionable programs to policy-makers. Greater engagement with the literature on policy implementation and the policy-action relationship (Barrett 2004) could be a useful first step, yet Lindquist (2006) reports there has been limited engagement with the implementation literature in the design and development of implementation units. In addition to their enthusiasm for project management techniques, those interested in building capacity for policy implementation would do well to revisit the scholarship and adapt some of its learnings to contemporary practice.

References

Bakvis, H. 2000, 'Rebuilding policy capacity in the era of the fiscal dividend: A report from Canada', *Governance*, Vol. 13, No. 1, January, pp. 71-103.

Bakvis H. and Aucoin P. 2005, 'Public Service Reform and Policy Capacity: Recruiting and Retaining the Best and the Brightest? in M. Painter and J. Pierre (eds.) *Challenges to State Policy Capacity*, Palgrave Macmillan, Houndmills, Basingstoke, pp 185-204.

Barrett, S. 2004, 'Implementation studies: time for a revival?' *Public Administration*, Vol. 82, No. 2, pp. 249-262.

Briggs, Lynelle 2005, 'A Passion for Policy?' paper presented Wednesday 29 June 2005 as part of the ANZSOG/ANU Public Lecture Series 2005.

Edwards, M., Ayers, R. and Howard, C. 2003, *Public Service Leadership: Emerging Issues*, APSC.

Howlett, Michael and Lindquist, Evert 2004, 'Policy Analysis and Governance: Analytical and Policy Styles in Canada', *Journal of Comparative Policy Analysis*, Vol. 6, No. 3, 225 – 249, December.

Forster, P. 2005, *Queensland Health Systems Review Final Report*, Queensland Government, September 2005.

Lindquist, E.A. 2006, 'Organising for policy implementation: the emergence and role of Implementation Units in policy design and oversight', *Journal of Comparative Policy Analysis*, Vol 8, No. 4, December, p 421.

Painter, M. and Pierre, J. 2005, 'Unpacking policy capacity: issues and themes'. In Painter, M. and Pierre, J. (eds.) *Challenges to State Policy Capacity: Global Trends and Comparative Perspectives*, Palgrave Macmillan, Basingstoke.

Palmer, Mick 2005, *Inquiry into the Circumstances of the Immigration Detention of Cornelia Rau*, Commonwealth of Australia, July 2005.

Parsons, W. 2004, 'Not just steering but weaving: relevant knowledge and the craft of building policy capacity and coherence', *Australian Journal of Public Administration*. Vol. 63 (1), March, pp. 43-57.

Peters, B.G. 1996, *The Policy Capacity of Government*. Canadian Centre for Management Development.

Peters, B.G., Rhodes, R.A.W. and Wright, V. 2000, 'The struggle for control' in Peters, B.G., Rhodes, R.A.W. and Wright, V (eds.) *Administering the Summit: Administration of the Core Executive in Developed Countries*, Macmillan, Houndmills.

Podger, Andrew 2002, 'Defining an Australian approach to the roles and values of the public service in the twenty-first century', *Canberra Bulletin of Public Administration*, no.104, June 2002, pp 1-5.

Pressman, J. and Wildavsky, A. 1973, *Implementation*, University of California, Berkley.

Savoie, D. 2003, *Strengthening the Policy Capacity of Government*, Report to the Panel on the Role of Government, Research Paper Series, Vol 1, pp 239-290.

Shergold, Peter. 2006a, *Pride in Public Service,* Address to the National Press Club, Canberra, 15 February.

Shergold, Peter 2006b, *Project Management in Public Administration*, Speech delivered to ANZSOG Conference on Project Management and Organisational Change, Canberra, 22 February.

Smith, M. and Richards, D. 2006, 'Central control and policy implementation in the UK: a case study of the Prime Minister's Delivery Unit', *Journal of Comparative Policy Analysis*, Vol 8, No. 4, December, p. 325.

Tiernan, A. 2006, 'Working with the stock we have: the evolving role of Queensland's implementation unit', *Journal of Comparative Policy Analysis*, Vol 8, No. 4, December. p. 371.

Walter, James 2006, 'Ministers, Minders and Public Servants: Changing Parameters of responsibility in Australia', Australian Journal of Public Administration, Vol 65, No 3, pp 22-27.

Wanna, J. 2006, 'From Afterthought to Afterburner: Australia's Cabinet Implementation Unit', *Journal of Comparative Policy Analysis*, Vol 8, No. 4, December, p. 347.

ENDNOTES

[1] The capability review process was announced by Cabinet Secretary and Head of the Home Civil Service, Sir Gus O'Donnell, at an appearance before the House of Commons Public Administration Select Committee in October 2005. Though details are still be worked through, the departmental capability reviews will focus explicitly on 'the underlying capability issues that impact on effective delivery'. For more information see O'Donnell's statement at: http://www.civilservice.gov.uk/publications/html/pasc_speaking_note.asp

[2] For detailed descriptions of the structure and activities of the Commonwealth and Queensland Implementation Units see Wanna (2006) and Tiernan (2006) respectively, while for a comparative assessment of these developments see Lindquist (2006).

[3] Immigration is due to report to Parliament in September 2006. Queensland Health must report formally on the implementation of the *Health Action Plan* by December 2006, but is posting regular reports on progress towards key promises on its website http://www.health.qld.gov.au/news/6mthchklist.asp

Section IV. Better Project and Program Delivery

11. Program Management and Organisational Change: New Directions for Implementation

Lynelle Briggs, Australian Public Service Commissioner

The Issues

Effective and responsive program management is not simply about *technique*. Rather, we are here concerned with the much harder job of changing our organisations. This leads neatly to the question of why do we need to change? What problems, what issues, what challenges are we responding to?

The answer to these questions will, of course, vary depending on the very specific contexts of our agencies, and the public sector jurisdiction in which we work. There are, however, a number of 'generic' factors common to Australia and other advanced countries that are driving change across Australia's public sector.

I want to look briefly at those that I regard as especially important for organisational change. They are:

- community or citizen expectations,
- challenges to implementation,
- organisational performance,
- complex, difficult and seemingly intractable, or 'wicked', problems, and
- political interest and will to improve the realisation of policy goals.

Community Expectations

Australians are much more sophisticated consumers of government services than they were only a few decades ago. They are much better educated, much wealthier and benefit not only from a supportive social safety net, but also from the convergence of new administrative law in the 1980s and widespread access to media and information and communication technologies. With this improvement in Australian's standard of living, our focus has switched from the Government providing the basic fundamentals of health care, shelter and welfare towards the overall quality and standard of government services.

Yet, as we have become wealthier and more sophisticated, we are no happier and we demand more from governments than ever before. The Australian community now expects high quality, seamless, accessible and responsive service delivery ... and that's how it should be!

Implementation Problems

At the same time, the Australian public sector has become more efficient, effective and innovative at delivering government services. It is, then, somewhat paradoxical that successive governments at all levels in Australia have been bedevilled by implementation problems, or by programs going off the rails.

There is no one particular cause, more a reflection of a multitude of sins—for example, where policy design has failed to properly take account of the challenges to implementation, resulting in cost overruns, unexpected delays and poor outcomes; or where officials have failed to get across to governments the problems of underinvestment in essential aspects of programs; or where we have not appreciated the time that it might take to get key stakeholders on side; or where officials have not kept their eyes on the target or have let the ball drop; or where we have simply failed to appreciate the higher standards demanded of us today.

Organisational Performance

Everyone knows that the world is changing constantly. Many of us have trouble just keeping up and, yet, the spot light is on all of our organisations' performances and how they might be improved, in the wake of productivity requirements, tighter budgets, higher community expectations and so on. Our goal really should be to move from a leading edge public sector, where we are now, to an outstanding one. That's why organisational change is so closely linked with effective program management.

'Wicked' Problems

Complicating the picture even further are what Peter Shergold describes as 'wicked problems'—complex and intractable issues, such as the health and economic well-being of Aboriginal and Torres Strait Islanders, balancing environmental protection and economic growth, social under classes and welfare dependency and national security; problems that are seemingly resistant to government intervention. [1]

These are the sorts of problems that urgently need to be *both* the focus of new thinking (informed by past experience) *and* subject to leadership that employs dynamic and citizen focussed techniques—that are integrated and coordinated across agencies and jurisdictions. On top of that, there needs to be a commitment to directing the right level of resources to the task.

It is in this context that we have seen, in Australia and around the world, a focus on connecting government; on whole of government solutions to hard problems; on working across agencies and across jurisdictions; and on horizontal governance that involves stakeholders in the design, planning and implementation of government programs.

We are, of course, also seeing new and innovative approaches in many areas, but the point is that there is more to do, and there are no one-size-fits-all solutions. Many of these 'wicked' problems—addiction, obesity, welfare dependence—require behavioural change. Much of the recent policy design in these areas is underpinned by notions of shared responsibility and self reliance, and an acknowledgement that governmnts cannot achieve their objectives without the support and involvement of the community, or without increased cooperation and collaboration between sectors and agencies—more 'co-productions' (as ANZSOG is known to describe them).

This approach is evident, for example, in remote Aboriginal and Torres Strait Islander communities where communities make commitments (to improve school attendance, reduce drug and alcohol use, for example) and governments undertake to provide services or funding to assist the community to achieve their objectives (through Regional Partnership Agreements and Shared Responsibility Agreements).

Political Will and Interest

Responsiveness to the elected government was a key theme of the watershed report of the Coombs Commission into Australian Government administration in the mid-70s, and was generally understood in terms of how the Government's intentions were translated into policy.

What we are seeing today is a determination by the Government to have greater influence on the timely and effective delivery of their policy interventions. Governments want to see some 'bang for their bucks'—clear improvements as a result of their interventions. They do not want to see their money fritted away or unspent through poor planning or bureaucratic time wasting or incompetence. Indeed, Peter Shergold said last week that '[e]very government knows that its future depends not only on how wisely it makes decisions but on how effectively its public service delivers them'.

It is, therefore, not surprising that the Australian Government has moved to push for a greater focus on Government outcomes and to make some important structural changes at the delivery end.

It has established the Cabinet Implementation Unit, within the Department of the Prime Minister and Cabinet, to encourage earlier and more effective planning for implementation of public policy decisions delivered through government programs and services.

It is implementing the findings of the Uhrig *Review of Corporate Governance of Statutory Authorities and Office Holders* to clarify lines of accountability between agencies and Ministers and relationships between agencies and their portfolio departments.

What we are seeing here is a determination to get the right governance arrangements in place, as a foundation for improved delivery and implementation of the Government's policy initiatives. This is not a shift away from devolution, but an enhancement, with a focus on achieving better results for the Australian community within a devolved environment.

To this end, in 2004 the Government created the Department of Human Services, which brings together six agencies, as a means to improve co-ordination between them, improve their responsiveness to Government direction, and to raise the quality of the services they deliver. The Prime Minister said at that time:

> [O]ne of the things we lack in the public service both at a Commonwealth and a State level is a consolidated focus on the efficient and timely and sympathetic delivery of services. We tend to look at service delivery as an afterthought rather than as a policy priority.

Of course, the political interest in the nuts and bolts of public administration is not limited to Australia. In the UK recently the House of Commons Public Administration Select Committee launched an inquiry into the place of strategy and planning in government. It will explore, among other things, whether strategic planning is too centralised, or not centralised enough; how people are best trained to carry out strategic planning; and whether Parliament should have a greater role in the strategic planning process.

It raises in my mind that classic question of when is it appropriate to bring project management skills into the policy process? I guess, the answer must surely be, as soon as possible—the two are, after all, part of a wider program management continuum.

The Focus of this Conference

These, then, are some of the complex problems, issues and developments that have inspired this conference. The focus of the conference is project management and organisational change. Its fundamental message is that implementation must be taken seriously, and that we can, and we must, do it better.

In the time that remains I would like to outline my views about what I think of as an evolved concept of program management.

A More Evolved Sense of Program Management

In the early 80s, when I was working in the then Department of Social Security, 'program management' was used in a limited sense of 'to run' a program. With the advent of the 'new public management' it evolved to reflect new styles of operating in the public sector. The use of the term very likely records the shifts and nuanced adjustments that have occurred in public administration in the last two to three decades.

Today, the sense in which I am using 'program' describes the overall intervention by the Government which is intended to bring about change that is consistent with a policy position. Welfare to Work, the Regional Partnerships program, or Australia's skilled migration program are classic examples.

In this contemporary sense, program management is the discipline of delivering, directly or indirectly, the outcomes and outputs that contribute to achieving a policy objective of the Government—for example, to support elderly people with low income in their retirements; or to assist business and community development in regional areas; or to provide more effective government services to Aboriginal and Torres Strait Islander communities.

The type of integrated and coherent program management framework that I see evolving in the Australian Public Service operates on two levels: the systemic or public service-wide level, and at the agency level.

At the agency level, officials manage particular programs and work with others to facilitate the delivery of Government policy objectives.

At the systemic level we are seeing a whole of government approach to the monitoring of implementation of Government policy decisions. This is happening through the Cabinet Implementation Unit is 'traffic light' report, and the 'gateway' review system being developed by the Department of Finance; a focus across the APS on learning from experience; capability building through development programs, and, importantly, by ensuring greater exposure of people to service delivery and implementation issues.

The discipline imposed by program management not only helps to articulate the relationship between aspects of the program's outputs, but seeks also to ensure that they are integrated so that 'the whole is worth more than the sum of its parts'.

A commitment to program management recognises that responsibility for developing and implementing the Government's major programs often crosses organisational and jurisdictional boundaries, and requires joint agreement about what is to be achieved and how that will happen.

As it has evolved, program management has taken on a 'change' focus. The term itself implies, in my view, a responsiveness to the environment (political, social, cultural, strategic) that drives change; but also changes to structures and processes, to a more strategic focus on expected outcomes and, if necessary, to culture—with a clear view to achieving the Government's policy objective. [2]

For program management to be effective in this new environment, organisations must change to move with it and to deliver on the Government's objectives.

Active Program Management

What I think this conference reflects is a determination to follow through on a cultural shift that has been taking place in the public sector—where we are finally shaken loose from our silos, where we move past the rhetoric of whole of government working, to what I think of as an active or dynamic form of program management.

What do I mean by active program management? I mean that it is not sufficient to simply have the elements of good corporate governance in place—to have ticked the boxes—corporate plan—tick; strategic plan—tick; service charter—tick. Rather, what is required is a framework that actively supports program managers (and project managers below that) to manage their piece of the puzzle and to understand and manage the intersections with other areas of their business. [3] Some of the important elements of such a framework include:[4]

- sophisticated scoping, planning and timing (including business case, setting of milestones etc);
- putting in place appropriate milestones, success criteria, and measures for quality assurance;
- proper and early assessment of risks and strategies for their handling;
- stakeholder management and communications strategy;
- ensuring all the resources are in place (human as well as financial);
- ongoing monitoring to ensure that the program continues to meet its objectives;
- we should also build into the management of our programs:
  - consideration of whether the program is having its intended effect and, if not, take corrective action (for example, suggest policy changes or changes to guidelines);
  - processes for advising the Minister of progress, developments and outcomes;
  - measures to achieve efficiencies or improvements in administration of our programs;
  - audit and evaluation processes, including sound management information systems, to assess how program and project outcomes are shaping up in relation to the objectives of the program;
- given the trend to increasingly work through others for the delivery of Government services, we also need to employ partnership approaches, effective contract design and management and procurement processes; and
- we need to come to grips with the new governance and accountability issues these approaches bring—to find effective ways of marrying vertical and horizontal lines of accountability, and to understand that ultimately (whether we like it or not) accountability for program performance and outcomes still remains with us.

Active program management promotes efficient and effective use of Commonwealth resources, particularly by ensuring that expensive rectification measures—for programs gone wrong—are not required.

We've been on a fairly steep learning curve in the APS as the financial management and related skills (including contract management and procurement) expected of us have expanded. I think there's been a tendency for over-confidence, followed by some predictable fall-out. Financial management is a core competency and has to be managed year in and year out to ensure not only that existing projects are supported, but that new projects—responding to new challenges and new policy directions—can be implemented well.

Program failures, through botched program management, result in damage to the reputation of the APS, and undermine the level of trust in government amongst those that are the focus of the program and amongst the community more generally. The snowball effect of unhappy customers equally applies to the public sector as in the private sector—word spreads quickly; therefore active and effective program management is essential.

Programs, in whatever form, are never static. They need to be actively managed with a critical eye for their nuancing and further development or even their replacement by something better—bringing us back to organisational change and project management. [5]

Program Management Capabilities

Peter Shergold describes implementation as the 'heavy lifting'—as opposed to policy advising which he says is often seen as the 'zenith of apolitical courage'. Implementation, he argues, is the point at which 'courage' is most needed, undertaken as it is in the public gaze and subject to intense scrutiny. [6] It is the point at which the policy is judged to have succeeded or failed.

It would, therefore, be remiss of me not to refer explicitly to the capabilities that we need in the public sector to achieve the integrated program management and high standard of outcomes we aspire to, and which the Government and the community demands.

Program management requires a diverse set of capabilities, including, but not limited to:

- financial management;
- risk management;
- contract management;
- change management;
- relationship management;
- strategic management;
- project management; and

- influencing skills.

Even a cursory glance at the Senior Executive Leadership Capability (SELC) Framework—the criteria against which senior executives in the Australian Public Service are selected and developed—gives a sense of the wide ranging skill sets required to perform the business of government.

Dynamic and integrated program management does not require a new super-breed of public servant—but we are clearly looking to recruit people with a different and more diverse mix of skills than we have in the past. It is not surprising, then, that the APS has become a 'graduate' workforce. Overall, about half of us have graduate qualifications, and 64 per cent of new recruits (who mostly do not enter through graduate programs) are graduates. [7]

Changing capability requirements are also reflected in the learning and development programs that the Australian Public Service Commission offers. I am committed to the development of programs by the Commission that are responsive to what agencies need, and to supporting agencies align their business objectives with their organisational cultures.

A common thread is the importance of a strong, strategically orientated APS leadership team. The Commission plays a central role in the development of APS leaders and over the next few months I will be unveiling a new suite of leadership programs for the SES. We have already begun reinvigorating our EL programs to focus more on regulatory activity, service delivery, policy development and program management. I am hoping to launch our new program management training programs by the middle of the year.

Attracting people with the right mix of capabilities is critical to the success of program management in the APS—we need the right people in the right jobs at the right time. A feature of the project management approach you will hear about today and tomorrow is the explicit focus on looking at what you're trying to achieve and actively matching the skills that are required to bring it about. I am very firmly of the view that we need to be much better at this in the public service.

The latest Management Advisory Committee report on managing and sustaining the APS workforce highlights some of the significant challenges we are going to confront in the coming decades, as we respond to population ageing and workforce constraint and as we compete to maintain our specialist and technical skills.

Added to this, though, is the need for public servants to reflect personally on what they can do to align their behaviours and attitudes with the changes evident in modern government program directions, and what they might do to work towards moving the cultures of entire public sector organisations towards greater alignment. It is this sort of thoughtfulness and action that is necessary, amongst other things, if we are to reach the gaol of an outstanding public service.

Program Management 'take-aways'

To sum up, the messages that I would like to leave you with about the evolving concept of program management are that:

- program management seeks to provide *coherence* in the context of (ever increasing) *complexity*;
- program management is a *dynamic* and *integrated* process that *drives change* in order to achieve the Government's policy objectives;
- program management provides clarity about the roles of people and agencies, so that *responsibilities* and *accountabilities* are also clear;
- program management often requires *responsibility and accountability across boundaries*;
- program management helps to *identify* and *resolve tensions* between different aspects of a program—including through the *alignment* of *business objectives* with *organisational culture*; and
- program management requires a *diverse set of capabilities* and *active engagement* to use them and to *change cultures and practices*;

Ultimately, good program management will impact positively on *trust* in government, *citizen engagement* and good *outcomes* for the Australian community.

Conclusion

We are all heading in much the same direction—looking to achieve better alignment of our organisational cultures and business objectives so as to achieve better outcomes for the communities we serve. The language we use to describe what we're doing will, undoubtedly, vary between agencies to some extent, and more so across jurisdictions and sectors. The fundamental message remains, however, that we must do implementation better and that we can do it better.

References

Bridgman, P. and Davis, G. 2000, *The Australian Policy Handbook*, 2nd edition, Allen and Unwin, St Leonards, NSW.

Marsh, I. 1999 'Program strategy and coalition building as facets of new public management', *Australian Journal of Public Administration*, Blackwell Publishers, December, 58 (4).

National Audit Office, 2001, Modern policy-making: ensuring policies deliver value for money. *Report by the Comptroller and Auditor-General*, HC 289 Session 2001–2002: 1 November.

Normington, D. *David Normington's 5 non-negotiable elements of program management*, Department for Education and Skills, United Kingdom, http://www.dfes.gov.uk/ppm/index.cfm?fuseaction= content.view &CategoryID= 30 &ContentID= 199 &SiteID=1.

Shergold, P, *Regeneration: New Structures, New Leaders, New Traditions*, speech delivered at the Institute of Public Administration Australia National Conference, Canberra 11 November 2004. http://www.pmc.gov.au/speeches/ shergold/regeneration_2004-11-11.cfm

Australian Public Service Commission, 2005. *State of the Service Report 2004-05*, Commonwealth of Australia, Canberra, http://www.apsc.gov.au/ stateoftheservice/ index.html

ENDNOTES

[1] Bridgman and Davis (2000: 43-44) describe wicked problems as 'issues that cannot be settled and will not go away'; they typically involve '[h]istorical factors, competing interests or sunk costs … mak[ing] all sides to a dispute unwilling to compromise'.

[2] Marsh (1999:54) has identified a range of elements required for strategic thinking in program management: continual monitoring of outcome effectiveness, identifying alternative ways in which to configure a program, and monitoring emerging issues and trends and the identifying the implications of those for the existing program.

[3] Marsh (1999:54) characterises program managers as 'legitimate change agents', and suggests that active engagement is critical to their role.

[4] Normington refers to '5 non-negotiables for program management': clarity on objectives, leadership and roles, boundary working, risks, timelines and milestones.

[5] The UK Auditor-General's 2001 report, *Modern policy-making: ensuring policies deliver value for money*, suggests some essential considerations for active management of policy delivery:

1. A program is not always relevant or effective in a static form, and as a result there must be continual monitoring of effectiveness
2. The needs of the group(s) targeted by a program may change or evolve
3. As time progresses, there may be opportunities for savings and efficiencies to be realised in the delivery of the program
4. Program managers working in a whole of government context must be aware of, and, where appropriate respond to, changes that partner agencies make to their parts of the program delivery.

[6] Shergold, P, *Regeneration: New Structures, New Leaders, New Traditions*, speech delivered at the Institute of Public Administration Australia National Conference, Canberra 11 November 2004.

[7] *State of the Service Report 2004-05*, p.150

12. What is a Project Management Culture and How do we Develop it and Keep it Alive

Kathleen Kuryl, Manager Better Practice & Project Services, Department of Premier and Cabinet, Tasmania

Abstract

In developing the Tasmanian Government Project Management Framework, the Project team relied heavily on the involvement and support of all Tasmanian Government Agency representatives. The stakeholders developed into a very cohesive group who believed in celebrating success! One result has been the development and adoption of a whole of government approach to Project Management methodology, as detailed in the Tasmanian Government Project Management Framework (TGPMF), supported by the Project Services area in the Tasmanian Department of Premier and Cabinet. Another result has been less tangible but manifests itself in a sense of shared ownership across government, leading to wider adoption. This sense of shared ownership and wide adoption of the TGPMF could be said to be a good indicator of a healthy project management culture across the organisation, but is it really? And if it is, how do we continue to 'grow' the culture and also how do we link it to supporting organisational change?

Background

In 1999 the Tasmanian Department of Premier and Cabinet, (DPAC) initiated a Project with the rather long title of Project Management Information and Resources Project (PMIRP). The Objective for the PMIRP was to improve accessibility to, and improve the quality of, information on project management tools and techniques and on available training for Tasmanian Government project participants.

Longer-term benefits from the Project were identified as:

- improved standards for project management across the Tasmanian State Service; and
- increased knowledge and skills in project management methodology, through training and development covering all project participants.

Outputs included a new website featuring electronic copies of all resources, including:

- Tasmanian Government Project Management Guidelines;
- glossary;
- templates;
- knowledge base;
- fact sheets;
- resource kits;
- interactive tools, such as a Project Sizing Calculator and an 'Ups and Downs' game;
- an *opt in* mailing list; and
- help desk function.

Other outputs included:

- a Communication and Marketing Strategy Plan;
- Project Management Forums;
- newsletters;
- agency information sessions;
- facilitation of planning sessions for project teams in agencies; and
- individual advice and support.

The Project was termed a 'Project about doing projects' as it modelled, tested and reviewed the Tasmanian Government's preferred project management methodology in its project management processes, as well as in the development of the outputs. It was to exemplify the application of better practice in the management of a project. This imposed extra constraints on the Project Manager and team as, not only did quality outputs have to be delivered, the Project itself, together with its outputs, had to stand alone as a model for projects within the Tasmanian State Government.

In developing the outputs, the Project relied heavily on the involvement and support of all Tasmanian Government Agency representatives. The project was typified throughout as people working collaboratively across Government to produce quality, useable and accessible resources. The goodwill and support experienced by the project team, in undertaking their project activities, was overwhelming. There was extensive whole-of-government consultation before the Project commenced and during its execution. The result has been the development and adoption of a whole-of-government approach to Project Management, as detailed in the Tasmanian Government Project Management Framework supported, by the Project Services area within the Tasmanian Department of Premier and Cabinet.

An external consultant, John Smyrk of Sigma Management Science, conducted a post project review in 2001 and again in 2003. In compiling the report, the Inter Agency Steering Committee, joint Business Owners of the Project, were surveyed. The report concluded, 'Information about project management is much easier to obtain than it used to be. The practical value of the toolset is seen as good. The impact on projects using the toolset is seen as very good' (July 2001).

Phase One of the PMIRP, which was the planning stage, involved the management of a large number of stakeholders in the form of project managers from all Tasmanian Government Agencies as members of the Output Working Groups. This exercise increased stakeholder expectations across Agencies and these expectations had to be managed during Phase Two of the Project, which was the production phase. This phase resulted in the early release of some outputs, such as project management forums and resources on the web site. It also resulted in a growing sense of shared ownership of the resources as opposed to being seen as DPAC imposed.

In the redevelopment of the existing resources, and identification of new ones to be developed, considerable changes were identified from consultation activities conducted in Phase One. The existing Guidelines, although fit for the purpose for which they were intended, were incomplete and focused mainly on IT projects. They had also only been available to a limited audience, mainly those projects that contracted the formal Quality Advisory and Review Service. The PMIRP worked collaboratively with project managers from all agencies to redevelop the Guidelines to become the Tasmanian Government Project Management Guidelines, which were then made publicly accessible through the Project Management website (www.projectmanagement.tas.gov.au).

The methodology as described in the Guidelines identifies 11 key elements, which must be considered in the management of projects no matter what the project size. The Guidelines are structured around these. The key elements include some relationship to PMBok , but also others identified by Tasmanian Government project participants. The core of the methodology focuses on the application of a scoping and planning model adopted from John Smyrk, Sigma Management Science. The model is termed the Input-Transform-Outcome model (ITO). It directs project planning processes that are focused on the outcomes/benefits, which the Project is aiming to achieve, and planning from this identification. The PMIRP modelled this approach. One of the results was the development of an Outcome/Benefits Realisation Plan, which was signed off by the Project Business Owners and committed, in principal, all Agencies to the utilisation of the outputs in order the achieve the stated outcomes/benefits. I will focus on this further in the chapter, as it is one way we link project management activities to organisational change management.

Existing templates were redeveloped mirroring the Guidelines redevelopment. New templates, identified from the consultation processes, were also developed. It was determined that if the Tasmanian Government Project Management Guidelines were the 'what' of the methodology, then they needed to be supported by products which detailed the 'how' of their application. This included templates that could be downloaded from the website and content added; Fact Sheets; Knowledge Base, including example documentation from Agencies; A Quick Guide to the methodology; interactive tools and games, help desk, and an opt in email list. A number of Forums were held where the draft resources were tested and project managers shared their learnings with practitioners from all agencies and also practitioners external to government.

It was deliberate policy to make all project management resources, tools and information available electronically, without restriction. It was recommended by the Project Manager, and agreed to by the Business Owners, that while the primary clients were Tasmanian Government Agencies, in the interests of fostering the Project Management Community of Practice, resources would be freely available on a public site.

A strong partnership was formed with the existing Quality Advisory and Review Service, later incorporated into the Project Services area, operating from the Unit and also the Training Consortium, which has responsibility for brokering training for Tasmanian Government Agencies.

Project Management Culture

The development of the Tasmanian Government Project Management Framework and subsequent publishing of all resources on a publicly accessible website has led to a greater focus on the practice of project management techniques within the Tasmanian State Government. This is evidenced, not only from the final review of the Project, but also from continuing feedback from Agency personnel, information from website usage, attendance at forums and the number of requests for information, support and advice. A requirement for project management knowledge and skills, specifically knowledge of the TGPMF, has also been included on a much more regular basis for project positions advertised within Agencies.

Not only has the profile of the project management profession been raised within the Tasmanian Government, but also emails received from around the world indicate increased professional interest and the use of project management tools and techniques. This area has received formal requests from organisations wishing to adopt the methodology and tools available on our website. The free online registration system for the download of the Project Management Templates provides an ongoing record of where these templates are being used, and therefore where there is the application of project management techniques.

Another result of the development of the TGPMF has been less tangible, but manifests itself in a sense of shared ownership across government, leading to wider adoption. This sense of shared ownership and wide adoption of the TGPMF could be said to be a good indicator of a healthy project management culture across the organisation, but is it really? And if it is, how do we continue to 'grow' the culture and how do we link it to supporting organisational change?

We are quite happy to admit that Tasmania is a small State and we are either all related to each other or know each other, or know friends of friends. This can be a disadvantage, but throughout my rather long career in the Public Service whenever we are working on a major change initiative it has proved to be a huge advantage. Certainly in gaining commitment to developing the TGPMF, it was of great advantage in helping develop and use our networks.

Key messages identified as part of our communication planning included stressing that the sharing of understandings and experiences of project participants was a vital element of any project management support activities. Another key message was that the project outputs had been produced as a joint effort between all Government Agencies and were therefore relevant across government. Both of these key messages still form part of our communication and marketing initiatives. We continue to 'sell' the message that the Guidelines and materials are not DPAC's, but belong to all agencies, as they were involved in the development of them. While most of the material is written within the Unit, the resources do capture the experiences of project participants together with research into better practice. Resource development involves a great deal of consultation with our practitioners and focuses very much on capturing their learnings.

While the PMIRP employed all of the formal project management approach including stakeholder management and communication strategies, a great deal of informal networking was also taking place. This has continued with team members currently spending many hours on the phone providing advice to project participants, meeting for informal chats over coffee and inviting agency project participants to drop in. We also put project managers in touch with other project managers. We organise formal forums and informal get togethers. No resources are published without going through our Project Management Advisory Committee (PMAC) who also circulates them to agency project participants for feedback. We are always conscious that Premier and Cabinet can be seen as an ivory tower and that we could lose touch with the realities of the everyday issues that project managers and teams face.

In recent times we have focussed on more organised 'community of practice' activities and on supporting other areas of government business to take a 'community of practice' approach under the Better Practice program. We now have other frameworks developed, such as Web Publishing and Information Security, which are supported by active communities of practice.

It is said that culture manifests itself in both formal ways, such as through the use of symbols, and informal ways. The TGPMF and related activities can be said to be the more formal manifestations of our Project Management Culture and are to a certain extent measurable. The community of practice and associated network activities are the less formalised manifestations of a healthy culture, but vital to its development and sustainability.

So, what is a PM culture?

Answers.Com, Wikipedia [1] defines organisational culture as 'comprising the attitudes, values, beliefs, norms and customs of an organisation. Whereas organisational structure is relatively easy to draw and describe, organisational culture is considered to be less tangible and more difficult to measure'. The same applies to defining what makes a project management culture. *Answers.Com* describes a strong culture as one where staff respond to stimulus because of their alignment with organisational (substitute project management) values. Where culture is strong people do things because they believe it is the right thing to do. If we were to take this as an indicator of a strong project management culture, within the Tasmanian Government, the TGPMF has not been mandated in any policy documents but accepted as the Tasmanian Government methodology through its application in practice.

If we were to try listing the criteria for defining a project management culture I would suggest that it would vary from organisation to organisation. The 'evidence' I use to make me believe we are a long way there in the Tasmanian Government is the following.

- the TGPMF is not mandated but accepted across agencies;
- we have high level sponsors including the Inter Agency Steering Committee (IASC), which has membership of Deputy Secretaries from all agencies;
- we have an active Community of Practice that extends outside government;
- senior executive within agencies expect to see projects planned and documented using the Framework;
- we have a whole-of-government training pathway for project managers;
- our workshops and forums are well attended (usually over 100);
- agency personnel know whom to contact if they have a project management issue, not just us but project managers in other agencies, networks are alive and well;
- we have two representatives from each agency on our Project Management Advisory Committee, (PMAC) and the majority consistently turn up for meetings, circulate information within their agencies and regularly provide timely feedback to us on resource development and service delivery issues;
- we continue to monitor and report activities and current issues, and there is still interest in us doing so;
- 90 percent of large Tasmanian Government projects use our fee-for-service QA;

- 100 percent of large Tasmanian Government projects use our guidelines and templates;
- several agencies have recently begun to look at the establishment of various forms of Project Support Office (PSO) using the TGPMF resources as the tools;
- several agency Corporate Plans specifically mention having applied the TGPMF;
- our team is well known across agencies and we are told we have a good reputation as being accessible and responsive;
- we currently have 650 subscribers to our email list (self-subscription process);
- we receive many requests to present at agency information sessions;
- agency personnel return from conferences and contact us to proudly mention that 'our' TGPMF has been referred to;
- current major projects across government – all of which include significant organisational change management challenges (OCM) – have elected to take a project approach, either by individual sets of projects or programs of projects; and *most importantly*
- there is a sense of shared ownership of the methodology on the part of practising project managers, who feel comfortable to comment and provide feedback on what works and what does not.

With regard to helping ascertain how healthy your Project Management Culture is, Project Management Maturity models exist, and organisations can be contracted to assist in assessing the maturity level of your organisation. The Australian Institute of Project Management (AIPM) proposes one such model. It proves a little more difficult to gauge whole-of-government maturity as opposed to individual agencies. While I have focussed on whole-of-government activity in this chapter, individual Tasmanian Government agencies are obviously at differing stages with their own application of a project management discipline.

One can also join Project Management Benchmarking Networks that provide valuable insights when you are benchmarked with like organisations. Many of these opportunities we are unable to take advantage of due to budgetary constraints. We therefore try to use our networks, both interstate and overseas, to as much advantage as possible. We continually seek to share our learnings with others and to learn from them. Our standard response to a copyright request is:

> Yes, with due acknowledgement, but it is 'warts and all stuff' and we would love to hear back from you about what you are learning about the usefulness of the resources and how they might be improved. More importantly lessons learnt from the projects you are undertaking and how these lessons might be captured and shared.

In summary, I believe we do have a healthy project management culture in the Tasmanian Government but the form it takes is probably different to how it would be seen in other State or Federal Government jurisdictions. For example, in some Commonwealth Departments it is a mammoth job to get agreement to common project management processes across individual units let alone across the whole of department or indeed government. In many cases Project Management frameworks or methodologies have to be mandated with other support activities aimed at creating the collaborative culture that will enable more than lip service to be applied. Gateway processes are gradually being implemented where projects have received large amounts of funding. I would contend that gateway processes need to be founded on particular project management methodologies. The UK uses PRINCE2 for example. It is much easier, and possibly more efficient and effective, to introduce a Gateways approach if the project management practices are sound and in place. In fact, why would we fund major change initiatives where there is no evidence of a quality project management framework within which the projects will be undertaken?

How do we continue to grow the PM Culture?

Our biggest challenge now within the Tasmanian Government is to fight the perception that (okay) we have done the project management 'stuff' we can go into maintenance mode with the Project Services' activities and focus on other things. I have responded by using a very female type metaphor of, 'if you give birth to a baby and nurture it to early adolescence, you do not suddenly leave the child to fend for itself, as it probably will not survive!' In our case the Community of Practice would certainly keep things going, but without strong support and continual revision and improvement of the TGPMF, the rot would soon start to set in.

Referring to *Wikipedia* once again, there is a stated risk that where a strong culture exists another phenomenon can emerge, *Groupthink*. This is a state where people think so alike that they do not challenge organisational thinking and there is reduced capacity for innovative thought. Having an established Project Management methodology could lead to missed opportunities for innovation through reliance on established procedures. We are very conscious of this and constantly seek feedback from our practitioners, based upon their knowledge and experience. We also do our very best to keep up to date with the latest research and to keep our own professional development current. We have tried to create a 'living' framework where we are constantly reviewing and endeavouring to make sure that our resources, advice and support meet the needs of our practitioners. We have been told that our resources are very practical and useful, and this is what we strive to achieve. We also strive to keep a high profile amongst the practitioners, keep them in touch with each other, and continue to generate the sense of shared ownership of the resources.

Our standard response whenever someone mentions the DPAC Project Management Guidelines is to say, (nicely) 'No, they are the Tasmanian Government Project Management Guidelines and were put together by practitioners from all agencies, not just DPAC'. This continues to be one of our key marketing messages. We now have an extensive network of practitioners across all agencies and we use constant communication, formal and informal to keep this network alive. We work in partnership with our Government Training Consortium to ensure Project Management training pathways are provided and information sessions are held for new recruits. Agencies can also request in-house training tailored specifically to their needs, and we assist with organising this, sometimes delivering it ourselves, depending upon the need.

Our local TAFE has introduced Project Management training as part of the Business Services and Public Sector Training Packages. We are collaborating with them and they are using some of our resources so that government employees receive similar messages. One of our team is delivering part of the course.

We have begun to work with our Department of Treasury and Finance to incorporate the requirements of the budget submission process into the Project Business Case templates. This includes assisting with designing of training modules for budget submissions and aligning that with project management processes.

A number of Inter-Departmental Steering Committees have been formed to oversight major Tasmanian Government projects, and these committees apply the governance structures and methodology as outlined in the TGPMF. This includes

- the Tasmania *Together* Program which is a long-term social, environmental and economic plan for the State's development for a period of 20 years; and an overarching framework for planning, budgeting and policy priorities for the government and non government sectors;
- eGovernment projects, including major changes to the Monetary Penalties and Motor Registry systems; and
- Social Policy Projects.

Our area has contact with each of these Inter-Departmental committees including the Inter Agency Steering Committee that also acts as the governing body for our Unit is activities.

We are beginning to explore, as a Government, the relationship between policy development and project management. As previously mentioned we already have good examples in government of major policy initiatives, which have taken a structured, project management approach in development and implementation. Tasmania *Together* has been mentioned as one such example. Our Social Policy

Projects Unit, within DPAC, takes a project management approach to implementation of social policy. It is arguable that good policy development and implementation is achievable by taking a structured project management approach within the context of the strategic direction of the organisation. If project management is all about the management of change, so is policy development.

Team members continue to make themselves personally accessible and practitioners come to us for support and advice. We can also assist by putting project participants in touch with each other across government. As I mentioned previously, being small has its advantages. We often refer to silos within government but I argue that through our project management community of practice (CoP) and other CoP activities we are drilling so many holes in the silos that they should eventually crumble.

The Project Services team has also gained credibility with Senior Executives and through the provision of the Project Management Quality Advisory and Review Services, Steering Committees take quality recommendations very seriously and in at least two recent cases recommendations to halt and review large projects have been accepted.

There is no easy answer to keeping the culture alive. I think it boils down to sheer perseverance and the need for a central group to continually support the practitioners out there in whatever ways they deem useful. Passionate commitment to 'the cause' is a must as is a belief in celebrating every whiff of success. A sense of fun is also important and that is why we include a 'fun' bit on our web site.

Project managers need champions as they ply their craft, often in the face of middle managers who put the pressure on to 'just get on with doing the project', none of this rubbish about taking time to plan and document before commencing the work. The Tasmanian Government Project Management Guidelines Version 6.0 (March 2005) state specifically that 'considerable time should be allowed in the *initiation* phase of the project life for initial planning and scoping activities, as this is often the most neglected key element, due to pressure just to get on with doing the project. This pressure should be vigorously resisted'. [2]

We still have a big job to do in winning over that group labelled 'middle managers'. We do have strong commitment from the practitioners, and strong support from the senior executive. But it is at the business unit level and with the business unit managers that we still have a challenge to convince of the usefulness of taking a structured approach to managing projects. There is still the perception that project management is all about documenting and far too much of it. We have to constantly fight that perception and stress that the purpose of the documentation is all about recording the decisions made for future reference.

How do we link Project Management to Organisational Change Management?

Having determined that we believe we have a reasonably healthy project management culture within the Tasmanian Government, how can we use this to support organisational change? We do this by building it into our project management methodology and supporting project managers and steering committees to clearly define the nature and extent of the changes the projects are aiming to bring about. We try to give them the tools and networks to support their efforts to do so.

We define project management in the Guidelines as 'a formalised and structured method of managing changes in a rigorous manner. The application of any project management methodology requires an appropriate consideration of the corporate and business culture that forms a particular project's environment'. [3]

One of the key fundamentals of our approach is that all projects bring about change. Our approach in planning and scoping projects is to begin with the fundamental question of 'why is the initiative being undertaken?' and 'what are the planned outcomes/benefits the project aims to achieve?'. Some of these are then defined as 'measurable' and we term these 'Target Outcomes'. We argue that every project, no matter what the size, should be able to prove at the end that they have achieved the planned business benefits/outcomes.

Our response to a recent Cross Jurisdictional CIO committee survey requesting information in relation to current/best practice associated with ICT project management and benefits realisation, stated that:

> It should be noted that the Tasmanian Government Project Management Framework stipulates that Departments frame Business Case funding requests and Project Business Plans in terms of the business drivers rather than solely technology or infrastructure requirements. In this sense, there are no 'ICT' projects as such, but rather projects with business drivers that may include an ICT component as part of the solution.

In recent times, the Tasmanian Government has chosen to manage change increasingly through the use of project management principles and practices. There are currently no cross-agency projects being undertaken in Government that do *not* employ the TGPMF to some degree.

Organisational Change Management (OCM) can be defined as the management of realigning an Agency/organisation to meet the changing demands of its business environment, including improving service delivery and capitalising on business opportunities, underpinned by business process improvement and technologies. It includes the management of changes to the organisational culture, business processes, physical environment, job design/ responsibilities, staff skills/knowledge and policies/procedures. Projects are used as the vehicle for implementing changes to an Agency/organisation. Projects are all about transformation and are intended to create change of one kind or another, no matter how small or large. [4]

While organisational changes are often monitored during project implementation, in the past not enough attention was paid to defining the organisational changes required to ensure project outputs are effectively managed after project closure and defining who is responsible for making this happen. For the changes to be effective and the full benefits achieved on an ongoing basis, planning for business/organisational change, at the beginning, during and after the project, is essential.

Very few projects are carried out in isolation in an agency, organisation or business unit. Overall strategic direction for the management of change within the agency/organisation may have been established already, and articulated in relevant corporate/strategic plans or similar documents. This should be considered in the light of the overall organisational approach and the extent to which the project is involved in bringing about change. We contend that project outcomes/benefits cannot be fully realised without the necessary organisational changes being made.

Owens and Owens state that organisational change management should focus on both tangible and intangible changes. The tangible being the physical organisational changes required and the intangible being the people risks to the project, i.e. cultural changes, buy-in and acceptance from stakeholders etc. While Owens and Owens suggest that it is the Project Manager who takes responsibility for this, we argue that it is the collective responsibility of the Project Manager, Project Sponsor, Steering Committee and Project Business Owners. [5]

James Carlopio (2003) states that, for a project to be successful, organisational change management needs to be integrated into project management, not just a bolt on. [6] In the TGPMF we have named Organisational Change Management/Outcome Realisation as one of the eleven Key Elements of project management.

There is a growing focus on being able to measure and secure benefits. We support the Outcome/Benefits Realisation planning approach where we argue that no project should be closed until it is very clearly documented as to whom the project outputs will be delivered, what business process changes will be needed to manage the outputs and who will be held accountable for Outcome/Benefits Realisation on an ongoing basis. We suggest that this planning commence with project initiation so that before the project commences there is at least an understanding of who the Business Owners for the project outputs will be on project closure.

The purpose of Outcome/Benefits Realisation planning, and its documentation, is to ensure that:

- the final stages of the project are managed in a satisfactory manner;
- the utilisation of the projects outputs are linked to the planned project Target Outcomes;
- the success of the project's outputs are assessed and corrective action performed if required; and
- the planned project outcomes/benefits are realised to a significant extent, prior to formal project closure.

Outcome/Benefits Realisation planning, we suggest, is all about gaining commitment from the Business Owner(s) to manage and maintain the outputs in a quality manner, and to ensure that reporting of progress against the realisation of the Target Outcomes occurs at agreed intervals after the project closes. In order to manage the project outputs in a quality manner, Business Owners must take responsibility for implementing the necessary organisational changes.

We advise that as part of the *initiation* phase of a project, the Business Owner(s) for each of the high-level outputs from the project should be identified and included within the governance structures. It is the Business Owner(s) who will accept responsibility for the ongoing management of the project outputs once delivered, the realisation of the Target Outcomes from the use of those outputs and subsequent flow of benefits to the agency/organisation and its customers.

Organisational change management programs are increasingly delivered by using a project management methodology with the aim of fully achieving the benefits of the project. Benefits cannot be fully achieved if the required organisational changes have not taken place. These include process change, technology change and most importantly, people change.

Conclusion

In conclusion, the development of a project management culture within the Tasmanian Government has meant a long-term commitment, mainly on the part of the project management practitioners, but also for senior executives and the Project Services team based in DPAC. One cannot really pinpoint in time when it began, but like most other organisations, the Tasmanian Government has progressed along a path of project management maturity. As a result of a major project failure in the early 1990's, there was recognition of the need for a structured approach to managing projects to increase their likelihood of success. The Tasmanian Government's project management methodology was developed and has evolved over the past ten years. It has been an iterative process with input from external consultants, international research including an analysis of the nine knowledge areas within the PMBOK® and pragmatic input from practising project managers within the Tasmanian State Service.

The Project Management Resources and Information Project (PMIRP) was an exercise in organisational change management. It resulted in the establishment of the Tasmanian Government Project Management Framework and a small Project Services team. This team continues to work collaboratively with our practitioners to keep our project management culture alive and healthy. This work does require passion, commitment and continual championship for 'the cause'.

ENDNOTES

[1] http://en.wikipedia.org/w/index.php?title=Special:Cite&page=Organizational_culture&id=38036666 (accessed on 7 February, 2005)

[2] Tasmanian Government Project Management Guidelines Version 6.0 March 2005, page 11.

[3] Tasmanian Government Project Management Guidelines Version 6.0 March 2005, page 3

[4] Tasmanian Government Project Management Guidelines Version 6.0 March 2005, page 30

[5] *Using Change Management to Achieve Business Benefits,* Steve Owens & Susan Owens, AIPM IRC, http://www.aipm.com.au/html/irc.cfm (accessed 10 February 2006).

[6] Carlopio. J, Changing Gears The Strategic Implementation Technology, Palgrave Macmillan, New York as quoted in *Using Change Management to Achieve Business Benefits,* Steve Owens & Susan Owens, AIPM IRC, http://www.aipm.com.au/html/irc.cfm (accessed 10 February 2006)

13. Project Management and the Australian Bureau of Statistics: Doing What Works

Dennis Trewin, Australian Statistician, Australian Bureau of Statistics

Introduction

Project management has to be a core competency for an organisation like the Australian Bureau of Statistics (ABS) and, indeed, for all our organisations. And I am not just talking about IT projects, I am talking about operational projects, particularly large projects like the population census which we are doing later this year. Now I said IT projects, but that is probably a bad term to use. What we really should be talking about is *business* projects with IT as an *enabler*.

I will first go through some of the reasons for needing a project management framework, that is, why the ABS decided to introduce one. I will then walk through the ABS project management framework before talking about some of our key learnings, both successes and failures. Finally I will describe a case study of the application of the project management framework, our Business Statistics Innovation Program.

My key message is the need for an agreed project management framework. This is not only to ensure that you have effective project management, but that it is done in a consistent and effective way. You can then support your project management framework with training programs, guidelines and so forth. If everyone is doing it their own way it becomes much more difficult. I will be talking about the ABS project framework, but I am not trying to sell that to you, what I am trying to sell to you is that it is important to have some form of project framework. And there is off-the-shelf software available. Microsoft Project is one example but there are many others that you might be able to fairly easily adapt for your own particular circumstances.

The ABS Project Management Framework

Why did the ABS implement a project management framework? There was a situation about eight years ago where we had too many projects running over time and over budget. And there also was a lot of creep in project scope and that's one of the reasons that they were running over time and over budget. Project responsibility was not always clear. There was insufficient ownership by the business areas of projects. There was also insufficient emphasis on identifying risks and how they should be managed. And, interestingly, we found there was too much emphasis on output rather than outcomes. This is quite common for projects that are based on new IT applications. There is a tendency to think the job was finished when the IT application had been developed.

Just to give you one example of the emphasis on outputs rather than outcomes, we had a major data warehouse project where the people that developed it said, 'it is built, it meets all the specifications and is fully tested". But the end users were not using it effectively. So the project was not really complete. There was a missing gap between the output of delivering a particular warehouse system and the outcome it being used successfully by the people who should be using it. And I think this is true of a lot of projects. People forget about the last step of assisting users to apply the new system effectively.

And also we did not have a universal approach to project management. A lot of people did take project management seriously but they did it in their own way. We were influenced by a representative of *Lend Lease*, a company that has a great reputation for project management. In fact they argue that good project management is one of the most significant contributors to their profit margins. At the time they were constructing a new building for us so we had an opportunity to talk to some of their senior people and project management was one of the issues that we talked about.

Our project management framework has seven key elements. These are set out in Table 1. It is not rocket science, but a lot of common sense. But actually having the elements documented and used to manage projects is very sensible.

TABLE 1: Key Elements of the Project Management Framework

- Project Planning
- Management of Risk
- Management of Issues
- Management of Change
- Project Quality
- Project Governance
- Project Financial Management

The first phase I will talk about is project planning. This phase sets out the business case including the specification of outcomes that you actually want to achieve. But also, importantly, it defines measures that determine whether you actually met these outcomes or not. It also sets out the project outputs and how they are linked to the project outcomes.

Management of risk is extremely important. The first step is to identify what the significant risks are and this really should be done in a brainstorming type of session. And sometimes it is very useful to bring in people who are not too closely associated with the project. You might bring in people who may not know much about the particular project but they have experience in project management and through this set of eyes they can see things that often those that are closer to the project cannot see. After you have identified the risk it is important to develop risk mitigation strategies, i.e. how might you reduce or even eliminate a risk. And then you have to make a decision on whether you will adopt the risk mitigation strategy or take the risk. In some cases its impact may be so low or the chance so low you decide, well let us take the risk and not expend the resources involved in reducing the risk. It is also an important part of project management to think about what the contingency plans will be where you are not fully taking account of a risk. And of course it is important to monitor risks all the way through the project. They can change.

We all know from our experience that issues crop up all the time. They need to be managed but it does not make sense to deal with them one by one as they occur. It would simply lead to chaos. I guess some are so important you have to and that is where judgement comes to play. But all issues should be recorded and it is important to examine if there are some patterns emerging so that you can address issues in a systemic way rather than just on a one by one ad-hoc way. And as issues are processed they become either tasks or risks or dropped as no longer an issue because they are not sufficiently important.

Management of change is another key part of project management. And this should be planned for early in the project rather than waiting until the commissioning stage, because it really can be the key to success. We all know that change is not always welcome by those who are most affected. A lot of people prefer to live in their comfort zone. So it is important to identify the people who might be affected by change, understand what their concerns are and develop plans to address these concerns. It is also important to win their hearts and minds and that they know and understand why you are making change. You need to convince people that it is not only in the long term interest of the organisation that it is also in their long term interest if that is the case. If it is not their long-term interest it is better that they know that sooner rather than later as well. It helps them plan their future. Job design is a very important part of this process. And if you can, you should allow the people who are most affected to influence the way jobs are designed. And training or reskilling of course is a vitally important part of the management of change, particularly if staff are changing responsibilities.

Project quality is largely common sense. For your outputs, determine how you are going to decide whether they are actually fit for purpose. What are the measures of success?

Project governance is important. Many projects fail because the governance arrangements are inappropriate or unclear. First of all, establish milestones and manageable project phases. A lot of projects are very big so it is important to break them down into chunks, manageable chunks. We have a rule that we do not allow any project phase to last more than 12 months or take up more than four staff years. Once you get beyond that, it is starting to get difficult to manage. Of course lots of large projects are much bigger than that. So you should try and break it down into manageable chunks that you can control much more easily, as well as being able to gain a full understanding of the links between the different chunks. These have to be managed as well.

As to setting up the actual governance arrangements, this is 'horses for courses'. Our project management framework suggests that a project board be set up. And generally you should make the business area provide the chair of the project board just to make sure the project ownership is appropriate and senior people from the business area are involved throughout the project. For smaller projects this might be overkill and the usual line manager, if you like, can take on the responsibility of the project board, i.e. the decision making responsibility: determining key strategies, monitoring project progress and so forth. But they may decide to set up a consultative or steering group to assist them even though they are taking the main responsibility. But no matter what the project governance arrangements are it is important to define and document the roles and responsibilities of all who are involved or confusion can reign. People can start getting involved in activities that are not really their business. Or the reverse can occur, that is they do not take responsibility for things that they really should be responsible for. The key role is the project manager. That is the person who has most responsibility for the things that happen from day to day. And the project owner is important. They often are the Chair of the Project Board or they may delegate their authority to someone else. But they must retain ownership.

It is necessary to make hard decisions that may change original project plans if things do not proceed according to plan. It may be that as things develop the original plan does not make sense anymore, that you should do something somewhat different. You may have budget blowouts or time table blowouts perhaps even in the early phases of the project. And making necessary adjustments to the project plan is a very important plan of the responsibility of the project board or whatever governance arrangements you establish. We try very hard to maintain budgets and timetables no matter what. So, if things are not going according to plan the preferred option is to modify our ambitions rather than just let things slip.

I will not say much about the project financial management except that it is largely common sense. We have found it useful to analyse variations to expenditure plans, particularly significant variations, because it can give you insights into potential problems.

Within our project management framework, there is a set of facilities that are part of the framework. First of all there is a software package. We have developed our own package within the Lotus Notes system. To support the package there are a range of templates (e.g. Issues Management, Risk Management) and Guidelines. And there are also support arrangements inside the ABS, experts on project management that people can talk to particularly in the early stages of a project but also in the intermediate and later stages if problems emerge. We have also contracted an external expert, a chap by the name of John Smyrk who helps us from time to time, particularly in the early stages of large projects. And the suite of tools is supported by classroom training and an online training package.

Just repeating something I said at the start of the talk, I am not arguing that you should use the ABS project management framework, I am just using it as an illustration of a framework and suggesting that something along these lines is important for all organisations. It is also important for all projects whether IT enabled or not.

What have we learnt from the use of the Project Management Framework?

I will first turn to a summary of the successes we have had since the introduction of the Project Management Framework. Since we introduced the project management framework we have experienced better control of projects. We have managed risks much better. For each project we go through a process of identifying risks and working out how they should be controlled. Problems have been identified earlier and therefore much easier to resolve. Also our financial performance on projects has been much better. There have been less budget blow outs. Quality has been built into project outputs – there has been greater collaboration between the project team and the project owners on what fit for purpose actually means. And that is partly because of the improved information flow between the different stakeholders and a better understanding of their respective roles. So we have reduced project creep. Project creep now is seen in a negative light and avoided. If there really is a need to add functionality to a particular project it is seen as a separate exercise, requiring separate justification.

There are some lessons we have learnt, particularly from our early experiences. The first one is getting the scale of project management in proportion to the size and impact of a project. The mistake we made was using the project management framework to its full extent on every project and for some projects that was a sledgehammer cracking a nut. So adapting the project management framework to fit the particular characteristics of a project is quite important. We've also learnt to monitor milestones better. And to take deliberate action once we realised that a milestone will not be met rather than just hoping that you'll catch up at some later stage in the project.

Some of the projects board got into *micro-managing* the project. The micro-management tasks are for the project manager and his/her team, not the board. So having a clear understanding of the respective roles of the project board and the project manager is something that has been refined with experience. And the other lesson is to kill-off projects or significantly modify projects if it is clear that they will not deliver. This is a very important role for the project board. Project managers can often fall in love with what they are doing and it is very hard for them to let go. But project boards are a step removed and should be in a position to stop projects if that is what is really necessary. It is not easy to admit failure.

A Case Study – The Business Statistics Innovation Program

Now I am now moving onto the case study. It is our Business Statistics Innovation Program (BSIP). It finished in June 2005. It was aimed at achieving multiple outcomes as described in Table 2.

TABLE 2: Outcomes Sought from the Business Statistics Innovation Program

- Improved efficiency/productivity
- Methodological and technological improvement (exploiting new data sources (e.g. taxation) and new technologies e.g. input data warehouses)
- Improved data quality
- Improved management of business respondents
- Increased capacity to respond to emerging needs
- Stronger statistical leadership
- Enhanced opportunities for staff

I will soon tell you a little bit about what we actually achieved through this project. What we were trying to do was adapt new technology and new methodologies to achieve desirable business outcomes. But to be successful we also had to move away from an organisational structure that was based largely on silos. ABS collection activities were largely vertically organised around particular statistical collections or groups of collections and that stopped us getting full advantage of new technologies, new methodologies where economies of scales matter as well as reducing the coherence of statistics across the silos. The following diagram illustrates what we did (Figure 1):

Figure 1

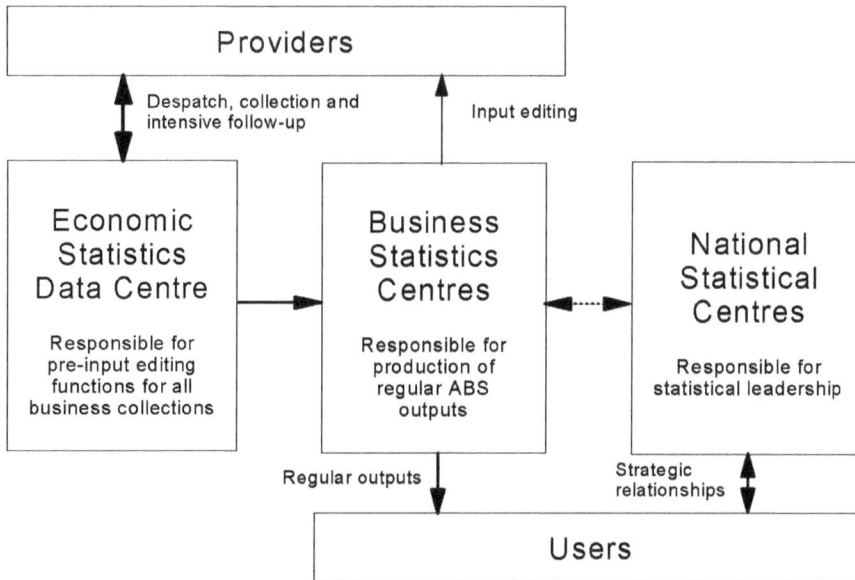

We changed from a vertically structured organisation that I just talked about to a more horizontal structure to provide greater functional specialisation and economies of scale. Starting on the left hand side of the diagram, we have the Economic Statistics Data Centre which undertakes all the data collection activities, all the front end processing activities and so forth. There is only a single data centre whereas there are multiple Business Statistic Centres (BSCs), shown in the middle part of the diagram. They are based around groups of similar business collections. For example we have one Business Statistic Centre (BSC) for all our sub-annual business collections, we have another BSC for all our agriculture collections. The third type of organisational unit is the National Statistic Centres (NSCs). There are multiple National Statistic Centres and they are based on particular statistics themes. So we have a labour NSC, for example, and its role is to get away from being solely based on internally focused labour collection based activity that it was responsible for to having a much greater alignment with the users and producers of labour statistics and to take an interest in all data sources that could be used for labour statistics.

BSIP was a significant program, taking a bit over three years to establish. But we went about it in a structured way. Firstly we consulted very broadly with staff, very early when we were first thinking of making changes. And we actually changed plans as a result of those consultations. I personally got involved in some of the consultations because I wanted to demonstrate my own interest in this major change program as well as hearing first hand the reactions of staff.

As I mentioned above, we exploited the available technology. It was new technology, but not leading edge.

A key objective of this whole program was to exploit new administrative data sources. The key source we had was taxation data and with the introduction of the GST all of a sudden we had available to us all the information on the business activity statements. So in effect we were getting a business Census every quarter. People may not have liked GST but statisticians did because they had this wonderful new data source that they could now use to produce new statistics or reduce the collection load we place on businesses. And BSIP was also an opportunity to introduce greater consistency across our statistical collections. They each had their own life and developed the way they did things independently. This may have been justified when looked at in isolation but they were different so we didn't have the degree of coherence that we would have liked across our statistical sources. Re-skilling staff was an important part of the 'how' and very early in the change program we identified the training needs. And consistent with the theme of this chapter, good project management was also very important.

I would now like to make a few more detailed comments on the involvement of staff. Before we actually started the program we developed a set of what we call strategic scenarios and they were the basis of the discussions we had with staff and unions. The key thing was not only that we did talk to staff about the scenarios but we weren't just lecturing, we were also listening. We actually made changes as a result of the feedback and that helped get greater ownership of what we were doing. Once BSIP was broken down into specific projects we also provided scope for staff to have an influence on exactly what was going to happen within each project, particularly on job design aspects. And there was continuous commitment from senior staff for the whole program. The end result was that, in terms of staff reaction, we moved from staff being very sceptical at first (understandably because there was concern about things like job tenure, what sort of work they were going to be doing, whether they were going to be made redundant, would they have the skills to do it) to reluctant commitment. By the end of the three years we really had most staff very committed and enthusiastic about the whole program and looking for ways to actually do new things that we hadn't actually thought of.

With respect to governance, we set up a BSIP management board. I will mention one thing that I think is quite important: we included an outside expert on the program management board. We thought it was important to have someone who was going to have a different perspective and that actually proved to be very useful. We also as I mentioned before used a chap named John Smyrk who did a review at the very beginning of the proposed arrangements and also mid way through the program just to give us some insights on some things that we might do a little bit better. The BSIP program was broken up into a series of projects and line managers took responsibilities for particular projects. Because of the size of BSIP we set up an implementation coordination team that provided secretariat and monitoring services and a range of other support activities.

In terms of achievements, I guess the one that we are most pleased about was that we more than achieved our productivity goals. We were planning to reduce from 1,029 staff employed on business statistics to 895 in fact we ended up with 856. And other good things happened whilst BSIP costs stayed within budget. The organisational change was completed but business continuity was important. In the early phases of the project we managers asked about measures of success and business continuity was at the top of the list. We did not want to implement the changes in a way that meant that particular statistics were going to be delayed or not produced for a particular period of time, or that there were serious discontinuities in time series. We managed to do this and being able to achieve this goal was very important to the success of the project.

There were a number of lessons learnt. First of all, the need to be clear and focused at the start about the outcomes being sought. A lot of the projects fail because the outcomes or goals that were being sought were not clear. This was a big program, involving a massive change. We had a number of projects that contributed to the program but they all needed to be inter-related. So having all that set out clearly and setting up the governance arrangements to allow it to happen and manage issues is important.

Keeping the amount of change manageable is another lesson. We actually cut back on some of our plans when we thought that it was going to be too much to achieve at one time. Communication is very important. We used our intranet to get messages, particularly from me, out to staff about what was happening and how progress was made. But there is nothing like face-to-face communication and we encourage the senior people who were involved in BSIP to get out and about as much as they could and let people know what was happening. This is a three-year program, and staff do not want to hear 'nothing' about it for those three years. People want to actually know what is happening as the project progresses. And just repeating what I said a few moments ago, address the skills development process early in the program. It is very important to involve staff in working out exactly what the skill gaps are and what you might do to address them. It also helps develop ownership.

14. Intervention Logic/ Program Logic: Toward Good Practice

Karen Baehler, School of Government, Victoria University of Wellington

Abstract

Although it is often possible to assess policy separately from service delivery, good final outcomes for citizens invariably depend on smart policies being effectively implemented. It makes sense, therefore, to look for ways of improving performance in both realms – policy and service delivery – simultaneously and collaboratively. A contrivance known as intervention logic or program logic is being recognised in Australasia as one such tool for bridging the policy-implementation divide and thereby contributing to organisational change and renewal. Logic models work by introducing a single framework for designing, managing, and evaluating programs and projects. This chapter will briefly describe that single framework and discuss recent applications of logic modelling in New Zealand's public sector, including lessons learned about good and bad practice in logic modelling.

Introduction

The pursuit of better government is unquestionably a noble pursuit, and one which springs, at least most of the time, from the better angels of our nature to which Abraham Lincoln once referred. Noble intentions do not necessarily guarantee good results, however, and so we find that many bright ideas for improving government processes and operations only barely see the light of day before fading into obscurity. My colleague Bob Gregory (2004) has called the roll of these now-forgotten innovations – zero-based budgeting, management by objectives (MBO), total quality management (TQM), and planning programming and budgeting systems (PPBS), for starters – and reminded us that current and future innovations of the same ilk are likely to suffer the same fate, despite their creators' good intentions.

The analysis presented here begins by acknowledging this important lesson of history, but then looks beyond it to see whether a more stable core of knowledge, insight, and common sense might lie below the surface of fluctuating public management fashions and political tastes for public sector reform. If such a core exists, and if it has the potential to contribute to long-term progress in government performance, then it is worthwhile trying to unearth it. One place to start doing this is with a disparate set of good-practice methods drawn from the fields of public policy, program evaluation, and public management, all of which reflect a common set of basic propositions about the nature of policy and policymaking.

This chapter has two main purposes: (1) to identify and describe a common core of common sense wisdom that unites recent developments in the areas of policy design, public management, and program evaluation, and (2) to plead the case for focusing our limited attention on developing, nurturing, and applying this core of ideas across the public sector, rather than perpetuating competition among new policy and management 'innovations' and their acronyms.

The Common Core

In today's fragmented and narrowly specialised public sector, different functional areas quickly develop their own distinctive language and practice. Thus, as public management theory and practice has settled into the current era of 'managing-for-outcomes' (MfO) and 'results-based management', the field of policy analysis and advice has been striving to become better informed by evidence, sensitive to community concerns and interests, forward-thinking, and outward-looking. Over the same period, program evaluators have been developing a wide array of methodologies suited to different kinds of evaluation tasks, as well as experimenting with and adapting techniques drawn from the fields of systems thinking and dynamics and dabbling in complexity theory, while those in charge of public sector service delivery have been seeking to lift their game by way of project management applications and other methods.

Optimistic outsiders gazing down upon this scene may see a rich abundance of public sector energy and creativity which is bound to generate improvement, but their pessimistic counterparts will be quick to note that continual proliferation of new techniques and methods within narrowly defined areas of public sector activity is more likely to build a bigger and better Tower of Babel than it is to improve actual government performance. With policy, management, evaluation, and service delivery experts all pursuing their own discipline-specific, smart-practice innovations, it is no wonder that practitioners in these fields are finding it hard to talk to each other and work together effectively. Intra- and inter-agency cooperative networks may be all the rage in public sector studies, but scant attention has been paid to the ways in which core, discipline-based practices actually impede such collaboration. Exhorting policy advisers, public managers, evaluators, and service deliverers to spend more time building networks, sharing information, and looking for collaborative opportunities will not yield fruit so long as the professionals in these fields are speaking different languages with respect to good practice.

Fortunately, beneath the buzzword-babble of outcomes, systems, complexity, and evidence, one can detect a common core of plain-language meanings from which shared understanding and action may emerge. What unites these various devices and techniques are two simple and familiar, but also revolutionary, ideas about means and ends:

1. policy means and ends, and the theories of cause and effect that connect them, should nearly always be considered together; and
2. where public purposes are concerned, only citizens can complete the process of converting public resources into real outcomes. Government cannot do everything; it constantly relies on the active cooperation of citizens.

New Zealand's embrace of managing-for-outcomes (MfO) was justified partly on the grounds of the first idea. Although the big state sector reforms of the 1980s clearly had accomplished much in the way of efficient delivery of programs and services and transparent governance, some critics concluded that the New Zealand model's strong focus on monitoring and reporting outputs was causing the public service to lose sight of policy objectives (Schick 2001, Steering Group 2002). With ministers officially accountable for outcomes and agency chief executives primarily accountable for outputs (and for reporting on the links between the two), there were concerns that these two essential actors, and their respective institutions, were slowly drifting apart into their own preoccupations.

The common language and shared mission of MfO was therefore needed to reconnect outputs with outcomes and to reconnect government departments with both ministers and the people whom they serve. Central agencies put considerable effort into helping agencies articulate their 'vital few' high-level outcomes in ways that would clarify links as well as gaps between the agency's outputs and intended outcomes, with the ultimate goal of helping agencies rethink and then reconfigure their output mix for greater effectiveness. It is too early to say whether or not MfO has had the desired effect yet. There is always the danger that a focus on outcomes will perpetuate or aggravate the artificial distinction between outputs (means) and outcomes (ends), rather than reconnecting them. Whatever the result, it is worth remembering that restoring the integrity of the output-outcome chain was at least part of the original intention. It is also worth noting that many of MfO's effects on actual departmental practice may be both powerful and unobservable; the fact that evaluations cannot pick up these effects does not mean they are not present.

The idea that means and ends always travel together also has roots in certain perspectives on policy analysis. Whereas the conventional view of public policy assumes that decision makers set policy objectives and analysts/advisers design various configurations of resources (in the form of programs and policies) for reaching those objectives, Aaron Wildavsky (1987) defined a public policy as a yoked phenomenon – a program together with its goals or a particular set of resources tied to particular objectives. We might call it a sort of means-and-ends package deal. In order to ensure the coherence of this package, it is also necessary to include some kind of theory, rationale, or causal logic that explains why those particular means are expected to generate those particular ends. For example, the policy of providing welfare benefits is linked to the outcome of improved family well being and social solidarity according to a typical social democratic view of causation, whereas a more conservative worldview links the very same policy to an entirely different set of outcomes that includes inter-generational dependency, declining well being, and resentment between the working poor and the beneficiary poor. Thus, means and ends are not enough to specify a policy; some sort of linking theory or logic is also needed.

Viewed in this way, policy choice becomes not only a choice among alternative programs, services, regulatory schemes, or activities, but also a choice among alternative objectives, the achievement of which would constitute each related program's aim, as well as a choice among causal theories. This redefinition of the policy choice process as a simultaneous and interlocking (rather than sequential or hierarchical) choice of ends, means, and causal theories has significant implications for those who give advice about improving government performance, because if Wildavsky was right, then determining which programs and services are 'best' cannot be done by reference to externally derived policy objectives. Instead, advisers need to present policy options in the form of alternative program packages, each designed to achieve a slightly different configuration of objectives via its own combination of multiple instruments and resources, and each supported by its own causal theory. Advisers also need to present decision makers with information that will help them compare the alternative packages in terms of feasibility, costs, risks, uncertainties, distributional impacts, and, where possible, likely overall effectiveness. Decision makers need to know not only what the program is meant to produce and how it is meant to do so, but also whose cooperation and/or compliance is required to make it work and the kinds of circumstances that are most likely to support or undermine it. This approach to policy advice recognises that policy choices are nearly always driven by a combination of technical, broadly political, and more narrowly partisan considerations. It does so by presenting program options as multi-dimensional packages and recognising that different actors and stakeholder groups inside and outside government will focus on different dimensions of the selected package.

Wildavsky's yoked definition of public policy also has implications for program evaluation. In addition to the familiar problem of attributing specific outcomes to specific actions by government, the desired outcomes themselves are seen as a matter of policy choice and, therefore, subject to interpretation and change over time. Among the various professional groups associated with the public policymaking process, evaluators have been leaders in thinking about how means-ends connections and causal theories should be studied amidst uncertainty and complexity.

Examples of yoked policy choices are not hard to find. In the area of drug policy, choosing between a policy of stricter sentences for drug convictions or a policy of decriminalisation also constitutes a choice between the objective of clearly communicating society's disapproval of drug-taking behaviour, on one hand, or on the other hand, loosening that message in order to pursue a different objective, that is, reducing the social and financial costs associated with drug law enforcement. In an area such as transport, choices among competing objectives are often much more explicit, as when government must divvy up its limited budget for road works among competing projects with different objectives, such as alleviating big city traffic congestion versus improving market access for rural farmers versus reducing road accidents and fatalities. Virtually all allocative policy choices have this simultaneous ends-means quality about them. This is why very few experts have even attempted to devise technical schemes for solving government's grand budget allocation decisions – guns vs butter or health vs education vs housing. Examples of competing causal theories are also plentiful. The invasion of Iraq was expected by some to liberate the Iraqi people from oppression and ultimately contribute to Middle East stability and development, while others expected it to fuel civil war in Iraq and destabilise the region.

A particular program or policy's intended links between means and ends can, of course, be strong or weak, direct or indirect, proximate or distant; the causal theory may be based on evidence, educated guesses, or flights of fancy. Whatever their features, it is these hypothesised links in the cause-and-effect chain that communicate government's intentions and thereby provide the platform from which policy designers, implementation planners, and operational units can go about their core business of marshalling resources and enabling people inside and outside of government to work together converting resources into desired outcomes.

This brings us to the second core idea signalled earlier. The second unifying theme from recent developments in good practice is that turning outputs into outcomes, or public means into public ends, is fundamentally a process of co-production that requires action by both government and citizens. This principle may seem obvious in cases such as social services, where the effectiveness of social work interventions clearly depends upon the receptiveness and responsiveness of the client. [1] But even the least touchy-feely of all public functions – national defence – depends upon people paying their taxes, refraining from gratuitous actions that would undermine the military (such as interfering with military exercises or bombing military bases), and keeping a watchful eye on government's use of military power. These sorts of activities, in turn, depend upon public support for the norms of parliamentary representation and oversight, a free press, and free speech, to name just a few of the essential prerequisites to healthy democratic governance. Although some of these citizen obligations are backed by laws and the threat of penalties for non-compliance (including voting in Australia and census participation in New Zealand), we assume that the vast majority of people will fulfil their obligations voluntarily. Production of the resulting goods can therefore be attributed in large measure to high levels of cooperation.

Examples of co-production are everywhere. Government determines eligibility for benefits and writes benefit checks, but it is up to individual beneficiaries how they will spend the money to sustain their families. Government builds roads, but citizens decide when and where to drive on them for purposes of work, recreation, socialising, etc. Citizens also choose how fast to drive (with or without regard to posted speed limits) and with what level of care and attention (with or without regard to legal definitions of reckless driving). Government funds universities, but citizens decide whether and what to study, how much effort to expend, and whether to join or resist the brain drain once they graduate. Understanding these co-production processes is central to designing smart policies that will encourage, enable, educate, persuade, bribe, or coerce citizens into making the kinds of choices that contribute most to aggregate public goals.

Although the principle of co-production is not often acknowledged explicitly, it is implicit in current conversations about accountability for outcomes, participatory policy design, and public trust in government. New Zealand central agencies have worked hard over the past several years to reassure chief executives that they are being held accountable for outputs and 'managing for outcomes' only (always in inverted commas), and not for actual outcomes themselves. This sort of approach acknowledges the complex web of factors that combine to determine any social or economic outcome, and recognises that government policy contributes only a few sticky threads to that web. It is a small step from this acknowledgment to embracing a co-production model of the output-outcome chain. Those who agitate for more participatory approaches to policy design, through more and better consultation for example, also seem to tacitly understand the role that citizens play (whether they are consulted or not) in the achievement or undermining of policy goals, although the pro-participation advocates often couch their arguments more in terms of democratic principles than co-production realities. Likewise, those who warn about citizens' declining trust in government clearly understand the central role that citizens play in the work of government even if they do not always acknowledge policy-specific cases of co-production.

Scratching below the surface of current public sector fashions reveals at least two core ideas – the principle of means-ends dependency and inseparability in public policy, and the principle of government-citizen co-production – which may be worthy of further development. A currently popular set of concepts known as program or intervention logic in Australasia (or the results chain in Canada) provides one possible avenue for this development.

Intervention or Program Logic

As noted above, the linchpin of a yoked approach to means and ends is the theory of causation. Such a theory consists of assumptions and propositions that lead from a policy, program or service idea – such as an immigration point scheme that favours applicants with certain job skills or a program of tax credits for research and development investments – to a policy goal, such as economic growth. It is very much like an argument, and the causal logic for any particular policy or program should, in fact, reflect the substantive arguments being made in favour of that policy or program in the political arena, while also addressing the substantive arguments being made against it. Causal theories or logics can be presented in many different forms ranging from a simple narrative that describes an expected scenario (textual) to a causal loop diagram (visual) to a decision tree model populated with probabilities of selected events (visual and mathematical).

In Australia and New Zealand, a linear form of presentation known as intervention or program logic has enjoyed some popularity over the last few years. This version of logic modelling is based largely on the work of Sue Funnell (1997), who focused on evaluation applications but also noted the potential for logic modelling to function as an ex ante policy design device, a point also made in the international development literature (Saldanha and Whittle 1998). In their 2002-2004 guidance to departments preparing Statements of Intent, New Zealand central agencies promoted the use of intervention logic as a tool for presenting each department's full array of output-outcome chains, thereby propelling logic modelling into yet another realm of practice, that of organisational strategic planning and public management.

Following Michael Quinn Patton (1997: p. 221), we can describe the logic of a government intervention in terms of a 'theory-of-action,' i.e., a set of assumptions and inferences about cause-and-effect that add up to a theory of 'how to produce a desired result'. Such theories may spring from academic work or they may be found among what Robert Gregory (1989: p. 141) calls the 'inchoate hypotheses' held by virtually all decision makers, or the rough-and-ready assertions by politicians that the future will be brighter if *my* preferred policies are pursued rather than *yours*. Douglas Arnold (1990: p. 18) views 'causal chains' as the common currency of citizens, legislators, and coalition leaders within legislatures, and therefore as the heart of policy debate:

> A large part of any policy discussion is a debate about cause and effect, and it is so whether the debate occurs on the evening news, in living rooms across America, in the halls of academe, or in the halls of Congress.

Unlike theories in science, policy theories are always normative; they describe the intended sequence of causes and effects associated with an actual or proposed policy, rather than the actual sequence. Thus, in order to understand such theories, logic modelling must start optimistically: It consults common sense and asks the policy's supporters how the policy is meant to work, ideally; in other words, it models the intentions rather than actual effects. The optimistic model is then subjected to relentless critical scrutiny.

A policy's intended theory-of-action may be illustrated by a sequence or chain of outcomes, each stage of which represents both an end (i.e., the outcome of the previous link's success) and a means (i.e., a prerequisite for reaching the next link). The particular policy, intervention, or output to be examined fixes the bottom of the chain; the policy's end outcome or chief goal provides the top fixture; and the mechanisms by which the intervention is expected to work form the middle links of the chain. In many cases, a single intervention or output will have more than one ultimate outcome, in which case the chains of outcomes leading to each form a sort of bouquet of logics. In other cases, a single intervention will link to a single end outcome via more than one rationale, in which case the chain of outcomes will sprout branches that rejoin at the top. A variety of configurations is possible.

The chain of outcomes and hypotheses provides a platform for the most important step in the intervention logic exercise: exposing what the policy seems to be taking for granted, that is, its assumptions (Cato et al, 1998). Every policy rests upon assumptions concerning the suitability of its 'technology' to the situation. For example, welfare-to-work programs assume that jobs are available for former beneficiaries; anti-smoking media campaigns assume that people respond in predictable ways to public-service advertisements; tax breaks for targeted industries assume that businesses take taxation into consideration when making location choices; devolution assumes that lower levels of government can absorb new functions effectively. In an intervention logic model, key assumptions will slot in at particular links in the chain.

Revealing assumptions about relevant social, environmental, economic, legal, or behavioural prerequisites to success is the shortest route to unearthing the risks embedded in any given policy proposal. Indeed, risks can be defined as what happens when assumptions go wrong. They are a combination of (1) factors that might derail progress along a chain of outcomes, plus (2) factors that might cause even a successful policy chain to generate unwanted side effects or unintended consequences. A chain of risks associated with a chain of outcomes and assumptions often adds up to an argument *against* the intervention in question – what might be called the pessimistic or opposition logic. As described later, studying the opposition's arguments against a policy is a highly efficient way to identify some of that policy's risks.

Other horizontal dimensions may be added to the logic model as well, and are described below.

Factors inside and outside control

As one moves up a chain of outcomes, the number of variables within government's control tends to diminish while those outside government's control expand (Funnell, 1997). Identifying factors within government's control helps analysts and managers pinpoint where an agency has some leverage over events, while identifying factors outside control exposes complicating factors. Together, these factors begin to define the boundaries for a systems view of the policy in question (Stewart and Ayres, 2001).

Opportunities for collaborating with other agencies either inside or outside of Government

Factors outside the agency's control may fall within the control of someone else who qualifies as a natural collaborator in the project. If that someone else is another government department or a community organisation, then the author of the logic has good reason to reach out to the specified organisation(s) to discuss possible partnerships or cooperation arrangements. Policy logics provide clear grounds for joined-up initiatives.

If the outside actors with control are the program's clients or just citizens in general, then the co-production element of the program can be seen as emerging, and program designers will want to think carefully about how the program is expected to interface with and potentially influence the behaviour of these key actors.

Enabling outputs

Managing the risks to a given intervention and keeping the outcomes chain on track may require additional interventions over and above the program being modelled. This step prompts the policy designer/adviser to think about the whole package of instruments and resources that may be needed to help a policy idea achieve its associated objectives.

Target outcomes (intermediate and final) versus 'actuals'

Funnell's (1997) approach expands from an output-outcome backbone to a management and evaluation matrix where resources can be allocated to various stages of the logic, the program's progress can be monitored at each stage of the intermediate and final outcomes, and operational risks can be identified and managed. This is the key point of overlap with project management techniques, which could usefully be applied to the program logic matrix.

Every policy idea will contain multiple competing logic models – one that expresses the *intended logic*, that is, the course of events or chain of results anticipated and promised by the policy's supporters (some version of this becomes the *official logic* once a policy has been adopted), and another that describes the chain of results most likely to unfold if the policy were adopted and implemented, that is, the *realistic logic*. The realistic logic is, of course, the policy analyst's *holy grail* – a glimpse of the policy's actual future. If policy analysts could accurately describe the realistic logic before a policy is implemented, they could advise more confidently about both the preferred course of action for government to take and the best way to manage risks in chosen policies. [2]

Unfortunately, analysts cannot generate accurate, realistic logics with any confidence, at least not in complex policy areas, but they can test official logic against its *opposition logic*. Opposition logic refers to the chain of failures or disasters that would result if a policy fulfilled the expectations of its critics rather than its supporters. Comparing official and opposition logics yields considerable insights about a policy's risks – both political and operational. This technique allows policy analysts to make use of political rhetoric – the language of both clients and clients' opponents – to structure and guide (but not pre-empt) analysis. It also helps clarify the principle of the inseparability of policy ends and policy means by emphasising the importance of clarifying causal theory. Starting from identical programs, different causal theories can lead to entirely different outcomes, and for this reason, logic models need to explain why and how they expect one particular set of outputs to generate a particular set of outcomes.

Some policies will arrive on the analyst's desk already sporting multiple rationales thanks to *coalition logic*. Because officials can bargain around means more easily than around ends, they often find it easier to agree on a particular activity than to agree on a goal for the activity (Kingdon, 1984). For example, supporters of wetlands conservation might assemble a coalition consisting of environmentalist groups, who wish to protect fragile species, and traditional hunting clubs, who wish to preserve duck-breeding habitats so that they can hunt the ducks. Although the groups' values and purposes diverge rather sharply at the top of the policy's outcomes chain, they coincide lower down the chain, and this coincidence of intermediate outcomes may be sufficient to sustain the political coalition. In this example, the politically astute user of intervention logic may decide to obscure the divergence in ultimate ends by truncating the outcomes chain somewhere in the middle, below the point of disagreement.

One of the most forceful of all logic models is the *analogy*. Analogies may take normative forms, for example, work is to welfare receipt what voting is to citizenship. Or they may take hypothesis-like forms, for example, the decriminalisation of marijuana is to expected marijuana consumption what repeal of prohibition was to alcohol consumption in the U.S. in the 1930s (MacCoun and Reuter, 2001). The analogical device informs policy by revealing and providing evidence about the mechanisms that cause outcomes – evidence taken from analogous, but not identical, times, places or policy sectors.

Intervention logic offers policy advisers a structured approach to critical thinking rather than a formula-driven decision tool. Whereas decision-based methods tell the advisor to recommend the option with the highest score on the top-weighted criterion or the highest benefit/cost ratio, intervention logic does not produce any recommendation at all. Instead, to borrow Sir Geoffrey Vickers' (1965: p. 40) term, intervention logic helps the analyst build and communicate an 'appreciation' of the policy's key features – facts, values, assumptions, mechanisms of intended cause and effect, and likely feedback effects. The practice of logic modelling seeks to promote a critical stance toward conventional wisdom but from an internal vantage point rather than a bird's eye view. Intervention logic assumes that, at least in some cases, a policy's key features, including both strengths and weaknesses, are easier to see at close range. It assumes that we often cannot judge the degree of divergence between intentions and reality until we truly grasp the intentions. Therefore, the skilled intervention logic user starts by taking conventional wisdom seriously (even when one thinks it is wrong), modelling the rationale behind a current or proposed policy, and then identifying its strong and weak links.

Toward Better Practice

Experience with applying intervention logic in the New Zealand public service has generated a few lessons about good and bad practice.

Learning v accountability

A common complaint about logic modelling is its vulnerability to being captured by conventional thinking. Once a policy or program backbone has been created, it tends to look authoritative and people may think twice about questioning it. Over the last several years, as New Zealand departments prepared their department-wide 'outcomes hierarchies' or logic models to be included in *Statements of Intent*, some concerns have been expressed about the tendency for departments to simply use the logic model format to rationalise and justify their status quo policies and outputs, rather than using it to examine critically their mix of outputs. The litmus test of outcomes-based management, and logic modelling, when used as one of its tools, is whether or not it gives departments a platform from which to make changes in their output mixes to boost effectiveness. It is not yet clear that such changes are occurring as hoped.

Does this absence of discernible impacts mean that logic modelling is either a bad idea or hopelessly unrealistic or both? On one hand, a methodological purist would have to condemn the kind of retrofitting application of logic models that departments are suspected of using in New Zealand. Good practice in intervention logic clearly emphasises the absolute necessity of revealing assumptions and risks associated with each backbone and critiquing each step in the causal logic. It is not meant to be used for rationalising or shoring up either current policy or someone's favoured proposals for change. On the other hand, no one should be surprised when departments respond to an official request for performance-related information by defending their existing programs. When faced with official reporting requirements, no matter how non-threatening the language of the requirement, rational departmental officials will always use whatever tools are available to weave the most positive picture possible of their department's development. Officials know that all reporting can and will be used to construct a 'performance story' tied to their departments (Mayne 2004), and it is natural for them to want to control that story to the greatest extent possible. [3] For this reason, central agencies probably ought to acknowledge quietly that some sugar-coating of departmental performance stories is tolerable, *but only if* robust procedures are in place for scrutinising these performance stories and asking the kinds of hard questions that will reveal areas of weakness. Parliamentary committees, auditor agencies, and other institutional actors will probably play big roles in this. It may be time for government to direct some of its attention away from making marginal improvements in departmental reporting and direct it toward building more effective scrutiny and feedback arrangements.

Gregory (2004) has argued that political imperatives will always swamp serious efforts by policy advisers to question the government's policy thinking. Therefore, according to his argument, expecting policy advisers to use logic modelling techniques even for internal policy advice may be unrealistic. Even if Gregory is overstating somewhat the obstacles to free and frank policy advice, it is probably hopelessly idealistic for us to expect departments to publish reports on their websites that contain logic models revealing their current program's deepest vulnerabilities, particularly if the department is still early in the process of addressing those vulnerabilities. Good practice in logic modelling, if it happens anywhere, is most likely to be found in policy and management teams that are working behind the scenes to improve program effectiveness.

Transparency and accountability are fundamental values in a democratic system, and therefore, central agencies must specify particular forms of reporting that will be uniform across agencies. But at the same time, the art of crafting an effective public sector reporting system requires a delicate balance between Parliament's and the public's need for detailed information for assessment, on one hand, and departments' needs for time and space to carefully analyse and sensibly address problems behind the scenes, on the other hand. Rather than requiring departments to report on current weak points and future risks, I wonder if it might not be better for central agencies to require retrospective reporting from each department about how it has identified and addressed weaknesses in the recent past and learned from them. Knowing that they will be held accountable for evidence of recent learning may encourage officials to look for genuine learning opportunities now and in the future. This sort of retrospective reporting of learning is surely not *game-proof*, but it may provide a stronger incentive for genuine risk assessment and change management than the more direct reporting requirements provide.

Central agencies in New Zealand (and those advising them, including the author) are learning from their own recent experiences with intervention logic. The guidance documents for agencies around *Managing for Outcomes* and preparation of *Statements of Intent* made sustained and explicit reference to intervention logic techniques in 2002, while the 2003 and later versions of these documents did not endorse any particular methods for articulating the rationales linking outputs to outcomes. The more vigorous promotion of intervention logic in previous guidance documents generated backlash among some officials who felt that they were being forced not only to learn a new technique at relatively short notice, but also having to apply it to the broadest possible canvas – a whole department. Although central agencies provided considerable support, the task was probably too much too soon, and there were probably too few positive, internal incentives for departments to really get stuck into the task rather than simply ticking the box.

In hindsight, it may have been better to allow the interest in and enthusiasm for logic modelling to spread at a more natural pace across public service agencies and departments in New Zealand, fuelled by word of mouth and evidence of effectiveness. In addition to being slow, this kind of dissemination is hard to control, of course, and difficult to harness for purposes of reporting and assessment. It surely would have generated a potpourri of practices, very little uniformity, and huge difficulties for anyone trying to compare the effects of logic modelling practices on different agencies. In this case, however, a natural proliferation of practices may have been just what was needed to generate innovation and change, particularly with respect to practical areas where logic models are only recently being applied – including policy design, public management, strategic planning, and project management.

Outcomes always happen to someone outside government

A mysterious and powerful force has often been observed in logic modelling exercises, drawing participants away from thinking about intermediate and final outcomes towards thinking about internal government processes, such as: have we followed procedures? are we setting up the right networks? are we on time and within budget? are the operations people doing what they are meant to be doing, according to the policy? is the minister happy? These are urgent internal matters, and the public management/project management matrix associated with a logic model is suited to addressing these, but they should not to be confused with intended outcomes themselves. Outcomes (intermediate or final) are the consequences of government activity, as experienced by something or someone outside government – such as health status, educational achievement, border security, sustainable fish stocks, and the like. They are not processes of government activity. Logic models should start by thinking about the chains of outcomes that a particular program or policy is meant to produce, before turning to questions of resource allocation, staffing, procedures, networks, and other essential ingredients for making the chain work.

Where logic models leave off and systems models begin

Department-wide logic models may quickly become unreadable if all logical steps are included for all core programs (not to mention assumptions and risks as well). These 'copulating spider' diagrams, as current State Services Commissioner, Mark Prebble, once described them, are a common pitfall of logic modelling practice. Not only are they hard to read, but they also tend to miss out on opportunities to cut to the chase. Some programs' and departments' causal theories can be summarised simply and elegantly in just a few basic propositions; using a logic model to make these more complicated than necessary is a poor use of time and resources. Logic models are most useful when a department or program group can use them to stay focused on a few vital outcomes and on key stages in the output-outcome conversion process. A good logic model should reveal these logical 'hinges' rather than obscuring them (Baehler 2003).

However, those who use logic models to portray policy intentions will often find themselves under pressure to include in their diagrams every possible feedback loop and causal variable that might influence the policy's effectiveness. This is where policy logic models begin to shade into systems models of the policy environment. The tendency to drift from one technique to the other is natural and not necessarily to be avoided, but at the same time, modellers should try to keep certain important distinctions between the two practices clear in their own minds. The two most important distinctions, in my opinion, are between intention and reality, and between a policy idea and the setting in which it is meant to function.

The world is obviously a very complex place. Much social and even economic behaviour is notoriously difficult to explain and predict. No one can be certain how events and developments will be influenced (if at all) by any single government intervention, much less a complex array of policies and programs. Public policy experts like to repeat the mantra that we are constantly besieged by 'wicked problems' that morph before our very eyes and cannot readily be defined let alone solved using standard analytical tools. Brave souls in the social science world are now exploring how insights from complexity theory can be applied to wicked problems to help us understand them. These truly are important developments and worthy of more attention.

At the same time, however, it is important to remember that the basic logic of most government interventions is relatively simple. Policy logic has to be simple and forceful because (1) politicians have to be able to explain policies to stakeholders and citizens in order to win their support, (2) government policy itself is a fairly blunt instrument and delicate operations involving complex interactions of multiple variables are generally the responsibility of frontline staff and implementers (the algorithms of judgment used by frontline staff are virtually impossible to incorporate into policy or to express in a policy logic), and (3) as implementation scholars discovered decades ago, the more moving parts a policy or program has, the more opportunities there are for things to go wrong. For all of these reasons, intervention logic seeks to keep the policy backbone model relatively simple and straightforward. Logic backbones are usually linear to reflect the linear nature of most policy arguments – for example, if we subsidise or otherwise facilitate X, people will consume more of it; if we regulate Y, the harms associated with it will decrease; if we provide a new service Z, the target population will be enabled to function more effectively. As described above, laying out the intended logic of these interventions allows us to test it against what we know about how the real world works. Intended policy logic and social/economic reality need to be closely related to each other, but they are not the same thing.

This is where systems models come in. [4] They allow us to map what we know about how a relevant piece of the world works, such as economic development processes, or family formation processes, or cycles of environmental degradation and repair. When policy analysts and evaluators are testing the logical chain of impacts associated with a particular policy or program, they must draw upon knowledge of the many complex and often chaotic influences and drivers that characterise the actual world into which policies and programs interject their resources and rules. Systems models are simply tools for describing what we know about this complex reality. The relationship between logic models and systems models is therefore a reflection of the relationship between intention and actual effect. Logic models plug into a systems model at one or more points with the intention of showing how a policy is expected to break a problem circuit or create opportunities for new patterns of interaction to emerge. Logic models plug into a systems model by way of influencing the system's incentives, changing the resource mix, reshaping the rules and norms governing the system, or otherwise influencing actors' tastes, preferences, and choices. This is where the co-production relationship described earlier becomes essential. Policy designers need to understand the ways in which each particular area of policy depends upon group or individual cooperation and action in order to generate outcomes.

Excellent practice in logic modelling, therefore, requires at least some use of systems modelling to map the context for policy intervention. At a minimum, good practice in logic modelling requires that practitioners keep the distinctions between intention and reality, and between the policy idea and its setting, as clear as possible. Confusing or ignoring these distinctions may produce a model that neither communicates the policy's basic theory nor describes the policy setting adequately.

Where systems are concerned, model builders also should be in regular contact with the department's operational staff, most of whom interact daily with programs, clients, and their real-life settings. Based on these interactions, operational staff are continually forming and revising their own, often unconscious, models of how various components of a program, service, or policy influence client behaviour, nudge economic trends, shape international relations, or alter patterns of environmental change. Head-office staff cannot begin to understand policy logic, policy systems, or policy complexity without regularly consulting the front lines and comparing what they find there with what the original policymakers promised to deliver.

Top down or bottom up?

Logic models are most useful when one has a particular program or policy in mind, but they can be used to generate policy ideas if one has a set of high-level desired outcomes and a working knowledge of the systems model. This approach is sometimes called top-down logic modelling because it begins by mapping the chain of outcomes that are known to contribute to a chosen outcome, rather than starting with a selected policy or program. The process of mapping these outcome chains closely resembles the systems modelling process (I sometimes call it 'systems lite') because the intermediate outcomes are simply variables that contribute to the final result. The process of producing the map helps participants organise what they know about the outcome and the conditions that contribute to or detract from it, and sometimes leads to creative ideas for interventions as the chains move down the page.

I have not seen very many departments using top-down logic modelling, and it may be that systems thinking is more appropriate in the kinds of blue-skies policy advice and strategic planning settings where this technique is most likely to be needed.

Too soon to tell ...

The frontier for logic practices – their potential contribution to both vertical and horizontal integration of public sector work – has yet to be explored. Can policy models be devised that allow policy designers, implementation planners, project managers, strategists, evaluators, and even ministers all to see at a glance how their separate activities fit together into a coherent whole? If so, what would these models look like? How much detail would they contain? Would they be expandable and contractible, depending upon the desired application? Can website-writing software help us think about the shapes and functions of these sorts of models? One can imagine an entire department's website organised around the intervention logic for its core outputs. It would say: Click here for the strategic view and high-level outcomes, click here for the intermediate outcomes associated with output X, click here for the research projects designed to test assumptions of this causal link, click here for the plan to manage the risks associated with these intermediate outcomes, click here for a list of partners need to co-produce this outcome, and so on.

Conclusion

It is still probably too early to reach any definitive conclusions about the effects of logic modelling practices on policy advice, public management, and good government in New Zealand, Australia, or anywhere else, partly because their recent association with performance-related reporting documents has triggered a bit of backlash against these methods. Despite these setbacks, various forms of logic modelling are likely to continue evolving (though probably with different names) so long as individual analysts and managers continue to find them useful. The same is likely to be true of recent good-practice developments in the same 'cohort,' such as managing for outcomes, systems-based evaluation, and project management. As public policy and management fashions move on to the next set of enthusiasms, now is a good time to pause and look at the core messages that underpin logic modelling and related practices: the principle that means and ends and their linking theories cannot easily be separated, and the principle of citizen-government co-production of outcomes.

This chapter has argued that logic modelling practices, combined with systems modelling, can help policy, implementation, and evaluation professionals harness these core insights and put them to use both within their own professional realms and also as a bridging device across functional realms in the public sector. Even if logic models are not the best solution to any single challenge posed by the outcomes-based approach to public policy and management, logic modelling may be worth further attention due to its distinctive capacity for crossing functional boundaries and speaking a language that unites the notoriously fragmented areas of policy, management, implementation, evaluation, and even politics. As the practice develops, it is not inconceivable that logic models may provide a common platform from which policy designers, public managers, project managers, and evaluators, as well as politicians and citizens, may begin to develop a shared understanding of government policy – what it is trying to accomplish and how – and a vision of where they fit in the overall chain of effective co-production. By this train of logic, the multi-dimensional package of principles and methods known as intervention logic or program logic deserves continued attention and development wherever governments are seeking to work across functional areas, across departments, and with citizens to convert public resources into public goods.

References

Arnold, R. Douglas 1990, *The Logic of Congressional Action*. New Haven, CT: Yale University Press.

Baehler, Karen 2003, 'Managing for Outcomes: Accountability and Thrust,' *Australian Journal of Public Administration* 62(4): 23-34.

Cato, Bertha, William Chen, & Shannon Corbett-Perez 1998, 'Logic model: A tool for planning and evaluating health and recreation prevention projects,' *Journal of Physical Education, Recreation & Dance* 69(8): 57-61.

Eoyang, Glenda 2004, 'Soft Systems Methodology'. W.K. Kellogg Foundation. Available on http://users.actrix.co.nz

Funnell, Sue 1997, 'Program logic: An adaptable tool for designing and evaluating programs,' *Evaluation News and Comment*, July, pp 5-17.

Gregory, Robert 2004, 'Political Life and Intervention Logic: Relearning Old Lessons?' *International Public Management Journal* 7(3): 299-315.

Gregory, Robert 1989, 'Political rationality or "incrementalism"? Charles E. Lindblom's enduring contribution to public policy making theory,' *Policy and Politics* 17(2): 139-153.

Harris, Bill and Bob Williams 2005, 'Systems Dynamics Methodologies'. W.K. Kellogg Foundation. Available on http://users.actrix.co.nz.

Kingdon, John W. 1984, *Agendas, Alternatives, and Public Policies*. Boston: Little Brown.

Maani, Kambiz E. and Robert Y. Cavana 2000, *Systems Thinking and Modelling*. Auckland: Prentice Hall.

MacCoun, Robert J. and Peter Reuter 2001, *Drug War Heresies: Learning from Other Vices, Times, & Places*. New York: Cambridge University Press.

Mayne, John 2004, Reporting on Outcomes: Setting Performance Expectations and Telling Performance Stories, *Canadian Journal of Program Evaluation* 19(1): 31-60.

Patton, Michael Quinn 1997, *Utilization-Focused Evaluation: The New Century Text*, 3rd edition. Thousand Oaks, CA: Sage.

Saldanha, Cedric D. and John F. Whittle 1998, *Using the Logical Framework for Sector Analysis and Project Design: A User's Guide*. Asian Development Bank. Manila, Philippines.

Schick, Allen 2001, 'Reflections on the New Zealand Model,' based on a lecture to The Treasury, Wellington, August.

Steering Group 2002, 'Managing for outcomes: Guidance for departments,' Managing for Outcomes Roll-out 2003-04. The Treasury, State Services

Commission, Department of Prime Minister and Cabinet, and Te Puni Kokiri. Wellington, New Zealand.

Vickers, Sir Geoffrey 1965, *The Art of Judgment: A Study of Policy Making*. London: Chapman and Hall.

Wildavsky, Aaron 1987, *Speaking truth to power*. New Brunswick, NJ: Transaction Books.

Williams, Bob 2005, 'Complex Adaptive Systems'. W.K. Kellogg Foundation. Available on http://users.actrix.co.nz

ENDNOTES

[1] I am reminded of the old joke: How many social workers does it take to change a light bulb? Only one, but the light bulb really has to WANT to change.

[2] Intervention logic shares features with many other approaches, such as scenario planning and decision trees, but should not be confused with either. Scenario planning (Schwartz, 1996) takes a very broad scope and seeks to anticipate major shifts in social, economic, environmental, etc. patterns. (Intervention logic is closer to providing a structured approach to Bardach's (2000: pp. 32-33) more modest 'scenario writing' process, which he offers as an informal antidote to 'excessive optimism' on the part of analysts.) Decision tree analysis (Kidd, 1991) resembles intervention logic insofar as it includes the probabilities of both chance events and particular types of outcomes along various trajectories in its model. It differs from intervention logic, however, in treating the nodes in the sequence as intermediate *choices* to be made rather than intermediate outcomes to be produced.

[3] It is important to note that when departments emphasise strong points over the weak points in their performance stories, this does not necessarily mean that department officials aren't interested in, or aren't aware of, the weak links in their output-outcome theories (although that is possible, of course). It may mean simply that department officials prefer to address these weak links internally, before exposing them to intense public and parliamentary scrutiny.

[4] Those interested in exploring policy applications of systems thinking should have a look at Maani and Cavana (2000), Eoyang (2004), Harris and Williams (2005), and Williams (2005).

Section V. Implementation Review

15. Implementing Gateway in the Australian Government

Department of Finance and Administration, Australian Government [1]

Introduction

This chapter examines the Australian Government's approach and experience to date in implementing the Gateway Review Process (Gateway).

The Australian Government undertook research in 2005 to identify ways to improve the delivery of major projects (as measured by successful project delivery on time and within budget) by *Financial Management and Accountability Act 1997* agencies (FMA agencies). From the options available to the Government for meeting this objective, the decision was made by Cabinet to implement Gateway, which had been developed in the United Kingdom by the Office of Government Commerce in 2000 and subsequently applied by the Victorian Government in 2003.

Gateway is a project assurance methodology designed to improve project delivery. The methodology involves a small team of independent experts conducting short, intensive and timely reviews at key decision points (referred to as Gates) during the life of the project. The reviews focus on the issues that are most important to the project at that stage of the project's life, with reference to an established set of areas to be considered for each Gate that address the proven and comprehensive Gateway methodology. One of the key benefits of Gateway is that the reviews are focussed and short in duration, allowing reports to be high level and action oriented, highlighting where corrective action may be required at that particular point in time.

Implementation of Gateway provides an opportunity for the Australian Government to apply an approach that is acknowledged to have delivered on its objectives. [2] Demonstrable benefits in respect to project delivery have been achieved in other jurisdictions through:

* identifying the skills and experience required to deliver successful projects;
* increasing stakeholder understanding of their role in successful project management and the factors which contribute to the achievement of project objectives;
* identifying early in projects where corrective action may be required; and
* improving project management and delivery skills.

Gateway also sits well with the Government's budgeting and accountability framework. [3]

The Phasing-in of Gateway

Drawing on the experience of other jurisdictions, the Australian Government decided to phase in the implementation of Gateway over three budget cycles to allow time to consider the nuances of Gateway and adapt it where appropriate. In taking this approach, FMA agencies have the time, support, and opportunity to be fully engaged in the establishment of Gateway in the Australian Government, thereby helping to realise the benefits of Gateway.

A particular benefit of this phased approach has been having the time to develop an Australian Government focused Gateway training program and to train suitable Australian Public Service (APS) staff and private sector personnel as Gateway reviewers. One of the main outcomes sought in introducing Gateway into the Australian Government was to share and improve upon the project management skills of the APS. The involvement of public servants as reviewers capitalises on this existing expertise and facilitates the development and dissemination of project management and other skills across the APS.

The Implementers

At the direction of the Government, the Gateway Unit was established within the Department of Finance and Administration (Finance) to manage the introduction and continued operation of Gateway. The Gateway Unit:

- provides guidance and advice to agencies and reviewers;
- coordinates gateway reviews, including the selection and assembly of gateway review teams and assisting with logistical and administrative arrangements;
- disseminates generic lessons learnt on the management of major projects throughout the APS; and
- verifies gateway assessment tool (GAT) indicative risk ratings for projects prior to cabinet consideration of the proposal.

Although the Gateway Unit coordinates reviews, they do not participate as reviewers, nor are they responsible for actions taken by agencies on Gateway Review Report recommendations. The Unit takes the confidentiality of Gateway very seriously and as such does not disclose project information provided to the Unit, even to other areas of Finance.

To assist participants in the efficient and effective conduct of Gateway reviews, the Gateway Unit has developed publications as part of Finance's Financial Management Guidance (FMG) and Reference (FMR) series. The publications are:

- *FMG No. 20, Guidance on the Gateway Review Process - A Project Assurance Methodology for the Australian Government (the Guidance)*; and

- FMR No. 7, Gateway Review Process – A Handbook for Conducting Gateway Reviews (the Handbook).

A high level Brochure on Gateway is also available. It provides a high level overview of gateway for those wanting to gain a general understanding of the Gateway Review Process.

The purpose of the *Guidance* is to provide an introduction and practical information to Gateway reviewers, project teams and other potential participants on the process and requirements of Gateway.

The *Handbook* complements the *Guidance* and is intended to be a resource document to assist with the successful preparation for, conduct of, and participation in, Gateway reviews. It includes material on:

- the purpose of the review for each specific Gate;
- a list of the likely project documents to be reviewed at each Gate;
- areas to probe and the evidence required at each Gate, including possible questions; and
- a Gateway Review Report template.

As each project is different, the *Handbook* is not an exhaustive reference. It provides information that will assist with promoting a consistency of approach for conducting reviews of different projects across government and should be used to complement the expertise of the Gateway review team.

The Gateway *Guidance, Handbook* and *Brochure* are all available at the Gateway website, at www.finance.gov.au/gateway. The website also contains advice on the Gateway reviewer training, the application process to become a Gateway reviewer, the GAT (discussed later in this chapter) and a Frequently Asked Questions section for potential reviewers.

The Review Points

The Gateway Review Process is tied to the key decision points (referred to as Gates) of a project's lifecycle. The Australian Government's implementation of Gateway closely models the United Kingdom's (UK) application of the process; however, there has been some alteration of the content focus of each Gate to accommodate the Australian Government working environment, policy and processes. The Gates are illustrated in the diagram on the following page:

Figure 1

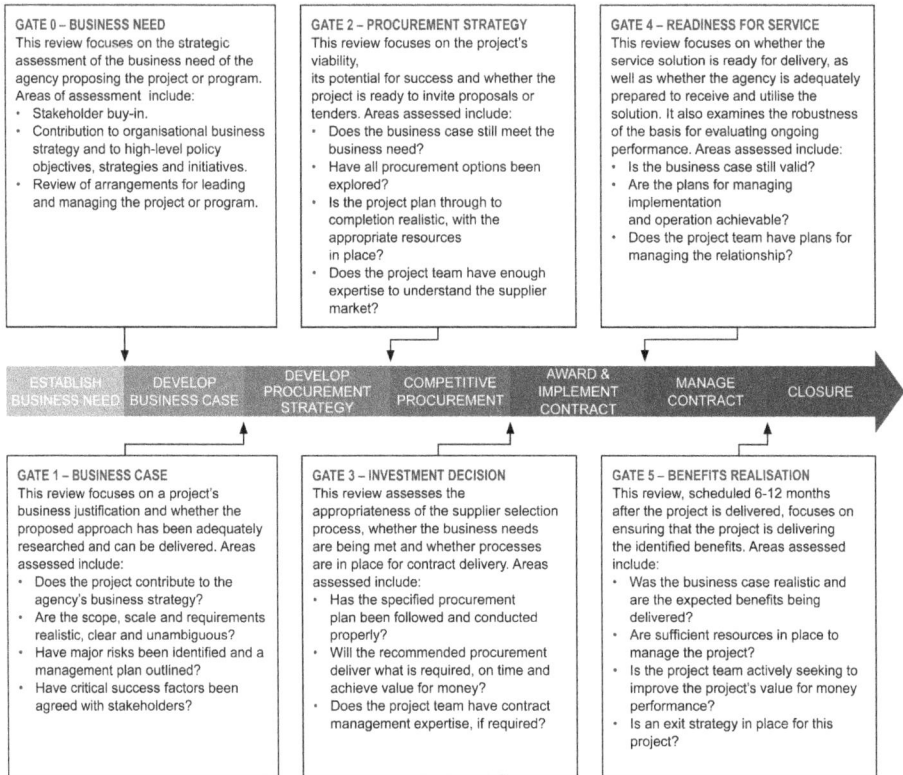

GATE 0 – BUSINESS NEED
This review focuses on the strategic assessment of the business need of the agency proposing the project or program. Areas of assessment include:
- Stakeholder buy-in.
- Contribution to organisational business strategy and to high-level policy objectives, strategies and initiatives.
- Review of arrangements for leading and managing the project or program.

GATE 2 – PROCUREMENT STRATEGY
This review focuses on the project's viability, its potential for success and whether the project is ready to invite proposals or tenders. Areas assessed include:
- Does the business case still meet the business need?
- Have all procurement options been explored?
- Is the project plan through to completion realistic, with the appropriate resources in place?
- Does the project team have enough expertise to understand the supplier market?

GATE 4 – READINESS FOR SERVICE
This review focuses on whether the service solution is ready for delivery, as well as whether the agency is adequately prepared to receive and utilise the solution. It also examines the robustness of the basis for evaluating ongoing performance. Areas assessed include:
- Is the business case still valid?
- Are the plans for managing implementation and operation achievable?
- Does the project team have plans for managing the relationship?

ESTABLISH BUSINESS NEED | DEVELOP BUSINESS CASE | DEVELOP PROCUREMENT STRATEGY | COMPETITIVE PROCUREMENT | AWARD & IMPLEMENT CONTRACT | MANAGE CONTRACT | CLOSURE

GATE 1 – BUSINESS CASE
This review focuses on a project's business justification and whether the proposed approach has been adequately researched and can be delivered. Areas assessed include:
- Does the project contribute to the agency's business strategy?
- Are the scope, scale and requirements realistic, clear and unambiguous?
- Have major risks been identified and a management plan outlined?
- Have critical success factors been agreed with stakeholders?

GATE 3 – INVESTMENT DECISION
This review assesses the appropriateness of the supplier selection process, whether the business needs are being met and whether processes are in place for contract delivery. Areas assessed include:
- Has the specified procurement plan been followed and conducted properly?
- Will the recommended procurement deliver what is required, on time and achieve value for money?
- Does the project team have contract management expertise, if required?

GATE 5 – BENEFITS REALISATION
This review, scheduled 6-12 months after the project is delivered, focuses on ensuring that the project is delivering the identified benefits. Areas assessed include:
- Was the business case realistic and are the expected benefits being delivered?
- Are sufficient resources in place to manage the project?
- Is the project team actively seeking to improve the project's value for money performance?
- Is an exit strategy in place for this project?

The Thresholds

Not all Australian Government projects will undertake Gateway. Gateway only applies to new projects conducted by FMA agencies, which satisfy certain financial and risk thresholds and which are being submitted to Cabinet for approval.

The current financial thresholds are:

- $10M and above for Information Technology (IT) projects; and
- $20M and above for other procurement and infrastructure projects

These costs are calculated over the life of the project (not just in one financial year) and include capital and operating expenses. These different financial thresholds were set based on the research and experience of FMA agencies, which established that there is generally a higher risk for IT projects than for other projects. The financial thresholds will be reviewed from time to time to ensure their appropriateness.

The second criterion, risk, is determined using the GAT. FMA agencies seeking Cabinet approval for projects costed in excess of the financial thresholds are required to submit a completed GAT to the Gateway Unit before the consideration of the project by Cabinet.

The GAT is a high level assessment tool that is designed to identify the indicative level of risk for a project. It provides a set of criteria against which an agency can assess the characteristics and degree of complexity of a proposed project, in order to develop an overall indicative risk rating. The risk rating is then confirmed in discussions with the Gateway Unit. The questions in the GAT allow for the provision of a written explanation for each of the responses to help inform the Gateway Unit in assessing the overall project risk.

As part of the phased implementation of Gateway, during the 2006-07 Budget process projects meeting the financial thresholds were required to complete the GAT. The Prime Minister and the Minister for Finance and Administration subsequently agreed to five projects undertaking Gateway. These five projects represent a cross section of projects of differing financial values and from both the ICT and infrastructure classifications.

Since May 2006, all projects meeting the financial thresholds and assessed as high risk are required to undertake the Gateway Review Process, if the project is approved by Cabinet. All projects assessed as high risk must have their Gate 1 Business Case Review scheduled prior to Cabinet considering the proposal. Commencing with the 2008-09 Budget process the risk threshold will be extended to include medium risk as well as high risk projects.

A subset of high risk projects have been defined by the Government as 'Mission Critical', and as such, the Government has decided that additional governance requirements be applied to these projects, on the basis that:

- such projects are essential to the successful delivery of a major legislative requirement or a major policy initiative committed to by the Government; or
- project failure would have catastrophic implications for delivery of a key public service, national security or the internal operation of an agency.

The classification of projects as 'Mission Critical' is expected to be rare.

The Reviews

A Gateway review is a highly interactive, cooperative and confidential process involving the Gateway review team, the Senior Responsible Official (SRO) [4] and the Sponsoring Agency's Project Team. It is neither an audit nor intended to be onerous for the Sponsoring Agency. The project can continue while the review is being conducted and the review should not require new documentation to be produced; it focuses on information already developed.

Gateway reviews are conducted by independent reviewers – people not associated with the project itself. Gateway reviewers are sourced from the public and private sectors and are selected for their skills and experience, not to represent their agency or firm. For high risk projects, the selection, engagement and funding of the review team is by Finance. For medium risk projects, the Review Team Leader will be selected, engaged and funded by Finance, but the remaining Team members (usually three) will be staff nominated from within the Sponsoring Agency who are not associated with the project.

As part of a Gateway review, the review team is provided access to relevant project documentation and to the stakeholders involved with and / or affected by the project. Stakeholders are encouraged to be as frank as possible in their discussions with the review team during the review in order to help the team gain an understanding of key issues or concerns.

There are three key stages in a Gateway review:

1. An Assessment Meeting between the Gateway Unit and the SRO and Project Manager for the project, to clarify the characteristics of the project, discuss the timing and logistics of the review and determine the skills requirements for potential reviewers. This meeting will generally take one hour.
2. A Planning Meeting between the assigned Gateway review team and the significant project personnel (including the SRO and the Project Manager) to clarify the project's characteristics and the requirements for the review. Requirements include the documentation to be provided, people to be interviewed and logistics associated with the review. This meeting will generally take no more than half a day.
3. The Onsite Review Activity, which involves examination of critical documentation and interviews with key Project Team members and other project stakeholders on the Sponsoring Agency's premises. Interviews will be carefully planned and scheduled to minimise the disruption to interviewees. The Onsite Review Activity typically takes four to five working days to complete. The Review Team Leader will brief the SRO on a daily basis regarding any findings to date. This briefing typically takes less than half an hour.

Gateway reviews should take approximately six weeks to complete from the Assessment Meeting to the conclusion of the Onsite Review Activity. To maximise the benefit attained from a Gateway review, the review activity should ideally take place four to six weeks prior to a major decision point to allow time to consider and implement recommendations emanating from the review.

Each Gateway review produces a short confidential report, which is provided to the Sponsoring Agency's SRO. To enable the review team to produce a report which is of most use to the Sponsoring Agency, there needs to be a willingness by all parties to share information openly and honestly. The Gateway Unit works to ensure this through:

- careful selection of review teams;
- ongoing liaison with review teams and FMA agencies;
- communication and dissemination of guidance material;
- ongoing training for the Gateway Review Process; and
- supporting the confidentiality of the process.

Communication with Sponsoring Agencies in the implementation of Gateway is a key focus for the Gateway Unit. That is why communication commences as early as possible in preparation for a review and continues through to the conclusion of the review. There will be a great deal of interaction between the Gateway Unit, the review teams and the FMA agencies participating in reviews.

Proactive involvement of the SRO is an essential element in a Gateway review. The SRO is important because they:

- oversee preparations for a review and take responsibility for meeting the agency's obligations;
- are the focal point for the work undertaken by a review team;
- own the review report and control its distribution;
- decide what, if any, action should be taken in response to the review team's recommendations; and
- are in a position to influence the people associated with the project, to help lay the foundation for a productive interaction with the gateway review team.

The focus of the review team's work is to provide a useful report to the SRO through the findings and recommendations they develop. Although they are providing a report to the SRO, the independence of the review is crucial to the success of Gateway. The review team is not working for the SRO, and the SRO can not dictate the way the review is conducted or what goes in to the report.

Gateway Reports

The product of a Gateway review is a Gateway Review Report which is handed over to the SRO on the last day of the Onsite Review Activity. Review reports are confidential, high level and action-oriented and around eight to ten pages in length. They are prepared for the Sponsoring Agency, not for the Gateway Unit. Because the review team meet daily with the SRO and a draft of the report is usually provided on the second last day of the review. The content and findings of the report should not be a surprise to the SRO but rather a summation of the advice and discussions that have been held during the review activity. Regardless of how critical its recommendations are, the Gateway report itself does not stop a project. It is the SRO's responsibility to decide the appropriate action to address the Gateway review findings.

The overall status for a Gateway reviewed project is indicated by a 'colour code' system of red, amber and green which allows the SRO to quickly determine how critical the recommendations are. It is emphasised to Sponsoring Agencies that a red rating does not indicate a project should stop; rather, it is critical to the success of the project that the issues raised in the report are addressed. An amber rating indicates that the issues raised in the report should be addressed before the next Gateway review. A green rating indicates that the project is on target, but may benefit from implementing the recommendations in respect to the issues raised in the review.

As part of the Gateway Unit is broader policy work in ensuring lessons learnt in projects are shared across the APS, a summary of the review recommendations are provided to the Unit at the end of the review for collation on a non-attributable basis. As part of this lessons learnt activity the Unit also receives a full copy of the Gateway Review Report but only once the next Gate is completed and in the case of the final gate review (Gate 5 – Benefits Realisation), the report is received three months following the review. The Unit does not receive a copy of the report to follow up what action was taken with respect to the recommendations, it is only for the purposes of developing the lessons learnt policy advice and to ensure the quality of reports is of an acceptable and consistent standard across reviews.

The Opportunities

In introducing Gateway to Australian Government projects, the Gateway Unit has been able to leverage off the experience of previous implementations of the Gateway Review Process in the UK and in Victoria, Australia. The Gateway Unit would like to acknowledge the considerable assistance both the Office of Government Commerce in the UK and the Gateway Unit of the Department of Treasury and Finance in Victoria have given Finance in establishing Gateway in the Australian Government.

The objective of Gateway for the Australian Government is to improve the delivery of major projects; however, Gateway does present other opportunities for the Government. The benefits of Gateway, effectively implemented, are expected to extend beyond the projects passing through Gateway so that learning and the dissemination of experience from the reviews can assist the development of improved project management across the APS.

References

Australian Public Service Commission 2004, *Connecting Government: Whole of Government Responses to Australia's Priority Challenges*, APSC, Canberra, available at www.apsc.gov.au/mac/connectinggovernment.pdf

National Audit Office Report (HC 877, 2003-2004): *Improving IT procurement: The impact of the Office of Government Commerce's initiatives on departments and suppliers in the delivery of major IT-enabled projects*, UK NAO, London, available at http://www.nao.org.uk/publications/nao_reports/03-04/0304877.pdf

ENDNOTES

[1] This chapter is an updated and expanded version of a presentation delivered at the conference by Robert Higgins, (then) Branch Manager of the Gateway Unit in the Department of Finance and Administration.

[2] National Audit Office Report (HC 877, 2003-2004): *Improving IT procurement: The impact of the Office of Government Commerce's initiatives on departments and suppliers in the delivery of major IT-enabled projects.*

[3] Australian Public Service Commission 2004, *Connecting Government: Whole of Government Responses to Australia's Priority Challenges - Chapter 5.*

[4] The Senior Responsible Official (SRO) is the official within the Sponsoring Agency that has overall accountability for the realisation of the project outcomes and objectives for the project under review.

16. Governments Can Deliver: Better Practice in Project and Program Delivery

Ian Glenday, Executive Director, Office of Government Commerce, London

Synopsis

The concept of independent peer reviews leading to improved benefits from major projects and programs is established by some leading enterprises. The British Government's Office of Government Commerce (OGC) have taken this concept and delivered it for nearly 2000 major reviews in British Government. Significant performance improvement has been delivered together with £3 billion savings.

This chapter examines the strategy for OGC Gateway Brand management, the lessons learnt from the large-scale roll out and the plans for the next phase.

The conclusion is that Governments can improve delivery of policy using this strategy provided robust political and senior official support is established.

Genesis of the OGC Best Practice

The Office of Government Commerce is the British Government Agency responsible for UK best practice in procurement and project and program management. When it was set up in 2000 it had to decide upon its priorities in the project management area. OGC made a fundamental decision early on to stop work on an already extensive library of project management best practices. Rather OGC wanted to work on how to move these existing best practices to the level it wanted to influence, that of the senior leaders of projects, the senior civil servants and Ministers, to help them understand their role in their projects and policies. OGC chose one service initially, with which it felt it could succeed at that level. That was the service of Independent Peer Reviews of projects by practitioners. This has been very successfully applied by the best of private sector and OGC wanted to translate it into a Brand which became a product and service, free at the point of delivery for Ministers and senior civil servants who were trying to run projects. A big challenge of course was communicating with these clients without any trace of techno gabble that was frightening to them and would have meant the material would have been blindsided immediately. Not because OGC didn't want a professional body of knowledge, but because it wasn't going to help with the selected audience. OGC has been highly successful, learnt a lot on the way, and had a lot of fun and excitement in making it work. It is exciting to note that, in Australia, both the Federal and the Victorian state governments decided to proceed on a similar basis. We have applied the service to IT Projects, construction and defence projects all over the UK. The early projects generated success stories which were remembered and used in OGC marketing of the Brand.

Establishing the Brand

OGC helped turn things around: 'it wasn't rocket science'. For example OGC Gateway helped turn around the Commonwealth Games in Manchester. The Stadiums were relatively straightforward at Manchester, but the project was not doing a terribly good job on getting the roads, rails and security links built on time. These tended to be in silos. It was easy for an independent team to suggest the need to think about these other things in an integrated manner. It was not about what concrete the stadium was made of, it was about whether or not anybody could even get out of the stadium. It is easy to fix when somebody comes in who has done it before, has been there before. Similarly, the UK has had helicopter projects without pilots when somebody forgot to train the pilots. These sorts of things do happen. But things like the Commonwealth Games became a medal on OGC's chest to say 'we've done something that really helped'. It is important when running out this sort of campaign not to be ashamed of the publicity involved in saying, 'hey, we do help'. So OGC were successful and said so.

How to Measure Success

So how would we measure success? Firstly by the large number of volunteer projects that came forward, totalling nearly 2,000. This is a phenomenal number. This suggests that OGC's reputation is high and the reputation is high because of who turns up, to do the Reviews. Teams include very senior civil servants that turn up to review other department's projects. They are not Review Team Leaders, they have a different contribution to make, mainly in the policy deliverability area. However, as part of a balanced team, they are valuable. This is very different to a less experienced person turning up. Ministers are now always interviewed on their projects by the review team and they have been very supportive and very helpful. We are now achieving a 6.5 per cent a year delivery improvement. Whilst we wish it was 100 per cent, there is nothing else that we are doing in Britain which is remotely providing 6.5 per cent across our big portfolio. In value terms the British Government gains 150 times more value out of this than it costs to run the Brand. It costs us five million pounds a year to run it and we make £1 Billion VFM savings every year. We make a lot of savings out of it but it is not why we do it. We do it because it is a better deal for the taxpayer in getting the benefits of projects. Nobody really questions the cash anymore, it is more about the benefits.

The Other Benefits of OGC Gateway

These sorts of initiatives have very surprising outcomes. One was that OGC learnt so many lessons from the reviews, that The British Government had to put into place a major initiative to set up project management Centres of Excellence (COE's) to embed those lessons in their own departments. The COE's take the lessons, and embed them up front in the next generation of projects, so that if a mistake happens it happens once but it will not happen too many times. So excellence became fallout. Rather fascinating fallout was that all senior civil servants are now required to do Gateway Review training and it is a career expectation to turn up to do Gateway Reviews. These reviews are now the project management training of choice for senior civil servants. So England has nearly 4,000 people now who, because they have been trained as review team members and have turned up on reviews, do their day job quite differently. That is a tremendous outcome, so we managed to get some short term outcomes, some medium term outcomes with the service of excellence and these terrific long term reskilling outcomes. And we have now built that in to the civil service standard career progression criteria. But it has taken five years to get to that happy state. So why did we succeed and how does it help other people?

Why did The British Government Succeed?

The UK had a clear business case for action. Politicians and the top of the civil service had had enough of failure to deliver. Therefore we did not have to generate enthusiasm. On the other hand OGC didn't have carte blanche. OGC said it could help, but we had to deliver something quickly otherwise support would have evaporated. We were very conscious when we put the program into action that we had to deliver the first set of results within six months. And we did so. So OGC didn't get a blank cheque, it got a blank cheque for a few months to prove a concept which helped make alliances successful. We had the right people involved, we had the head of the civil service literally on the phone every week asking, 'what's going on next?'. Politically, we had our Cabinet minister, the Chief Secretary of the Treasury, Chancellor Brown's deputy, involved in pushing the concept. So we had political support, we had the top official support. Next, we did not delegate this activity of getting the Gateway program underway to a low level. We ran it at a senior level, senior practitioners wrote the procedures as well as getting the reviews done. That was important. The productivity gain was enormous and we spoke the management language of the people we had to communicate with. Not to delegate too far would be a lesson. Of course we did have an important thing, the right structures, to stick with us long term. This was not a short-term program. We made mistakes, learnt, and adjusted direction. The board that runs this program, the Office of Government Commerce Supervisory Board is chaired by a Cabinet Minister, and has eight Permanent Secretaries. They lived with OGC and this process for all the meetings and took commitments as to what they were going to do next. It is a very good structure. So we had all the building blocks but we still had to produce a product that mattered. So what about the products?

The Products

The OGC Gateway product was the first trademarked product, and that's led to other services. The purpose of a product or service is that it is absolutely repeatable, if you have to do it one thousand times the quality will be consistent a thousand times. We could not invent it each time we did it because the UK is a very large-scale business, We had to have something good, repeatable and high quality. We were pursuing a very simple concept. We said there is a life cycle of a project or a procurement which starts with a strategic assessment, moves through a business case, then you choose a contractor from a long list, you check it is ready for service and you get some benefits, pretty easily. We chose six stages as the stages at which an independent review team would look at the project, during its life cycle (Fig. 1). The process emphasises early intervention. The opportunity to improve a project starts when the project begins, it is almost hopeless half way through to try to rescue it.

Figure 1

Opportunity to Influence Project Outcome

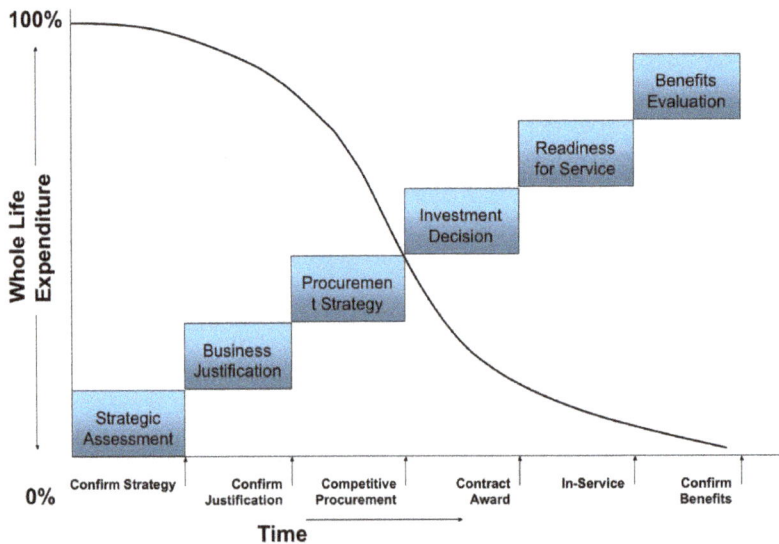

192

The issue was 'how does one use this as a discipline that is encouraging for the top of the office and for a Minister or anybody else?'. One of the most interesting outcomes of this process when we first used it was the project team sitting down and saying, 'well, actually I thought we were just about to start this project up'. And somebody else would say, 'no actually I have not seen a business case yet'. And somebody else would say, 'I think we'll let the contract tomorrow' and somebody else would say, 'well, actually we have not even agreed a business case or a short list of contractors'. The ability of this sort of diagram and the checklist that goes with it to tell a wide spread number of stakeholders where they actually are was a big win early on. So, using it as a route map just by itself proved very interesting. And then each of these stages had about ten criteria that helped people decide where they should be and what gaps they might have to fill in order to move on.

We thought about how to promote that message to a population who is not used to project management. We decided we wanted this to be a Mars Bar. You know it looked good, it tasted good and my goodness it did you good. It had to deliver every time. So we had no shame in saying, this is a Brand, it is going to be established as a Brand leader and we had a clear strategy to promote it as a Brand from day one. The Brand documentation was purposely world class and is written in plain English which includes no unique project management speak. OGC know it is world class because people have stolen it all over the world. We had high-class multi media promotion to promote the brand because it was not going to promote itself fast enough. And like a Mars Bar, we controlled the quality. We determined the team members, what they did and how they acted. People do not turn up because they are good people. They turn up because they have passed the accreditation test for being allowed to turn up. And that was very important. Now did we win the brand battle? Yes we did. If you flick on the BBC website and listen to the transcripts for the BBC news, you will hear every month a Minister on the radio being asked something like, 'okay Minister, how do you know this particular defence project is going to work?'. And he will say, 'because I've been working it with OGC Gateway team and they tell me we're on the right track'. Now that is Brand success. Each Minister has been given one of the Gateway brand management check lists and there's about 40,000 copies of these have been used. That is what comes of five years of branding. And people now know the term. The Prime Minister will use the term on radio. Ministers will use it. And they actually will understand what they are talking about too, which is even better.

Establishing Brand Criteria

In order to control the quality of this Mars bar, we had to decide on the quality elements. For us it was free at the point of delivery and then meeting the criteria shown in the slide. Because if you have a brand it is important to say how would you recognise it if you fell over it in the street. There are two issues to particularly emphasise (Fig 2). One is *independence* and the next is an *accredited practitioner team*. Who turns up is vital, and they are very distinguished people for the big projects. It will be somebody from the Sydney Olympics who does the Gate Zero review of the London Olympics. They have been there before, they are not scared of big decisions and have learnt from their mistakes. These are very impressive people and they are tuned to the projects size and complexity. The teams who turn up will have been there before and will recognise what is going on in minutes. And that is what is impressive. Next, fast delivery–five days maximum for a review, including writing the report. Even for an aircraft carrier project this is doable. It assumes it is an 80/20 process. It is very important to note that an OGC Gateway Review is not an audit and it is not quality assurance – it is an 80/20 top down management process, massively well received as a result of it being a short and focused review. The last thing to mention on criteria is access to stakeholders. That means all stakeholders. If it is a ministerial priority the Minister will be interviewed, they usually want to be interviewed but, if for some reason they are not available, we just simply will not do the review rather than fail to understand the issues. Good advice would be to stick to the elements that matter in the Branding.

Figure 2

Key Elements of the OGC Gateway Brand

- Project Lifecycle assessed versus best practice
- Independent and accredited practitioner team
- Short focused Review
- Open, plain English process
- Access to all stakeholders
- Candid recommendations
- Ownerships of follow-through rests with client
- Confidential client – team partnership

You can only get away with all of these process of course if it is based on reality. So it is a fact that the real successes have helped us preserve our position today. The sort of repeat issues that come up at each of these six gate reviews are shown in Figure 3. We know eight or nine things that, if we could stop them going wrong on every project, life would be more successful. At each Gateway review we are limited to ten or twelve points only that the team will be examining. What they will do is rapidly home down on three or four. Typically some of these repeat points, such as leadership, business case, adequate skills and resources will be amongst them. That's fairly normal and enables OGC to focus project help.

Figure 3

NAO & OGC Gateway™ Review - Key Lessons

Essentials for Programme/Project Success include:

- Robust Business Case (with pre-agreed Critical Success Factors)
- Adequate skills and resources
- Ongoing risk management process
- Clearly defined roles & responsibilities
- Effective stakeholder communication

- Sound financial controls
- Market knowledge and procurement advice
- Contract Management and delivery skills
- Scheduling and Planning
- Benefits realisation process

Mission Critical Projects

The UK had a problem to solve. We were producing 6.5 per cent improvement rates on our project portfolio. That actually hid the fact that for the small projects (50 to 100 million-dollar projects) we were achieving 20 per cent improvement. For the very largest ones, the ones that were nearest the heart of political change, we were only achieving 3-4 per cent. So we did a study to find out why and then more importantly try to decide what to do about it. Figure 4 shows the results of our study and of Gartners worldwide study of what goes wrong with the very largest government projects. Not everyone may agree with it.

Figure 4

Causes of Failure in Highest Risk Programs

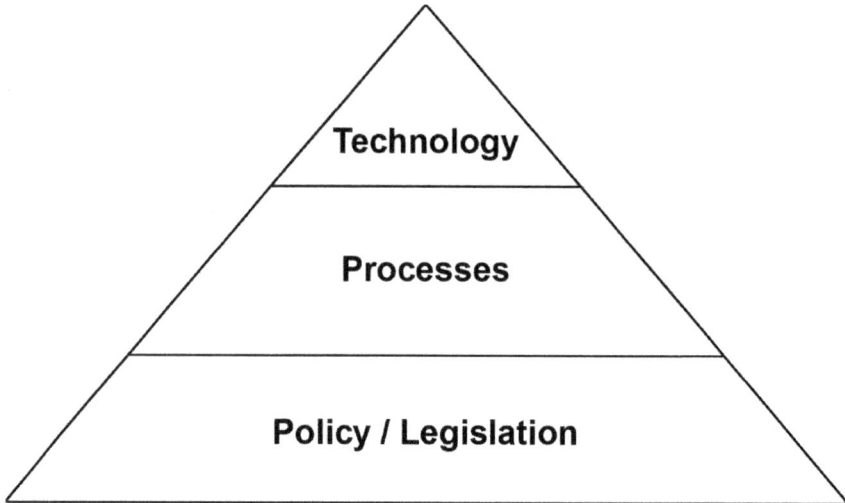

```
                    Technology

                     Processes

                Policy / Legislation
```

What it suggests is that technology is not the problem on the very largest projects. Project management processes are not the problem on the very largest projects, but the clarity of policy interpretation, the scope of it and understanding the political intention is the crunch that causes the very largest to either succeed or fail. OGC realised that we were not putting enough effort into the early stages of policy development and policy deliverability. And so we are moving on to getting involved with the policy developers before it even becomes a policy. What we did on the London Olympics, was to be involved with our project management teams as the bid was produced. So there were no excuses for the bid not to be right. We worked out a program where all the Ministers and Permanent Secretaries got involved and identified their key success indicators, which varied widely. Then we pulled them together and fed that back to the ministers as a group. The better news is we have also set up for the first time ever, a cross-functional ministerial group with a role in running the Olympic program. There are six Cabinet Ministers chaired by an independent Cabinet Minister who run the Olympic program. Please note the word 'run', they are not there as a safety valve, they have a job to do in setting priorities, and resolving escalated problems. So that is a real success. And we're now going to bring that success into all of our cross-functional projects. So what we now do is before the Gateway review program even starts we run an activity with the project at the stage of policy development. It can be done but only because of who turns up to help and their credibility in crossing the divide between project management and policy. The sort of people who do that, some retired Chief Executives of FTSE 100 companies, some ex-Permanent Secretaries in the UK, are all distinguished people who have been around and carry the credibility to talk to policy makers and are independently minded.

Conclusions

The Gateway program itself is now internationally trademarked to protect its integrity. So if it is not a Mars Bar it is a *Coca Cola*. You know it arrives tasting good, at the right temperature and it arrives in the same shape all of the time. And like Coca Cola, OGC do not distribute the products unless we are quite sure they are in good hands. There is more to do, since there is an ever-growing need to keep building capability at very senior levels. The policy makers and the politicians have shown great enthusiasm and patience in being involved with this Gateway process and they want to continue to be involved.

The UK Cabinet Secretary, Sir Andrew Turnbull gave the nicest accolade the Gateway program has had. He said, 'The OGC Gateway program is one of those more rare initiatives that has permanently changed Government'.

17. The Gateway Review Process in Victoria

Wayne Sharpe, Executive Manager, Gateway Unit, Department of Treasury and Finance, Victoria

Government policy rationale

The Victorian Government spends billions annually on procuring infrastructure, information systems, real property, goods and services. Contemporary government procurement is now well accepted as a strategic management function requiring a commitment by departments, large and small, to effective procurement planning, innovative contracting strategies, active contract management and continuous improvement of procurement processes.

Implementing the Gateway Review Process is a key strategy for improving infrastructure and Information and Communication Technology (ICT) project development and delivery across government. The initial focus of the Gateway Review Process is on high-risk and medium-risk infrastructure, procurement and information technology/change management projects. The aim is to help departments ensure their investment is well spent, meets business objectives and achieves value for money outcomes.

Successful procurement projects depend on aligning service outcomes with project objectives in all phases of the procurement process. A project based on a sound and tested business case is more likely to achieve the planned benefits.

The Gateway approach is a structured process that examines and confirms critical decision points from concept development through to project benefit evaluation. It probes the adequacy of the risk management framework to ensure that government procurement of construction, information technology and other services or projects is successfully delivered and that learnings are fed back, so that future projects can be managed better. It does this by enhancing the discipline of project delivery, for example, ensuring ongoing alignment of project objectives throughout the various stages of project development.

Why a Gateway Review Process?

The Gateway Review Process (GRP) is part of a broader Gateway initiative endorsed by the Victorian Government in March 2003. The initiative is a project management/development framework with three underlying objectives:

1. reduce budget/time overruns and scope changes in the delivery of initiatives by departments;

2. improve alignment of initiatives with government strategic objectives and departmental corporate plans; and

3. better assessment of portfolio initiatives across government ('joined-up government').

Applying to major capital investments across the General Government sector, the Gateway Initiative consists of:

1. a **multi-year strategy** with a long-term view (5-10 years) of general Government sector asset investment projects or initiatives – aligned with the Victorian Government's strategic objectives;

2. development of consistent general Government sector project lifecycle guidance, with an initial focus on preparing **better business cases** to support asset investment proposals;

3. independent **Gateway Reviews** built around six key decision points in a project's lifecycle, with the aim of assuring successful project delivery; and

4. **reporting** focused on exceptions – identifying issues early enough to keep projects on track or get them back on track.

Evidence suggests that a primary cause of cost and time overruns in asset investment projects is a failure to identify and manage project risks at all stages of the project's lifecycle, including the particularly critical initial project planning stages. Gateway Reviews focus on addressing this issue.

The process has been developed and adopted by a number of major corporations and progressive governments.

Characteristics of the Gateway Review Process

The Gateway Review Process has been developed from tried and tested practices in industry and in the public sector in the United Kingdom [1] and has the following key characteristics:

*   it uses short, focused independent reviews;
*   it uses a team of experienced and independent practitioners;
*   it includes all key stakeholders;
*   it is not an audit;
*   it is undertaken in consultation with the project team; and
*   it is confidential, and independent from the project approval process.

Reactions to Gateway Review Processes in other jurisdictions

The characteristics and benefits of the Gateway Review Process have ensured that it is well received throughout central civil government in the United Kingdom. The process has been successfully applied to projects undertaken by all its central civil departments including the Ministry of Defence. Departmental and industry reaction to the introduction has been extremely positive, with improvements to project delivery already demonstrated. Consultation with Gateway practitioners and other contacts in other jurisdictions has highlighted reactions and experiences.

United Kingdom

A number of benefits have emerged from the UK experience of implementing the Gateway Review Process, including increased assurance that the expected service delivery outcomes will result, delivery of projects within budget and time constraints, better management of risks inherent in projects, increased stakeholder satisfaction, and a snapshot of the procurement health of key projects for Senior Responsible Owners. [2] Specific comments include:

- project owners who have received Gateway Review reports on their projects are supportive of the process and have benefited from recommendations contained in the Review report;
- it is of paramount importance to keep the Gateway Review Process separate from capital approval sections of government. Gateway Reviews are about 'helping projects succeed'. They are not part of the approval process;
- the Gateway Review Process must add value and support to projects, with the initial focus on high-risk projects; and
- the need to improve project delivery for projects which cut across departmental or jurisdictional boundaries is not well recognised or accepted (a common misperception is that 'all physical-build projects are low risk').

The cost of the Gateway Review Process to the central civil government in the UK is reported as approximately 0.01 per cent of the overall cost of projects. Office of Government and Commerce Value for money reviews have confirmed that average cost avoidance of 3-5 per cent are being achieved when best practice recommendations from review reports are implemented. The cost avoidance result from early implementation of actions needed for successful project delivery. For example a project with a total estimated investment of $100 million would generate an average cost of $10,000 to undertake a Gateway Review that could result in average cost avoidance of between $3 and $5 million.

Practical benefits of Gateway Reviews

Some Victorian Government departments and agencies have implemented excellent internal processes for obtaining better value for money spent on procurement. As a major procurer of projects, government recognises that processes can be further enhanced to improve project outcomes and services to the community.

In other jurisdictions and in the private sector, experience has demonstrated that reviews at critical decision points in the procurement cycle add value and improve the outcomes of procurement and minimise the risk of project failure.

The Gateway Review Process involves targeted application of structured reviews, with the appropriate level of independence at critical decision points in project delivery. Implementation of Gateway Reviews can be expected to support a disciplined approach to the application of proven procurement processes leading to better outcomes.

Gateway Reviews will consolidate learning and procurement across the sector and give government and departmental Secretaries/CEOs confidence that high to medium-risk projects have had a level of expert independent review. The GRP provides three key benefits for government:

- a consistent, whole-of-government, disciplined process to help ensure that projects are delivered on time and within budget;
- increased confidence by departments, agencies and the Expenditure Review Committee of Cabinet in the health of a project; and
- an increased skill base across government through the development of review skills.

Implementing and operating the Gateway Review Process in Victoria will also help provide:

- successful projects delivered in a timely, efficient and appropriate way;
- best practice techniques in project delivery;
- lessons learned that are disseminated and incorporated into new projects;
- increased competence and valuable development opportunities for individuals involved in review teams; and
- enhanced project management capability within the Victorian public sector.

Scope

The Gateway Review guidelines apply to all new or existing high to medium-risk government projects that procure services, construction/property and information technology/change management projects.

At the earliest stages, if procurement is likely to be the chosen means of satisfying an identified need, departments and agencies should:

- assess the complexity and risk profile of the project;
- if high or medium risk, decide on the type of Gateway Review required and the timing; and
- schedule reviews to ensure discipline in the procurement process and an optimum value for money solution.

The Gateway Review Process is not designed to duplicate existing approval processes, but should assist and enhance outcomes from these processes. The GRP generally serves a different purpose than internal approval or reviews processes.

Establishing the Gateway Review Process

As noted, the Gateway Review Process is based on established industry practice comprising short, structured, independent reviews at six key stages in the life of the project.

Figure 1

Stage in project lifecycle

Establish business need: Identify business need; Develop program or project brief

Gate 1
Strategic assessment

Develop business case: Options identified, appraised; Affordability, achievability, value for money established

Gate 2
Business case

Develop procurement strategy: Develop procurement plan; Specify requirements; Update business case

Gate 3
Procurement strategy

Competitive procurement: Evaluate bids; Select or confirm supplier or partner; Update business case

Gate 4
Tender decision

Award and implement contract: Award contract/statement of work or transition to new contract; Asset/service ready for delivery

Gate 5
Readiness for service

Manage the contract: Service delivered; Benefits achieved; Performance and value for money maintained/improved

Gate 6
Benefits evaluation

Closure: End of procurement/Work package

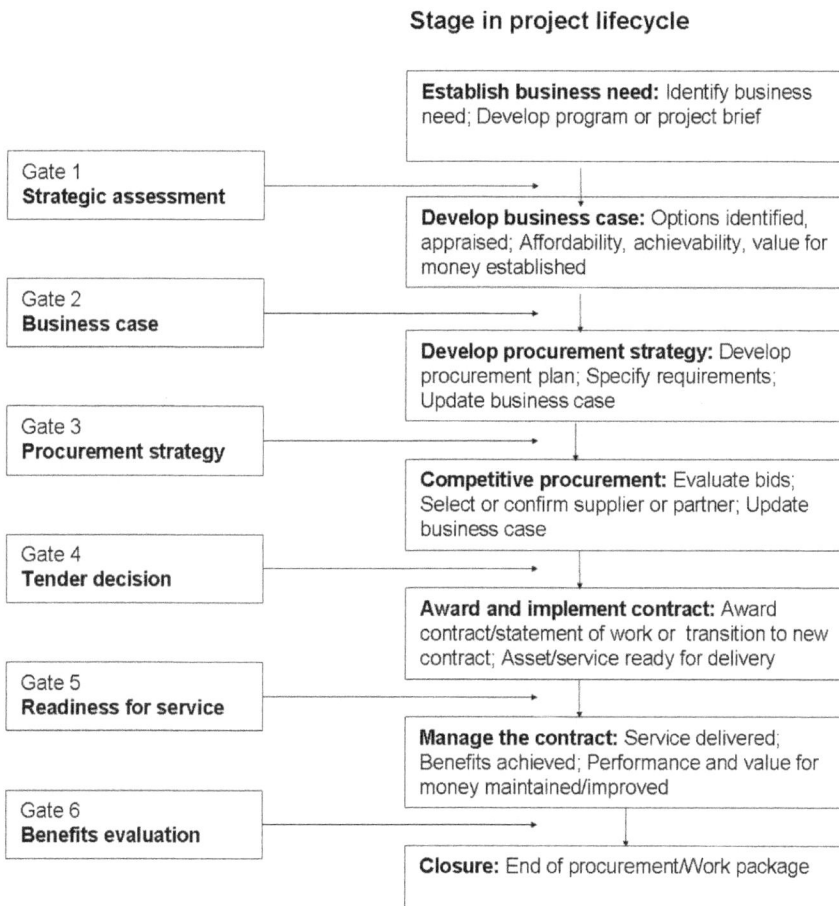

The reviews are conducted for and reported to the Senior Responsible Owner. The reviews seek to identify issues to ensure the successful delivery of the project.

The key to delivering objective high-quality reports is the independence of the review team from the project, and, in the case of high-risk projects, the independence of the review team from the project's department.

The review teams consist of senior government staff supplemented where necessary by external consultants. The interchange of senior staff between departments and agencies undertaking Gateway Reviews should improve project delivery across government.

Setting up – the steps

Several steps were involved in setting up support systems for the Gateway Review Process in Victoria. The plan involved establishing:

- an independent Gateway Unit with the role of developing, implementing and overseeing continuous improvement of the Gateway Review Process. The Gateway Unit has been initially incorporated into the Commercial Division of the Department of Treasury and Finance's organisational tree, with the operational and resourcing costs funded by Treasury, not on a cost recovery basis;
- a multi-department Gateway Supervisory Committee to oversee the implementation of the Gateway Review Process (including lessons learned and continuous improvement);
- Gateway Reviews for all projects classified as high risk for the 2003-04 Budget, with voluntary review of medium risk projects, and prioritised high risk projects to be considered at part of the 2004-05 budget process;
- feedback to the Gateway Supervisory Committee six times a year and quarterly to the Premier and the Treasurer on generic lessons learned from the findings of Gateway Reviews;
- encouragement of participation by senior experienced staff within the Victorian Public Sector as Gateway reviewers, particularly for high-risk projects;
- an accreditation and training regime to develop skills of Gateway reviewers in portfolio departments; and
- a database of accredited staff to participate in Gateway Reviews.

What is required by departments?

Government departments and agencies, managers, reviewers and particularly Senior Responsible Owners have a number of responsibilities in relation to the GRP.

Understanding the Gateway Process

Government departmental and agency staff involved in procurement or project delivery should familiarise themselves with Gateway Review responsibilities and processes including:

- ensuring that the Project Profile Model (PPM) is completed and sent to the Gateway Unit when the project is first considered during the strategic phase or the business case generation phase;
- ensuring the conduct of reviews necessary under the Gateway Review requirements;
- considering review outcomes and recommendations in decision-making on the project; and
- understanding the independence of reports issued by the Gateway Review Teams.

Departments and agencies are expected to establish a mechanism for coordination with the Gateway Unit and to make all arrangements for the venue and equipment required for Gateway Reviews. In addition, departmental and agency staff involved in the Gateway Review Process should be familiar with government policies and guidelines relating to asset management, procurement, construction and information technology.

Role of Senior Responsible Owner

A Senior Responsible Owner, who is either a Senior Executive or Senior Manager, is to be nominated by the departmental Secretary or Chief Executive Officer for each procurement project subject to a Gateway Review. Senior Responsible Owners ensure that Gateway Review requirements are implemented for the project for which they are responsible. This includes:

- managing the implementation of the Gateway Review requirements;
- arranging for completion of projects' complexity rating using the PPM and classifying them;
- liaising with the departmental Secretary or the Senior Executive nominated as responsible for procurement on the risk rating for the project;
- providing a copy of the completed PPM risk assessment to the Gateway Unit; and
- coordinating Gateway Reviews of the project with the Gateway Unit.

Selecting Gates for Review and nominating reviewers

Gateway Reviews are conducted before key decisions are taken in the procurement cycle (see Figure 1 a more detailed version).

As noted, Senior Responsible Owners from departments and agencies are expected to communicate with the Gateway Unit at least six to eight weeks before a

Gateway Review for all medium to high risk projects to ensure that the correct resources can be assembled and that the pre-Review work is completed.

The Gateway Unit assembles the review teams for all high-risk projects. The Unit will seek departmental nominations of potential review team members to be trained for medium and high risk projects. When trained, these people are considered accredited for Gateway Reviews of medium and high risk projects across other departments and agencies.

Application of Gateway Reviews

The primary purpose of the Gateway Review Process is to realise better value for government asset investment decisions. The process provides government and departmental Secretaries with assurance that:

- the best option to achieve a service objective is being pursued;
- independent review at key stages will help avoid potentially costly mistakes;
- the best available skills and experience are being deployed on the project;
- all stakeholders involved in the project fully understand the project status and the issues involved;
- the project can progress safely to the next stage of development or implementation;
- predictability of time and cost targets for the project is increased; and
- knowledge and skills are improved through participation in review teams.

Project profile model

The decision about conducting a Gateway Review is based on the complexity/risk assessment using a Project Profile Model (PPM). This assessment is done by departments.

The PPM is intended to provide a standard set of high-level criteria against which Senior Responsible Owners can assess the intrinsic characteristics and degree of complexity of a proposed procurement project, in order to establish the appropriate:

- control structures (including Gateway Reviews);
- risk profile and corresponding risk strategy; and
- design approach (for example, delivering the project in several increments or modules to help reduce complexity).

Using the project profile model

Three spreadsheets are provided by the Gateway Unit that are appropriate for:

1. Information technology/change management projects: all business change projects involving an IT element which, if not delivered, would significantly impact upon the project's ability to deliver its intended benefits.

2. Property and construction projects: projects procuring property (existing or to be constructed) as a supply of works or service.
3. Other services: (e.g. environmental management, facilities management, property and estates advice etc).

Senior Responsible Owners should use the spreadsheet most appropriate for their project. [3] The PPM should be used as a starting point in assessing the likely levels of risk associated with the project. It is a high level indicator, not an exhaustive project risk analysis model, although it can form the basis of a fuller project risk analysis. The model requires the Senior Responsible Owner to assess the project against a number of criteria to provide an overall score for the project. These initial scores will be validated by the Gateway Unit. The current approach is that:

- a total score of 20 or less indicates that the project is relatively low risk and Gateway Reviews will be managed from within the department or agency;
- a total score in the range of 21–40 indicates that the project is medium risk. Gateway Reviews for this category will require a review team leader, nominated by the Gateway Unit, who is independent of the department or agency. Review team members are sourced by the department or agency, outside of the project team for medium risk reviews; and
- a total score 41 or more indicates that the project is high risk and will require the review team leader and the review team members to be nominated by the Gateway Unit and to be independent of the department or agency.

It is important to stress that the PPM is designed as a guide to help the Senior Responsible Owner make their assessment. There may be issues that are not explicitly covered by the model but which affect the assessment. In particular, there may be other factors that increase the risk to the project and therefore warrant a higher rating. If in any doubt, Senior Responsible Owners should discuss these issues with the Gateway Unit.

Senior Responsible Owners are asked to notify the Gateway Unit (after confirming the PPM details with the departmental Gateway Coordinator) if the proposed project is medium or high risk. (The Gateway Unit does not record information for low-risk projects.)

The Gateway Unit needs a minimum of six to eight weeks from the receipt of the PPM to undertake the necessary planning and team selection. However, PPMs may be sent to the Unit in advance of this minimum period.

Procurement types

Gateway Reviews may be conducted at the six key decision points in the procurement cycle for all types of procurement, but the Gateway Process does not apply to all government projects, and not all Gateway Reviews are necessarily applied at all stages of projects. The need for and level of review required will be assessed on a complexity/risk basis. Core Gateway Reviews apply to specific procurement types, depending on the level of risk assessed via the PPM. Specific Gateway Reviews are required for different types of procurement. For instance, a post-completion Gateway Review would be appropriate for an information system project assessed as high risk with wide impacts across government, but may not be considered appropriate for a project procuring capital equipment assessed as low risk.

Gateway Reviews – The Six Gates

As noted earlier, there are six Gates, or key decision points, for reviewing projects. Gateway Reviews may be conducted for all types of procurement at any of the six key decision points (Gates) in the project (procurement) lifecycle: strategic assessment, business case, procurement strategy, investment decision, readiness for service and benefits evaluation. The detail in each Gateway Review is based on the results of workshops and tests on pilot projects.

Strategic assessment (Gate 1)

Gateway Review 1, strategic assessment, assesses whether the proposed procurement project is the best value means of servicing the identified need and whether it aligns with government and relevant departmental or agency strategic plans. To achieve this, the strategic assessment:

- confirms the need for the delivery of the service outcomes proposed;
- confirms that there is government and departmental/agency commitment to meeting the service need;
- ensures that the service and project objectives are fully enunciated;
- ensures investigation of all alternatives to procurement projects for meeting the perceived need;
- confirms whether a procurement project or program is the appropriate means of providing service outcomes;
- confirms that there has been a comprehensive investigation of alternative procurement methods including integration with service outcomes required of other departments or agencies ('joined-up' government);
- reviews plans for developing a business case, including financial and economic analysis, value management, risk management, stakeholder consultation, project management and change management; and
- confirms resources (including funding) are available to develop a sound case for government consideration for approval.

Business case (Gate 2)

The business case review assesses whether the project options have been fully canvassed and evaluated, whether the recommended option is the best value solution, and whether government should proceed with it.

To achieve this, the business case review aims to:

- confirm that the business case is robust – that is, in principle it meets service needs, is affordable, achievable, that appropriate options have been explored, and that the project is likely to achieve value for money;
- establish that a feasibility/options study has been completed satisfactorily – including financial analysis meeting Treasury requirements, and that a preferred way forward has been identified;
- confirm that the implementation of the project is based on open and active communication with all major stakeholders represented;
- ensure that the major risks have been identified, that outline risk management plans have been developed and estimated costs of risks are included in the project budget;
- confirm that, for major asset initiatives, alternative delivery methods have been evaluated, for example. *Partnerships Victoria* private/public operation versus a government-funded project;
- confirm that the scope and project objectives are realistic, clear and unambiguous;
- establish that, in formulating the proposed project, impacts on suppliers and their ability to deliver has been fully considered;
- establish that robust plans for managing the next stage of the project are in place;
- establish that stakeholders were considered in formulating the project;
- review stakeholder opinions and establish that plans are in place for ongoing stakeholder consultation;
- review and validate assessment of assumptions made about the project; and
- review the analysis of economic, social and environmental impacts and confirm that the project meets government's current objectives.

Procurement strategy (Gate 3)

The procurement strategy review aims to propose the optimum methods for delivering the project within budget and time constraints and to allocate risks to the parties best able to manage them. This review is undertaken before committing to a procurement methodology and contracting system. To achieve this, the procurement strategy review aims to:

- confirm that the proposed project aligns with the business case and will deliver the service outcomes within the budget allocated;

- ensure that the procurement strategy is robust and appropriate and has been established through authorised departmental/agency processes;
- establish that comprehensive plans for managing the project during the delivery process have been developed and are implemented;
- review risk management plans and establish that all major risks have been considered and plans for risk management are established, including budgetary provisions;
- ensure that supplier capacity and past performance have been realistically evaluated in developing the proposed procurement strategy;
- review benchmarks established to evaluate the project's success in delivering service outcomes;
- assess the appropriateness of the proposed contracting methodology and likelihood of its success in delivering the project and satisfying broader government policies;
- ensure the procurement method is in place; and
- ensure the site has been secured and all other pre-procurement actions are in hand.

Tender decision (Gate 4)

The tender decision review assesses whether the business case is valid once costs are established. The review also assesses whether the investment decision process was conducted with due probity and fairness to tendering parties.

To achieve this, the tender decision review aims to:

- confirm the business case and benefits plan when the bid information is confirmed;
- check that all necessary statutory and procedural requirements were followed throughout the procurement process;
- confirm that the recommended contract decision − if properly executed within a standard lawful agreement − is likely to deliver the specified outputs/outcomes on time, and within budget and will provide value for money;
- ensure that management controls are in place to manage the project through to completion;
- ensure there is continuing support for the project;
- confirm that the approved procurement strategy has been followed;
- confirm that the development and implementation plans of the client and the supplier or partner are sound and achievable;
- check that the business is prepared for developing any new processes where required, and has prepared for implementation, transition and operation of new services/facilities;

- confirm that there are plans for risk management, issue management and change management (technical and business) and that these plans are shared with suppliers; and
- confirm that the technical implications, such as 'buildability' for construction projects and, for IT-related projects, the impact of e-government frameworks, have been addressed.

Readiness for service (Gate 5)

The readiness for service review assesses the state of readiness to commission the project and implement the change management required.

To achieve this, this pre-commissioning review is designed to:

- check that the current phase of the contract and all documentation is properly completed;
- ensure that the contractual arrangements are up-to-date;
- check that the business case is still valid and unaffected by internal and external events or changes;
- check that the originally projected business benefit is likely to be achieved;
- confirm that there are processes and procedures to ensure long-term project success;
- confirm that all necessary testing is done to the client's satisfaction (e.g. commissioning of buildings, business integration and user acceptance testing) and that the client is ready to approve implementation;
- check that there are feasible and tested contingency and reversion arrangements;
- ensure that all ongoing risks and issues are managed effectively and do not threaten implementation;
- evaluate the risk of proceeding with the implementation if there are any unresolved issues;
- confirm the business has the necessary resources and that it is ready to implement the services and the business change;
- confirm that the client and supplier implementation plans are still achievable;
- confirm that there are management and departmental controls to manage the project from implementation to operation;
- confirm that all parties have agreed plans for training, communication, roll-out, production release and support as required;
- confirm that all parties have agreed plans for managing risk;
- confirm that there are reciprocal plans for managing the working relationship, with reporting arrangements at appropriate levels on both the department/agency and the supplier side; and
- check that lessons for future projects are identified and recorded.

Benefits evaluation (Gate 6)

The benefits evaluation review assesses whether the benefits expected in the business case have been achieved. The review will ensure that post-completion and post-occupancy reviews are conducted and the findings communicated, to improve future projects.

To achieve this, the benefits evaluation review aims to:

- confirm that post-completion review and post-occupancy evaluation have been carried out and the findings disseminated to participants in the procurement chain;
- assess whether the project has met business case goals and whether claimed operational benefits have been realised;
- review the adequacy of funding arrangements for ongoing operation and management of the project;
- establish the benefits of applying Gateway Reviews and government procurement processes to the project;
- identify improvements that might be made to existing procurement processes, as a result of experience from this project;
- if ongoing contract management is required, review the adequacy of client and supplier resources for the task;
- identify any deviations from the business case for the project;
- confirm that plans are in place for future renewal of the procurement project;
- review the adequacy of risk management plans for the project;
- review the adequacy of project change management plans;
- review the extent to which the project met stakeholder requirements; and
- review the project one year after it has been completed, and on a three-year cycle for the life of the project thereafter, to ensure the ongoing benefits of the project.

Gateway Review Reporting and Support

Review Guidelines

Guidelines to assist the review team conduct a review are available for each Gateway Review. The Gateway Unit can provide documentation and presentations to assist at any particular Gateway or for the general review process.

Reports

As project personnel, clients and other stakeholders may be interviewed about issues arising in the Review, review teams produce a short report summarising the review activities undertaken and the conclusions of the team about the health of the project. Review reports are provided to the Senior Responsible Owner only. If a copy of the report is sought it is at the discretion of the Senior

Responsible Owner if he or she releases the report. The report will not be released or circulated by the Gateway Review Team of the Gateway Unit.

Gateway Review reports provided to the Senior Responsible Owner, like all other government documents, are subject to the *Freedom of Information Act 1988*. Freedom of Information (FOI) requests for Gateway Review reports will be handled through the Senior Responsible Owner's department and not through the Gateway Review Unit. Certain information contained within the Gateway Review reports may be excluded from release as part of the various exemptions in the FOI Act.

The Gateway Unit retains a copy of the each Review report, to compile lessons learned for reporting generically to the Gateway Supervisory Committee and back to relevant departments or agencies. The Gateway Review Process uses Red, Amber and Green (RAG Status) classifications for assessing projects at each Gate:

Red – To achieve success the project should take action immediately.

Amber – The project should go forward with actions on recommendations to be carried out before the next Gateway Review of the project.

Green – The project is on target to succeed but may benefit from the uptake of recommendations.

Review Team Status

Review teams have no decision-making powers. All decisions arising from review recommendations are made by the Senior Responsible Owner.

Supporting Gateway Reviews

Importance of the review team

Any Gateway Review relies substantially on the independent expertise of the review team. Reviewers are required to have high-level skills, through training and extensive or relevant experience of aspects of the projects under review.

Review team members will be chosen from the private sector or other government jurisdictions when necessary to supplement skills and experience within the Victorian public sector and the Gateway Unit. Registration of Interest advertisements and other methods are used to compile a database of experienced private sector people to supplement review teams.

Training reviewers

Training is provided on 'Preparing to carry out Gateway Reviews' and 'Leading Gateway Reviews'. The training is designed to equip participants with the knowledge and skills to plan, prepare and undertake Gateway Reviews as team members and team leaders of high, medium and low risk reviews. Training is delivered by a external organisation, utilising modified OGC Gateway Training material from the UK. For details on how to undertake training please see the Gateway Review website.

Accreditation and skills – reviewers and team leaders

There are different levels of training for review team members and team leaders. The database of accredited departmental and agency reviewers as well as the private sector reviewers (established by the Gateway Unit) will include details of their skill base and experience. New nominees will be assessed and considered for inclusion on the database of reviewers. The reviewers details in the database are subject to the Privacy Act and are only utilised by the Gateway Review Unit. Nominees for Gateway Review team membership are expected to meet certain minimum requirements.

This outline recognises three levels of skills or expertise:

Level 1: Awareness. The participant is able to understand the key issues and their implications for the client, and ask relevant and constructive questions on the subject.

Level 2: Knowledge. The participant has a detailed knowledge of the subject and is capable of providing guidance and advice to others.

Level 3: Expert. The participant has extensive and substantial practical experience and applied knowledge of the subject.

The Gateway Unit will advise nominees and their departments or agencies of their inclusion on the database.

(i) Team leaders – There are particular requirements for team leaders of reviews of medium and high-risk projects.

(a) For high-risk projects, team leaders are:

- typically executive level in the public sector and the equivalent in the private sector;[4]
- substantially experienced (minimum of 15 years), with a background in managing business aspects of major procurement projects and/or programs with a typical value of $50 million or more;
- familiar with handling major strategic initiatives and managing business change;
- excellent communicators; and
- experienced in connection with sensitive and complex or unusual projects.

(b) For medium-risk projects, team leaders are:

- minimum level – Victorian Public Sector level 5;

- substantially experienced (minimum of 10 years), with a varied background, particularly in procurement or project/program management typically valued at $20 million; and
- excellent communicators.

(ii) Team members – Team members need a certain level of project management experience and/or experience in business change, business analysis or other operational or procurement areas. They include:

(a) Project managers with the following experience:

- professional project managers, who are accredited in Prince 2 (UK Office of Government Commerce project management methodology) or PMBOK (the Project Management Body of Knowledge Guide);
- successful managers of significant projects/programs or procurements;
- good team players and communicators; and
- 5^+ years relevant experience.

(b) Business analysts with:

- in-depth financial assessment evaluation experience; and
- experience in preparing business cases, strategic assessments and business requirements.

(c) Specialists in management in the following areas (minimum five years experience):

- business change;
- electronic documents and records;
- facilities; and
- construction and property.

(d) procurement professionals (minimum 5 years experience):

- professional procurement practitioners;
- with experience in managing contractual relationships; and
- with responsibilities for best procurement practice.

(e) operations experience (minimum five years) in:

- operations support;
- property portfolio management; and
- service management.

No fees are paid to departmental/agency personnel for participation in review teams.

Conclusion

Since the introduction of the GRP in 2003, over 90 projects with a total estimated investment of over $14 billion have had more than 120 reviews completed.

Of the SRO's that have provided feedback (greater than 80 per cent), all agreed that the Gateway Review undertaken on their project was beneficial and will impact positively on the outcome of their project.

A recently completed independent review of the Gateway Initiative, has also determined that:

- the Initiative's first component, the Gateway Review Process, helps identify problems early to allow time for their remedy;
- the Initiative's second component, the Multi-Year Strategy, has improved the alignment of asset projects with Government strategic objectives and department plans but, importantly, the lack of sharing of the Multi-Year Strategies among Departments is weakening Gateway's objective of better whole-of-government planning;
- the Initiative's third components, Business Cases, are useful decision-making tools for Departmental Secretaries and Government to determine how asset procurement should best occur; and
- based on the lessons learned from over 100 Gateway Reviews a publication entitled *'Commonly Identified practices that limit project success*', has been produced to share generic lessons learned.

Annex: Commonly Identified practices that limit project success can be downloaded from:

http://www.gatewayreview.dtf.vic.gov.au/CA256EF40083ACBF/WebObj/Gateway LessonsLearned/$File/Gateway%20Lessons%20Learned.pdf

Glossary

Gateway Review: Review by a small team of people, independent of the procurement project, undertaken at key decision points **(Gates)** in the project (procurement) lifecycle

Government department: The terms government 'department', 'department' or 'funding department' are used interchangeably. Agencies are included in the Gateway Process.

Infrastructure: Fixed assets that support economic and social development in a fundamental way.

Milestone: Significant events or outcomes that mark the progress of a project.

Monitoring: Process of regularly collecting information to review performance against specified criteria.

Outcome: Measurement against specified criteria of the extent to which objectives are achieved.

Project profile model: The project profile model (PPM) is a high-level assessment of the risk of a procurement activity. It provides an indication of the project's complexity/risk rating: high (category 3), medium (category 2) or low (category 1).

Procurement: Process involving all activities following the decision that goods, assets, facilities or services are required. It involves defining the scope, the acquisition and the disposal of goods, assets, facilities and services.

Project: An undertaking with a defined beginning and objectives by which completion is identified. A project may be completed using one or a number of contracts.

Risk management: A structured methodology for identifying and analysing potential risks and implementing an appropriate plan to manage them.

Senior Responsible Owner: The Senior Responsible Owner is a generic title for the senior individual who takes personal responsibility for the successful outcome of a program or project.

Service provider: Includes contractors, sub-contractors, consultants, professional service contractors, suppliers, agents and employers who provide goods, assets, facilities or services to a client.

Skill development: Any work-related learning or training activity that results in enhanced skills, knowledge and aptitude to perform a job.

Training: The development of skills, knowledge and aptitude to perform a job.

Value for money: Value for money is determined by considering all factors relevant to a particular purpose. It includes experience, quality, reliability, timeliness, service, capital costs, whole-of-life costs, innovation and value-adding components such as meeting government's economic, social and environmental policies.

ENDNOTES

[1] Office of Government Commerce. For more information, see www.ogc.gov.uk.

[2] The Senior Responsible Owner is a generic title for the senior individual who takes personal responsibility for the successful outcome of a program or project.

[3] Please note that the first two spreadsheets are applicable to IT and construction/property management projects procuring services. While such projects may be seeking to pass responsibility to service providers for some of the criteria addressed within the PPM (e.g. the degree of innovation used) these factors will still be fundamental to the ultimate success or otherwise of the project and will need to be monitored throughout the project lifecycle by the Senior Responsible Owner.

[4] This will vary depending on the requirements of the Gateway Review under consideration.

18. The Australian Government Cabinet Implementation Unit

Peter Hamburger, Department of the Prime Minister and Cabinet

My purpose is to address a particular managerial initiative in the Australian Public Service − the Cabinet implementation Unit − an initiative that is now about two-and-a-half years old and that reports to me.

One might, therefore, expect me to talk about the management role of the Unit but, in fact, I am going to start with the politics.

I will do that because, contrary to the expectations and hopes of many public servants, the Cabinet is primarily a political, not a managerial, institution and a body called the *Cabinet* Implementation Unit will therefore be located at the boundaries of politics and management. The political dimension will always affect what the Unit can do and how it can do it.

I gave a talk on Cabinet processes to senior officials of the Department of Finance some months ago and emphasised − to the point of tedium, I thought − that Cabinet is a group of politicians, performing the hugely valuable role of politics in a democratic society and that as a result they might not always appear rational to public servants. Their first question was 'why do they so often ignore our good advice?'

I had clearly failed to convey the message that politicians, when they collectively consider the political aspects of government decisions, are likely to take into account factors beyond costs and benefits, probabilities, and the nitty gritty of how to implement the decision. They are quite properly interested in the politics as well.

In our system Cabinet is about decision-making, coordinating government activity building and maintaining cohesiveness all at the political level. Cabinet decisions will naturally be based on the political judgments of the leading members of the political party that has been given a parliamentary majority by the people of Australia − and this is perfectly proper.

They will also be made under a constitution in which the responsibility for managing rests with the Queen's Ministers of State and the Departments of State they administer not the collective Cabinet which, like the Prime Minister, is not mentioned in the constitution. In practice, as well as in law, the responsibility for making a change in policy happen after the collective Cabinet has decided on it rests with individual ministers and their portfolio agencies.

So the two big impacts of the political dimension are:

- Government will always have an eye on the politics; and
- the politics within the Government involve tensions between individual responsibility of ministers and collective responsibility of Cabinet.

The size and complexity of modern government has greatly increased the amount of managerial work that has to be done at the ministerial level. I like to draw the contrast with the Australian Public Service of 1901: seven departments, eleven-and-a-half thousand public servants, 89 per cent of them in the Post Office.

The figures show that on size grounds alone Cabinet needs to be interested in implementation, however, size is not the only issue. Delivery is now a lot more complex:

- in many cases it has been moved outside government altogether, with government becoming a purchaser rather than a direct provider of services;
- very often, and increasingly, there are partnership, joint provision, or complementary provision arrangements, often across jurisdictional boundaries;
- even where government is the sole provider, that is often contestable or open to challenge;
- technology has very greatly widened the capacity for policy makers and implementers to interact, both in terms of the data processing that can happen and the extent to which higher level policy makers can by pass hierarchies (I have elsewhere used the 'strategic corporal' analogy); and
- customers for all sorts of services, including those provided by government, have become more demanding as they experience what can be provided in other areas.

Expectations have moved from the Model T Ford, with no options, even for colour, to the latest Fairlane which, if you buy it new, you can almost have built to your own specifications. Government service delivery has moved from the old clerical factories to complex networks like Centrelink and Job Network.

Cabinet and ministers are all held accountable in this very complex managerial environment and implementation failures often do lead to large difficulties for governments, for example:

- the Customs cargo management system threatened to leave everyone's Christmas presents on the wharves last year and bankrupt retailers;
- the Pay TV licensing in the later years of the previous Labor government caused enormous problems for that Government;

These are just two examples where ministers found that ignorance was no excuse, or at least did not ease the political pain very much.

It is self-evident from all this that we need much stronger support structures for Cabinet decision-making and much stronger linkages between the political and the managerial levels of government now than our forebears did in 1901, or even in 1970.

That is where the CIU fits in. It gives Cabinet a capacity to oversee implementation and an opportunity to be involved in, or at least in control of, the learning and adaptation that occurs in the implementation process.

In principle also, Cabinet is well suited to this:

- coordination is one of the central functions of Cabinet and many of the most difficult implementation problems arise at boundaries between agencies, portfolios or jurisdictions where Cabinet coordination occurs anyway;
- implementation is in part a learning process in which the policy and delivery elements interact to produce improvements in policy as well as delivery, and cabinet is high-level forum for collective policy making in government; and
- if an issue is important enough for Cabinet to have decided it, the issue should be important enough for Cabinet to keep track of how it is going.

But, whatever the in-principle arguments might be, in practice it is very much up to the Prime Minister of the day, having regard to the dynamics of the Cabinet they chair and the party they lead to decide whether and how something that is desirable in principle should actually happen: it is certainly up to the Prime Minister to lead on whether the practical system that is located with Cabinet and not somewhere else in the governmental structure.

The fact that this topic is on your program today and that it is me talking to it is proof that the present Prime Minister has decided that:

- the Government should pay more systematic attention to implementation; and
- that it should be done through Cabinet.

The Prime Minister has clearly set out his preferences and there is no doubt that the recent interest in implementation planning and monitoring very much follows a prime ministerial lead. Consequently, the arrangements that I will be talking about are, in the end, contingent not only on how well they work but also on personalities in the top political positions and the way particular personalities choose to operate.

That said, it is often useful to see Cabinet as a broader entity than the seventeen ministers who meet every week or two and an entity that consequently has elements that last beyond the tenure of particular prime ministers. The broader concept of Cabinet is that it includes the set of processes and procedures and the direct bureaucratic support that centres on the meetings of ministers:

- the history in Australia has been that the elements of the broader Cabinet system beyond ministerial membership tend to be sticky;
- procedural innovations that work have tended to survive and the greater part of our current Cabinet system is an accretion of past procedural innovations that have long survived their political parents.

There is good reason to think that if we build within the broad concept of Cabinet a workable and useful set of processes that focus on implementation, they will survive the inevitable future changes of personnel in the Cabinet narrowly conceived. That is our driving ambition anyway. We hope that the system we have set up has a degree of sustainability beyond the term of the present Prime Minister. One of the arguments for having a permanent public service is the capacity for thinking about the longer term.

So what are we actually doing?

One of our key initiatives has been to set up a Cabinet Implementation Unit, which has had a staffing level in the range of six to 12 for the past two-and-a-half years.

Our work so far has been of three broad types:

- ensuring that better information is put before decision-makers at the decision-making stage – a modest extension of the traditional cabinet support role;
- organising selective and targeted follow-up of decisions;
- and, partly as a spin-off from the other two, helping to change the way people think about implementation relative to policy and how they plan for implementation.

How are we doing it?

First, we have tweaked the cabinet drafters guide to require that proposals coming forward that have any significant implementation implications cover off on standard implementation issues:

- policy objectives;
- deliverables;
- milestones;
- the range of stakeholders (an important indicator of implementation complexity);
- risks; and
- governance arrangements.

The CIU, as matter of routine, checks draft proposals on their way to Cabinet and improves the quality of the information and argument going forward on implementation. Generally we end up with reasonable summary information on the important things that bear on implementation.

I should note at this point that Ministers do not have to read the implementation summary for the system to work, although it is clear that many do read them in important cases. But, most importantly, they can draw some comfort that these issues are being addressed and that, crucially:

- that the proponents of proposals, including ministerial proponents, have had to think through the issues and the defensive arguments as they prepare the document; and
- that the staff and public service *briefers* of ministers having studied the implementation attachments;

We are satisfied that the discipline is producing better outcomes.

If a key proposal is accepted, the implementation assessment must be expanded into a full implementation plan, lodged with the CIU. We work collaboratively with agencies in finalising the plan to ensure that it treats the relevant issues appropriately. We then use the plan to support structured follow-up of decisions. This gives us a basis for:

- assessing whether the project and its risks are such as to warrant keeping the Government informed of progress; and
- an agreed statement of the key milestones at which information will be potentially useful.

Essentially we pick up the higher-risk/higher-interest initiatives and provide a summary report every three months to the Prime Minister and then to Cabinet:

- the core of the report is a table presenting Green, Amber or Red traffic lights against the selected initiatives and measures within them;
- on top of that is a short summary of the Ambers and Reds and any notable points from the Greens;
- the number of initiatives being covered has risen as decisions are made that come into our net (there are currently about 70 initiatives comprising about 180 individual measures) but we expect to plateau about 10 to 15 per cent above this;
  - to put some scale on this, the Cabinet makes something over 300 substantive policy decisions in a typical year;
  - not all of them pose significant implementation issues and implementation does not last a full year in all cases (although sometimes it takes longer); and
  - the 70 that do is a significant number but one that is both a manageable preparation task for us and a comprehensible product for ministers.

The early experience has been that this is a very effective communications system:

- from the point of view of our Cabinet-level leaders:
  - it presents information in a manageable format; and
  - it quite rigorously filters a lot of information so that the bits that interest them are at the top and helpfully colour coded.
- from the public service point of view:
  - it is not frightening since it provides an early and hence usually fairly low-key opportunity to point to problems;
  - confessing at that stage means one's misery has company since there are always a number of Amber and Red lights across a good spread of portfolios;
  - there is a strong incentive not to hide looming failure since it is not generally career enhancing to assure the top of government that things are going well shortly before the train falls off the bridge; and
  - you are able to look good if things are travelling well.

Beyond the follow-up activity on initiatives being monitored, the Unit also has authority to conduct larger scale reviews in areas where we think there might be implementation issues worth pursuing. The Prime Minister's Delivery Unit in the UK has this function and has pursued it vigorously and, as far as I can see, with some success.

As far the CIU's review role is concerned, I think it is fair to say that so far it has been pretty much a flop:

- there are obvious sensitivities about the Prime Minister sending his Department officers in to review work in other portfolios;
- the Unit is not sufficiently staffed to do serious reviews and the Unit itself does not have the clout to do the sort of work the UK Delivery Unit does;
- we have not yet developed an approach to or methodologies for review activity that show any promise.

While I have not yet given up on finding a proactive role for the Unit in review work, I have yet to find a way to do it.

What I know, however, is that if we are to successfully undertake this function, we will need to be very selective, to focus on successes as well as failures, and work with the relevant line departments and agencies to get the best possible advice to the top of government.

The Unit has, however, been active in looking at systemic issues and played a significant role in the development work that led to the Australian Government adopting the system of Gateway Reviews discussed elsewhere in the program.

Also discussed elsewhere in the program is a better practice guide to implementation of program and policy initiatives. We have been working with the Australian national Audit Office on this and expect it to be released in a few months.

I mentioned that changing the way people think about implementation is also an explicit part of the Unit is charter. We get out a fair bit in a variety of forums to spread the message about the need to keep implementation issues in mind at all stages of the policy cycle.

Some of that effect comes anyway from the work people have to do to meet the new planning and monitoring requirements:

- there is a useful discipline of having to deal explicitly with implementation in the initial proposal to Cabinet:
  - then and in the later monitoring phase, the system forces the policy proposers to talk to the intended implementers, if they are not the same people as they often are not (i.e. it is good to see the left hand working with the right);
- we have had some suggestions that our processes have helped people drafting proposals to think beyond the details of delivery and place their proposals into the context of broader government policy;
- we think that the process changes have also nudged the policy people in PM&C to pay a bit more attention also to implementation issues.

In a few cases departments have set up project management or similar units to improve and monitor their own implementation activities and we do quite a lot of work with those counterpart units to improve the implementation of new and existing measures.

I started by noting that Cabinet's interest in implementation has been pretty much led from the top and the durability of anything flowing from it is consequently vulnerable in the medium to long term.

It is pretty much axiomatic that getting government policy properly implemented is going to be important to whomever is in government and that the sorts of things we are doing should be done:

- however, no-one can rely on things happening in government just because they make sense;
- and we cannot expect them to result simply from declaration of their importance; and
- the test will be whether the structures we have set up deliver something of value *and* survive well into the future.

So what are some of the key things we have found so far?

- most of the initiatives that are selected for this sort of high-level visibility start off as Green lights and stay that way;
- most of the others do not get beyond a watching brief;
  - we are able to tell ministers that something will be a bit late or fall a bit short of target in some other way but ensure that expectations are managed and no real damage occurs ;
- a small proportion clearly need follow-up and our monitoring system is being successful in starting action on these a bit earlier and a bit more vigorously than would otherwise be the case;
- we have produced some empirical evidence for various points that probably could have been taken as *bleeding obvious*:
  - within an agency, top level commitment to, and attention to, delivery is crucial;
  - many projects that depend on alliances within or beyond the APS get into difficulty because there has been insufficient attention paid to whether such alliances will work;
  - cross-jurisdictional or cross-sectoral, urgent, and politically sensitive initiatives are usually harder to do than initiatives completely within the control of a single minister and agency;
  - some things get in the way of other things, for example when you add up the huge amount of ICT procurement that underpins every Budget, it is hardly surprising that a lot of these projects have to re-phase their expenditure, because they just cannot get their procurement process for the contractors or specialists to line up with their Gantt charts. This is an area the Unit now pays considerable attention to, in reviewing new policy proposals;
  - the greater the uncertainty, the harder it is to do things; and
  - *shit* happens.

But even if these seem to be platitudes, a system that keeps a whole-of-government perspective on the progress in implementing key decisions offers a lot of advantages in terms of both an early adjustment of expectations and early corrective action.

For this reason, I have high hopes that the changes the Unit has introduced will stick, largely because the changes we have made are not only simple and robust but they are also small, bureaucratic, low-cost, non-threatening and add value to both government and taxpayers alike.

That may not sound glamorous – members of the Unit sometimes chide me for not taking a higher tone in describing their work:

- but minor bureaucratic changes that have slipped into the cabinet process over the years tend to be the changes that have stuck once they got there;

- also, of course, our changes self-evidently do good things and we should not be so cynical as to assume that that will be discounted; and
- usually, in fact, political decision-makers set out to do good rather than harm.

The changes are quite well-pitched strategically: although small and bureaucratic, they are located at points in the cabinet process where they cannot very easily be avoided and they set up incentives that are wholly positive.

Perhaps most importantly, after a relatively short time in operation we are beginning to see the Unit add some value to the policy process.

In particular, it is no longer enough for those advocating major policy to have a good idea. We know that there are many good ideas that originate in Canberra! We are now constantly reminded that the Government demands that that we think through our ideas and how they are going to be implemented. Overall, we are pretty optimistic that we are doing good things and that what we are doing is being well received. But you can bet your bottom dollar that we will not be resting on our laurels.

19. Organising for Policy Implementation: The Emergence and Role of Implementation Units in Policy Design and Oversight

Evert Lindquist, School of Public Administration, University of Victoria, Canada

Introduction

Over 40 years ago the spotlight was put on gathering scholarly interest on policy implementation with the publication of Pressman and Wildavsky's (1973) seminal book on *Implementation: How Great Expectations in Washington Are Dashed in Oakland*.[1] In its slipstream came Bardach's (1977) *Implementation Game* outlining the myriad ways in which policy initiatives could be diverted, deflected, dissipated, and delayed. Despite his pessimism about the promise of big policy solutions more generally, and the prospects for improving implementation in particular, Bardach nevertheless suggested creating capabilities related to implementation in two institutional locations for the purpose of 'game-fixing': in staff policy analysis and evaluation units in pertinent department budget offices and, in an environment of policy-capable US legislatures, in policy or appropriation committees with low turnover in staff and representatives. There, he speculated, officials might have the incentive, perspective, expertise, and resources to mitigate dysfunctional implementation dynamics.

40 years later, in very different institutional contexts, the leaders of governments in several jurisdictions – the United Kingdom, Australia, and Queensland – have created 'implementation' or 'delivery' units at the centre, ostensibly to advise, monitor and ensure better implementation of policy initiatives. In the UK, the Prime Minister's Delivery Unit was established by Prime Minister Tony Blair government in the Cabinet Office in 2001. In Australia, a Cabinet Implementation Unit was installed by Prime Minister John Howard in the Commonwealth's Department of the Prime Minister and Cabinet in 2003, and an Implementation Unit was established in March 2004 in the Queensland Department of Premier and Cabinet under Premier Peter Beattie.

The emergence of policy implementation units is intriguing, if only because they seem to have been at the instigation of prime ministers and premiers, and not the result of a recent call by policy scholars to build new capacities. Indeed, although implementation analysis has long been a staple in the tool-kit taught in graduate policy programs and textbooks, and should be an essential feature of decision briefs prepared for ministers, arguably the implementation literature has lost considerable profile and steam, with a small band of insightful contributors refining and elaborating theoretical propositions (Hill and Hupe 2002). Relatively little attention has been paid to question of capacity and doing better at making initiatives work in ever more complex policy environments. This, of course, has been a top concern of political leaders, who have adopted new performance regimes, the language of the New Public Management, and project management techniques to ensure priority initiatives are realized. Against this backdrop, the emergence and nomenclature of policy implementation units, however intriguing, seems like a throwback – one would have thought that the wave of such units would have hit in the 1980s in response to the original insights of Bardach, Pressman, Wildavsky, and many others writing at that time.

This chapter explores the emergence, roles, functions and accomplishments of policy implementation and delivery units, as well as their prospects. It does not argue that such units should be established as a feature of modern central government, but rather, that their emergence is worthy of note and understanding. Proceeding under the auspices of first ministers, these capabilities can be seen as a critique of existing management, implementation, and monitoring capabilities of the larger governance and public service systems where policy priorities are concerned, and the latest instrument unsheathed by some first ministers to design, assist and embed critical policy initiatives. But policy implementation units join the panoply of different capabilities leaders have experimented with to drive policy agendas and coordinate government activities, and, in the modern era, where policy is often recognised as inherently complex, share some similarities with capabilities intended to manage horizontal and whole-of-government initiatives. Indeed, a key goal of this collection is to ascertain what policy implementation units actually do, and whether they will endure, recognising that capabilities with the same names may play completely different roles in different systems, presumably reflecting the ecology of their respective institutional environments and the strategic needs of their progenitors.

The cases considered in this chapter (Richards and Smith, 2005; Wanna, 2005; Tiernan, 2005) reflected the universe of known 'named' policy implementation units in late 2005. [2] Despite the preponderance of Westminster systems serving as backdrop for these cases (with the exception of the European Union case), they have considerable diversity with respect to the motivations of political leaders who established them, the bureaucratic capabilities and roles that were installed, and the governance environments in which they have operated (unitary, federal, and multi-level governance). This chapter seeks to provide a framework for analysing and assessing the work of these units to date. It begins by with a brief synopsis of the evolution of thinking on implementation, and then considers the new environment for governance, policy development, and implementation.

Against this backdrop, the chapter casts policy implementation and delivery units as one of several 'adhocracies' that populate the centre of government (Desveaux, Lindquist, and Toner, 1994; Lindquist, 2004), and distinguishes among different functions because, despite their labels, implementation units may take on quite different roles and could be seen as rival capabilities and processes to other central capabilities. The chapter then provides an overview of the case studies and key findings. It provides a preliminary analysis of the patterns of these units, seeks to explain their arrival and mandate, and considers whether functional equivalents might exist in other jurisdictions. The chapter identifies lessons for establishing central implementation units and concludes by considering the prospects for these units and calling for more engagement with scholars on these developments.

Evolving perspectives on implementation

There has been no shortage of reviews of the implementation literature. Generally, it is suggested that the modern literature has moved through three phases (for example, Goggin et al, 1990; Hill and Hupe, 2002; Howlett and Ramesh, 2003; Schofield and Sausman, 2004). The first phase was triggered by the contributions of Pressman and Wildavsky (1973), Bardach (1977), and others. A flurry of writing emerged on the gap between policy intentions and the reality of program delivery in the US and other jurisdictions, considerable introspection about the limitations of social science research and ambitious ideas and solutions informing policy-making and the design of programs, and strong interest in discerning what interventions worked. Recognition of and debate over the implementation challenge was a defining moment for the modern policy literature, producing important strands of inquiry on implementation, evaluation, and knowledge utilisation that further defined the field and became insinuated into the 'policy cycle' heuristic (see Howlett and Ramesh, 2003; Pal, 2001; Bridgman and Davis, 2000; Hogwood and Gunn, 1984) but distinguished it from the early policy sciences approach (Lerner and Lasswell, 1951).

A second stream of writing focused on searching for useful theoretical perspectives and frameworks on implementation. This included work seeking to determine the most productive vantage points for thinking about how to anticipate and work through implementation challenges, which included the interesting debate over 'top-down' (forward-mapping) and 'bottom-up' (backward-mapping) approaches (Elmore, 1979; Berman, 1978), increasingly sophisticated efforts to develop frameworks and more sophisticated analytic tools that addressed the complexity of implementation (Mazmanian and Sabatier, 1983), and the sustained efforts to find better efforts to monitor and measure the impact of policy interventions (e.g. Williams et al, 1982). Arguably, this latter stream of research has built the most momentum over the years, particularly in the US, leading to a huge consulting industry dedicated to evaluation and quasi-experiments of program implementation, and effectively has defined the work supported by the Association for Public Policy Analysis and Management for the last two decades.

Like all fields, many of its early strands of writing endure as important lines of thinking in their own right. Howlett and Ramesh (2003) have suggested that more recent inquiry in implementation has tapped into game theory, public choice and principal-agent models to frame implementation challenges and guide empirical research. Considerable attention has focused on how instruments can be wielded and used in combination to achieve policy goals as well as different sectoral and national styles for approaching design and implementation (Linder and Peters, 1990; Howlett, 1991; Howlett, 1993). Recently, there has been renewed interest in implementation in the context of whole-of-government and multi-level governance perspective (Schofield and Sausman, 2004) and the challenge of managing complexity and networks more generally (O'Toole, 2004).

However, like the knowledge utilisation literature (though not as thoroughly), one senses that the literature on implementation has dissipated as a coherent field into specific lines of inquiry, effectively a victim of its success. Despite its status as a foundational stone in the policy tool-kit, many of the themes associated with implementation are taken up under different rubrics, such as horizontal management, whole-of-government, evaluation research, governing instruments, network analysis, etc. (Hill and Hupe 2002). Relatively few scholars march forward waving the implementation flag. And, despite the interesting theorising still occurring, and recent resurgence in interest in implementation (Schofield and Sausman, 2004), there is little evidence of applying implementation theory to practice and engaging practitioners in the emerging challenges of implementation, a style that was the hallmark when the literature first burst out (O'Toole, 2004).

This sketch of the implementation literature should suggest that contributors have done a good job of recognising complexity over the years, and thinking carefully about the analytic challenges of anticipating implementation issues; the mix, qualities and merits of different policy instruments for an implementation perspective; and the evolutionary and emergent quality of handling implementing policies and programs, a process of negotiation, adjustment and learning as managerial strategies. All of these themes and lessons should resonate even more in today's arguably more complex policy-making landscape. However, Bardach's early musings about building the right organisational and institutional capacities to mitigate implementation challenges has not received much attention over the years, and at best is only implicitly addressed in the field. This, combined with the lack of dialogue with practitioners on implementation challenges in recent years and the fact that several governments have recently considered or created units in their core executive to inform the upstream of policy development and to provide central oversight of implementation, suggests that the study of implementation units at the apex of governments is a timely and potentially fruitful line of inquiry.

Evolving contexts, new rationales for Implementation Units

Innovations like policy implementation and delivery units do not spring out of thin air: they are responses of first ministers to perceived challenges, signals about how they expect policies should be designed and implemented. Whether such innovations are well-conceived and live up to their promise is one matter, one that will be addressed by the case studies. Here we consider how the policy environment might have changed to stimulate such action in several different jurisdictions.

In the late 1980s and 1990s, a common challenge for many OECD countries concerned stemming the growth in the size of government budgets and either cutting or rationalising programs. Public bureaucracies were depicted as having their own incentives, resistant to efforts by governments to control growth in programs, and political leaders unwilling or unable to take decisive steps. This led to the argument that governments should assert political priorities and control over public service institutions, buttressed by theoretical perspectives such as public choice and agency theory. As tough fiscal decisions were made by many governments, their focus was less about implementing new policies and more about scrutinising and changing existing policy regimes, and meeting aggressive expenditure targets and reorganisation timelines. In this context policy implementation naturally received less attention, executive careers were increasingly based on managerial performance as opposed to policy shrewdness, and policy capabilities (not to mention labour negotiation capabilities) in public service institutions waned in many jurisdictions. For similar reasons focused less on the challenges of policy design and implementation (Barrett, 2004) and more on scrutinising alternative ways to deliver government services, ensuring that big service transformation projects were on time and budget, and adopting performance regimes.

As some governments turned the corner in their efforts to stabilise deficits and climb back to surplus positions, this raised the possibility of investing in new policy initiatives. With the pain of cuts fresh in the minds of decision-makers, there were likely higher tests for what constituted prudent and worthwhile spending, and for ensuring that the funds led to intended results. Arguably, too, by the end of the 20th century policy-makers had a much better sense of the interconnectedness of issues, the need for alignment in the use of different governing instruments, and the reality that many policy solutions required working across the boundaries of departments and agencies within and across levels of government. Whether such appreciation for complexity and the need for horizontal and whole-of-government thinking emerged from lessons from downsizing and restructuring, the frames emanating from hypertext and we-based models, or systems thinking from the likes of Peter Senge and others does not matter. The important observation is that more citizens and policy-makers sought to be more careful about how new policy initiatives were designed, how well-aligned new instruments were with existing ones, and how quickly such initiatives could be put in place.

With this sketch of the recent evolution and swings in the governance environment for many OECD jurisdictions, we can venture several different hypotheses for establishing policy implementation and delivery units. They include:

- *Meeting government commitments.* During the 1990s many political leaders as they campaigned for office committed to policy platforms with specific program commitments (i.e., the Liberal *'Red Book'* in Canada; Gingrich's *'Contract with America'*, British Columbia's *'New Era Commitments'*, etc). Here delivery and implementation units can be seen as an additional tool for first ministers and their government to ensure that top political and government commitments get met – a means for ensuring that governments kept focused on its agenda and message.
- *Asserting political control.* This hypothesis would be rooted in the presumption that departments and agencies would resist adopting new policies because they might compete with existing programs or not reflect the preferences of public service leaders. The goal of an implementation unit would be to bring pressure to bear and a spotlight on the public service.
- *Anticipating design challenges.* This hypothesis would argue that there is a need to vet policy proposals from departments and agencies for whether they fully account for the complexity of problems and the interaction of pertinent policy instruments, perhaps wielded by other governments or with other sectors.
- *Navigating implementation challenges.* The more complex a policy initiative, the more likely it will require capacity to manage and coordinate implementation in a multi-level governance context.
- *Addressing political optics.* Given the loss of credibility of government with citizens, and the perceived need for governments to become more 'business-like', implementation units might be established to project a new image and focus on getting programs in place on time and within budget.

Interestingly, each hypothesis implies that a government might staff an implementation or delivery unit with different kinds of talent and expertise, where they are located at the centre, and what processes they engage with. That said, the case studies may reveal that governments had overlapping and reinforcing reasons for creating the units, and that, no matter the initial goals driving inception, they evolved over time.

Implementation Units and the ecology of central capabilities

The 'centre' in most governance systems is comprised of a constellation of central agencies and secretariats dedicated to serving first ministers, and supporting and coordinating the government and the public service as corporate entities. Implementation units cannot be understood and evaluated on their terms because they are insinuated into an *ecology* of capabilities at the centre of government.

This observation is important for three reasons. First, implementation units may have emerged as a critique of other central units in the systems. Second, in a complex and 'congested' central state apparatus, such units have to compete for resources and the attention of ministers and departments alike. Third, any unit may be called on to take up different tasks and roles in the upstream or downstream of the policy-making process. In what follows we consider the ecology of capabilities that such units have to navigate and consider the different roles that implementations units might play.

Traditional cabinet secretariats

Perhaps the most important, if the least exciting, central capabilities are the secretariats that handle the upstream and downstream logistics for the meetings of cabinet and its committees. Typically, these units are dedicated to ensuring that proper notice, sign-off, consultation, and proper documentation and analysis occur before initiatives are tabled for ministers to consider. Depending on the size of the cabinet and its jurisdiction, there can be many secretariats, some serving cabinet as a whole and others serving particular standing and ad hoc committees. Usually, these units function as gate-keepers and process managers, and do not have the capacity to undertake policy and implementation analysis, nor to monitor or hold to account the performance of ministers and departments assigned responsibility for implementation.

Other standing cabinet secretariats

Cabinet offices typically have responsibility for advising the first minister and cabinet secretary on the overall direction of public service institutions. In this connection there usually are secretariats that provide advice and support on the appointment of top executives across the public service, the overall structure of ministerial portfolios and the machinery of government, and broader reform initiatives such as renewal and public service reform. Finally, there will be secretariats dedicated to coordinating the assessment and evaluation of ministers and top officials.

Coordinating secretariats

First ministers often establish several policy units at the centre of government, such as national advisors or secretariats on security, science, Aboriginal affairs, and the environment. These are different from the traditional standing secretariats responsible for supporting cabinet and its committees (although coordinating secretariats may support ad hoc committees of cabinet). These secretariats can function as focal points to move issues higher on the government agenda and clear the path for policy development; what Bakvis and Juillet (2004) have depicted as a 'catalytic' or champion role. However, Lindquist (2004) suggests that without strong political will, such capabilities will quickly become seen as 'symbolic' (Myer and Rowan, 1977).

Policy adhocracies in departments

The lead responsibility for developing, framing, and advocating a major policy initiative – even one that is clearly horizontal – will typically be assigned to a lead department or ministry, unless it is determined by the first minister that is prudent or necessary for a central coordinating units to be established. Such units are responsible for assembling expertise and undertaking analysis, developing a coherent and politically sensitive policy plan, and deal with and manage the central agencies and cabinet. It is in this latter role that such policy units will encounter and perhaps clash with policy implementation units.

Scrutiny and challenge

Central agencies may tend to defer to departments for their policy and operational expertise, but one time-honoured role of the centre is scrutinise and challenge new proposals and often their implementation plans, even if approved by the cabinet. Such scrutiny emerges from the responsibilities of departments of finance and treasuries – particularly in the expenditure management and budget office functions – to ensure that funds are well-spent and provide good value-for-money. This challenge role can be exercised as part of informing cabinet deliberations when considering proposals, but it can also take place once policy decisions have been made, and finer-grained budget and human resource allocation decisions have to be made in the downstream to decisions. The extent to which this takes place will also depend on how potent the budget office and finance ministries are in the implementation process; in some jurisdictions, managerial flexibilities and traditions of autonomy may circumscribe this role.

Facilitation advice

In some systems, central capabilities are established to support horizontal initiatives, either by providing advice, training or lesson-drawing. They could facilitate learning, the dissemination of best practices, and function as a 'centre of excellence'. This could be relevant to implementation initiatives since there could be learning and support informed by previous experience. Such capacity could assist officials leading a horizontal initiative at the formative stage, but such a role should be seen as distinct from the catalytic, champion, and implementation roles identified above.

Downstream coordination

The implementation of policy initiatives are usually assigned to lead departments, but sometimes their complexity and horizontality may require that the centre establish a coordination secretariat, either located with a lead department and sometimes in the cabinet office. In a parallel way, central agencies may often agree to coordinate across 'service' lines, particularly if key oversight functions and policies are distributed across different central agencies, to streamline the approvals and reporting associated with a particular initiative.

Monitoring and evaluating performance

The line between monitoring progress on specific implementation initiatives and evaluating the performance of ministers and their executive teams can be blurry, but the latter activity focuses on more global assessment and reporting, whereas the former may involve remedial steps by the centre to ensure that implementation occurs. This might involve working with ministers and their departments to identify milestones and performance indicators for specific initiatives, and more generally, developing accountability frameworks for departments and executive teams, and reviewing indicators to inform the annual assessments of executive performance. It may also involve identifying broad outcome indicators for gauging the impact of government policies and programs in different domains over a longer period of time.

The forgoing leads us to see that there is a significant difference between creating capacity to promote priorities, assign responsibilities for horizontal initiatives, design significant policy interventions, coordinate approvals, facilitate progress, provide information, monitor implementation, and assess outcomes. These are distinct roles for coordinating units to play in government, and itemising them in sequence lays bare the inherent complexity for properly managing policy initiatives from the centre. It is in this context that we need to consider the role of policy implementation units at the centre for government. But even here we can have functional differentiation, and in this connection it is useful to identify two different potential roles that such units could play:

- *Upstream implementation.* First ministers in Australia and Queensland have created implementation units in cabinet offices seemingly intended to ensure that *when* new initiatives are proposed, the administering organisations are properly identified, constructed and located, and that the right questions have been asked about a variety of implementation issues (Shergold, 2003). These implementation units provide *ex ante* quality control, to ensure the priority issues of government are properly addressed.
- *Downstream implementation.* A related, but distinct, function is to monitor progress on implementation and, when necessary, invoke central authority to clear the path for horizontal initiatives as they evolve. The best example

of dedicated capabilities for this purpose is the Delivery Unit in the British government, initially attached to the British Cabinet Office along with other policy and reform capabilities, and later moved over to the Treasury (Burch and Holliday, 2004).

It should be understood that implementation units could play one or both of these roles, or their focus could evolve over time depending on the interests of first ministers, and, of course, the competition and comparative advantage of other central capabilities.

More generally, we can see that there is great potential for implementation units, however defined and mandated, to overlap with and perhaps assume the responsibilities of other central actors in governance systems. Indeed, implementation units may have been established precisely to compensate for and as a critique of existing central capabilities. This implies considerable potential for overlap and rivalry for implementation units, and suggests that other central capabilities may exert pressure or attempt re-build capabilities to compete with or absorb implementation units. Moreover, there is no end to ongoing demand to create adhocracies and secretariats at the centre, and considerable pressure and incentive – particularly symbolic in nature – to retain them (Lindquist, 2004). However, prime ministers and top advisers also have to ask, 'How do you cull and re-align the centre?', so that governments can maintain their focus, and the time of central actors, departments and agencies can be utilised more effectively. In short, this canvassing of central capabilities suggests a degree of precariousness for these new units and suggest important empirical questions to explore in the case study contributions.

The Cases: Summary of findings and key themes

The three case study papers were presented recently at the Second Annual International Comparative Policy Analysis (ICPA) Workshop on October 3, 2005 in Vancouver. They included the following papers:

- David Richards and Martin Smith, 'Central Control and Policy Implementation in the UK: A Case Study of the Prime Minister's Delivery Unit' (2005) chronicles the emergence of the Delivery Unit (PMDU), but first considers larger trends in the governance of the core executive in the UK. The authors show how the design of the PMDU and its direct reporting to the Prime Minister (even though it has been located in the Cabinet Office and the Treasury) can be seen as a response not only to the arrival and challenge of New Public Management themes to the Westminster style of governance but also to significant fragmentation of delivery of service. They see the PMDU as a concerted effort of the Prime Minister to work *directly* and negotiate with delivery agencies on implementation of priority initiatives because the departments of the core executive had failed to bring about a necessary culture shift to improve delivery performance. Richards and Smith see the PMDU and its monitoring activities as reflecting Tony Blair's 'personalism' in carrying out the duties of the Prime Minister.

- John Wanna, 'From Afterthought to Afterburner: Australia's Cabinet Implementation Unit' (2005) examines the decision of Prime Minister John Howard and his top political and public service advisors to create a capability to encourage ministers and public servants to focus attention on the delivery or implementation aspects policy decisions. This interest arose close to the second term of the Howard government, and was addressed as part of the transition planning for his third government. Wanna describes how Prime Minister Howard and top officials learned from the UK experience with the PMDU and located a small Cabinet Implementation Unit (CUI) in the Department of the Prime Minister and Cabinet. The CUI can be seen as one of many strategies that Howard employs for running a 'disciplined' cabinet system. While the officials do not seem to be the high-flyers found in the PMDU with direct access to the Prime Minister, the unit does review all proposals going to cabinet for implementation analysis and risk assessment, and the unit maintains a 'traffic light' system to the Prime Minster and cabinet for about 30 per cent of all proposals that the cabinet has approved.

- Anne Tiernan, 'Working With the Stock We Have: The Evolving Role of Queensland's Implementation Unit' (2005) provides some background on Queensland's history and governance challenges, including efforts of the last couple of decades to modernise public sector governance and administration. The interest of Premier Peter Beattie in implementation arose as a result of several embarrassments during the second term of his government that revealed a disconnect between cabinet decisions and on-the-ground service delivery. This interest emerged as he shifted from a collaborative style of governing with colleagues to a far more directive and populist approach, running against the performance of the public service and working hard to keep his ministers in line. Beattie and his top officials were very well aware of Blair's PMDU and Howard's Cabinet Implementation Unit. However, they chose to re-organise standing policy and reporting capabilities to establish an Implementation Unit in the Department of Premier and Cabinet' Policy Division. An interesting feature of the Queensland experience is the extent to which the Premier sought to have this capability work through the 'desk officers' in DPC responsible for liaising with departments and agencies.

The annex to this chapter contains the list of the questions sent to contributors to guide the drafting of the cases. Table 1, inserted below, summarises many of the details from the cases studies along several dimensions. The rest of this section considers the similarities and differences in the experience to date with the three implementation units.

Table 1 – Highlights from Case Studies

Dimension	United Kingdom – Prime Minister's Delivery Unit	Australia – Cabinet Implementation Unit	Queensland – Implementation Unit
Genesis and Context	Prime Minister's Delivery Unit arises in 2001 from the PM's disappointment in lack of follow-though of policy initiatives on the ground, such as Joined-Up Government. Challenge was to create coherence and coordination in highly de-concentrated and fragmented delivery system. Cabinet Secretary designed the unit as part of transition planning before 2001 election.	Part of third term approach of the Howard government. Put in place in February 2004 at behest of Cabinet Secretary with a business background determined to assist in effort to consolidate and ensure implementation, incl. project management. Part of a larger reorganisation of the DPMC.	Emerged after June 2004 election as result of second term difficulties of Beattie government concerning Cabinet decisions that had not been implemented and led to a campaign promise to 'fix' the problem. Queensland public service yet to modernise. Created room for bureaucratic entrepreneur to create unit.
Exemplars and Precursors	UK Prime Ministers have a tradition of creating central units in the Cabinet Office for driving major public service reform strategic initiatives. Typically staffed with a mix of central, departmental and private sector officials. Blair ran a highly personalised government and created many central units relating to policy and implementation issues.	The Australian government established strong policy and coordination units in the 1920s, 1940s, and mid-1970s. Informed by UK's PMDU as result of Australian DPMC staff on interchange in the UK Cabinet Office. Secretary of DPMC went to UK to learn more about PMDU. Sought a bureaucratic as opposed to political-based capability that would be more collaborative.	Strong premier tradition with traditional structures, and a brief dalliance with a higher capacity Cabinet office during the 1980s. Beattie established central units in Department of Premier and Cabinet (DPC) on Strategic Policy, Reporting for Government, and Policy Research. Beattie moved from collaborative to directive role by end of second term. Design of IU informed by Queensland officials on exchange with UK Strategy Unit, and by Australia's CIU and UK's PMDU.

Stated Goals	To 'ensure the delivery of the Prime Minister's top public service priority outcomes'. To work directly with delivery units, rather than departments, to identify reasonable delivery schedule and outcomes. To monitor whether goals in the Public Service Agreements, first introduced in 1998, are getting achieved.	The Primer Minister sought a more strategic approach to managing the government's mandate. Key facet of this was to ensure timely and effective implementation of decisions, early warning if initiatives off track, awareness of best practices, and better design of significant policy and horizontal initiatives.	To monitor key election and cabinet policy commitments of the government, and to ensure that implementation takes place. To encourage considering implementation when policy is determined, to identify and remove obstacles. Underlying goal was to avoid previous failures.
Capacity, Skills, and Leadership	PMDU consists of 40 staff reporting directly to the PM. Comprised of a mix of central, department, agency, officials and private sector consultants. It is led by a Chief Advisor on Delivery, and has had two leaders to date.	CUI started in 2003 with 5 staff; by mid-2005 had 10 staff. The unit does not include high-level executives. Came from several policy and reporting units in DPC; no special expertise in policy or project implementation.	Queensland unit has 15 staff with strong central expertise in policy and reporting, but no expertise in implementation per se. Initial leader came from experienced pod of central officials who knew the Premier. Succeeded by a Treasury official with strong interest in risk management.
Location	First physically located in the Cabinet Office; PMDU moved in 2002 to the Treasury to ensure a good relationship with the Treasury's Civil Service Division. However, PMDU continued reporting directly to the Prime Minister. In 2005, PMDU became part of Building Capacity Section of Cabinet Office including EGU, OPSR, and the Better Regulation Unit.	Inside the Department of the Prime Minister and Cabinet.	Inside Policy Division of the Department of Premier and Cabinet.

Dimension	United Kingdom – Prime Minister's Delivery Unit	Australia – Cabinet Implementation Unit	Queensland –Implementation Unit
Ex Ante Modus Operandi	Worked with Treasury and agencies to develop targets associated with the bilateral Public Service Agreements. PMDU works with the PM on his priority areas – health, education, crime and transport – which involves 20–25 of the approximately 130 negotiated PSAs, and five departments.	Review cabinet proposals at the design and development stages. Goal is to ensure that proper risk assessment and implementation analysis has been undertaken by sponsor departments. Identifies the milestones to guide reporting. The CUI can also negotiate the implementation plans of departments.	Involved in announcing key government priorities; developing and circulating Ministerial charter letters; reports on 'Top Fifty' to Cabinet; developed the Implementation Assessment Template and revised the handbook for submissions to Cabinet. Goal is to educate DPC and department staff.
Ex Post Modus Operandi	Once targets are agreed on, PMDU reports on progress. This includes the Delivery Planning Process (links targets to deliverables), the Delivery Report (assesses whether targets are realistic), and the Prime Ministerial Stock-take (agency representatives meet directly with the PM). If there are problems, a Joint Action program is negotiated.	Progress reports and early warning should initiatives get off track. Includes a traffic-light warning system of about 30 per cent of initiatives to the Prime Minister; he sees all of them, departments see reports that involve them. Quarterly roll-ups are sent to Cabinet. The reports do not have qualitative assessment, but there have been a few reviews of whole-of-government initiatives.	Monitor and pursue the implementation of all Cabinet and Cabinet Budget Review Committee decisions, election commitments, and key policy initiatives. Produces reports on milestones, Top Fifty, and Key Initiatives. Reports to Premier and twice yearly to Cabinet on Charter Letters.

Interactions with Central & Other Actors	PMDU intrudes in an area previously the domain of the departments. PMDU must also navigate complex central terrain. Blair had also created a Forward Strategy Unit in the PM's Office, a Policy Innovation Unit in Cabinet Office, and the E-Government Unit (EGU), Office of Public Sector Reform (OPSR), and a Better Regulation Committee.	DPMC Secretary consulted portfolio secretaries about the CUI concept. Few tensions have emerged because CUI is essentially a reporting unit and does not connect to the budget process, nor to the priority-setting process, and therefore does not compete with other central units.	Premier concerned about not overburdening departments with more central interactions; therefore IU required to work though DPC desk officers (PCOs) for each department. No link to budget process and highly dependent on data and information from departments. Treasury, however, does have very public outcomes for each department on the web. Often IU staff pulled off to deal with crises due to expertise.
Degree of Precariousness	Clearly driven by the Prime Minister, and has regular engagement with him. Not a support for Cabinet per se; a means for the PM to interact and negotiate directly with agencies – effectively an end run around ministers and departments.	Unsure of role at first, largely because of departure of its progenitor. However, has emerged as a 'ginger group' informing PM of status of initiatives. Another tool used by an experienced PM running a disciplined cabinet. It seems that portfolio secretaries do not mind the reporting— helps with delivery agencies. In part, CUI exists due to disinterest on the part of DOFA on program management, implementation, and program evaluation in recent years.	Key challenges: dependent on departments for information; early identity crisis because did not report directly to the Premier; had to work through PCOs, so had low profile, and, because of staff expertise in policy and research, often were pulled off to fire-fight on crises engaging the Beattie government. Gap in leadership for four months.

Dimension	United Kingdom – Prime Minister's Delivery Unit	Australia – Cabinet Implementation Unit	Queensland –Implementation Unit
Impact to Date	Perhaps the best evidence of impact is the amount of time that the PM spends with the PMDU and the agencies in priority areas, but this is not the same as indicated that better performance has been secured with agencies. However, it has fostered a shift in emphasis from process to outcomes, and from relying on departments to the PM to oversee agencies in the priority areas.	PM-driven process; ministers not keen to be 'shamed' in Cabinet. However, increased awareness and discussion of delivery and implementation, particularly among policy and delivery staff in departments. More project management units in agencies. PM likes the regime – part of running a disciplined Cabinet system. Led to collecting more data on delivery, such as third parties.	Mixed reviews: evidence of raising awareness of PCOs and departments, but could be another check-off provision.
Prospects	Appears highly contingent on proclivities and energy of the current Prime Minister. One possibility is for the capability to move more squarely into the domain of the Treasury.	Clearly driven by current PM and DPMC Secretary. Three possibilities are the status quo, for CUI to move to DOFA, or emerge as a joint central unit to connect reporting to budget decisions, risk assessment, and the challenge function.	Depends on the Premier. Might persist, or capabilities may be directed to take up other suite of tasks. Its new leader is moving IU more into realm of risk assessment.

The case studies suggest several similarities in how the implementation units came to be created, how they were conceived and initially located, and what have constituted their 'bread and butter' activities. All of them were introduced by experienced first ministers with had considerable experience running their respective governments, and therefore had a good sense of implementation issues and gaps. For two, lesson-drawing was at play, with Australia tapping into the UK-PMDU experiment, and Queensland officials learning from both the British and the Commonwealth of Australia initiatives. Each first minister had top political and bureaucratic support and engagement for building capacity to improve implementation, but this implicitly reflected either disinterest or insufficient capacity on the part of other central agencies in the respective systems, such as budget offices or management boards, to take up this responsibility. The units each appeared to have relatively narrow scope – their creation did not entail, for example, absorbing other functions from other central units and they were carefully kept separate from the budget process. None of the units played exclusively in the upstream or downstream of policy implementation; rather, they were all in vetting policy proposals before cabinet decisions ere taken and in the downstream monitoring of implementation. Monitoring involved a strong focus on identifying milestones and reporting on priority initiatives; the horizon for the milestones seems to be around a year, and this functioned, as intended, an early warning system for first ministers. This vetting and oversight was motivated by the aspiration of educating and raising the awareness of ministers, central agencies, and the leadership of departments and delivery agencies about the need to anticipate and deal with implementation issues.

Despite these similarities there were differences. The size of the implementation units vary considerably – PMDU (40), Queensland (15), and Australia (10) – and so does their composition, with the Australian and Queensland units tapping more into public servants with generalist policy skills, whereas the UK PMDU assembles expert teams for each of the priority areas from central agencies, departments, and the private sector, presumably reflecting the specialist expertise for certain priority monitoring. The more substantial size and composition of the PMDU reflects an oversight regime that, in addition to the monitoring of milestones and general reporting to cabinet, is deeper and more aggressive, working with the Prime Minister to plan, negotiate, and oversee the performance of delivery agencies, circumventing the traditional roles of departments. Not surprisingly, the PMDU is very prominent, clearly an agent of the Prime Minister in dealing with delivery agencies. In contrast, the Queensland IU has a low profile, working through other parts of the DPC to liaise with departments. This represents an interesting anomaly, since the Premier has made much of the need to improve the quality of the public service and to ensure follow-through on service delivery. However, the Queensland IU has a latent function, assisting the Premier with crisis issues, because of its staff capabilities also included policy and 'fire-fighting' experience.

Finally, notwithstanding the engagement of first ministers with the implementation units, and evidence that they seem to be playing significant transactional and education roles, the case studies seem to indicate their existence is somewhat precarious. Implementation units are inventions of particular first ministers, who often reorganise or structure their central capabilities in their personal and cabinet offices. It is not clear that these units have built a strong constituency beyond the respective first ministers – it seems unlikely that ministers, central agencies, or executives in departments and agencies would strongly argue for the offices to be maintained once the current first ministers left office.

Implementation Units: What and why?

One purpose of the case studies is to determine more precisely the role and functions of implementation units that have emerged in recent years, realising that the label could encompass a variety of activities. Accordingly, this section returns to the hypotheses set out earlier in the chapter to determine whether implementation units emphasise one stream of potential activities over others, and whether this differs significantly across the cases. This section also ventures ideas about why implementation units have emerged in the way they have, and at this particular juncture.

Table 2 demonstrates that, based on the evidence provided in the case study papers, the implementation units do not seem to focus on only one or two aspects of implementation, such as only monitoring government policy commitments or fixing delivery problems as they emerge. Rather, they seem multi-functional, designed to accomplish multiple goals. To be sure, the accounts suggest that each unit has different emphases: arguably the UK PMDU is more squarely focused on challenging agencies to develop robust timetables and to address problems, and has the capacity to do so; Australia's CUI devotes more time in the upstream reviewing cabinet policy proposals for the quality of implementation analysis; and Queensland's IU seems more focused on ensuring more complete cabinet proposals (as opposed to closely vetting proposals) and reporting. These emphases get revealed not only in the balance of activities, but also the number and staff capabilities associated with each implementation unit.

Table 2 – Findings on Hypotheses re Rationale and Roles

Hypotheses	UK – PMDU	Australia – CUI	Queensland – IU
1. Meeting government commitments	Yes – a monitoring system for tracking progress on top policy commitments	Yes – a monitoring system for tracking progress on top policy commitments.	Yes – a monitoring system for tracking progress on top policy commitments.
2. Asserting political control over bureaucracy	Yes, asserting control was an important motivation behind its creation, work, & staffing arrangements.	Somewhat: its focus is on reviewing and monitoring – it does not problem-solve like UK's PMDU.	Not really: designed not to over-complicate the work of departments, yet send a message about priorities.
3. Anticipating policy design challenges	PMDU focus more on identifying targets and realistic timetables than implementation analysis.	Implementation analysis in upstream an important role for CUI – reviews all Cabinet policy proposals.	Hired staff with policy and reporting background; not hired for implementation analysis; focus on better cabinet documents.
4. Navigating implementation challenges	PMDU involved not only in monitoring but also in negotiating and making adjustments through JAP.	Mainly provides an early warning system for PM; issues likely addressed by the portfolio secretaries.	Provides an early warning system; presumably the DPC-PCOs and ministers deal with delivery issues.
5. Addressing political optics	Not simply optics, but does seem a factor – PM invests considerable time negotiating milestones for priority initiatives.	No, other ways to secure optics…about injecting better analysis, avoiding surprises, and less about solving delivery problems.	Does seem more symbolic and IU diverted to fight political fires. However, there is an educative and monitoring roles at play.

It bears repeating that the goals encapsulated by these hypotheses can be achieved by governments using other capabilities and processes; in other words, there could be central units and processes that are very much concerned about implementation but undertake the work without the 'implementation' label. Identifying such functional equivalence does not fall within the scope of this exploratory study.

Having explored the patterns in genesis and modus operandi of implementation units, we can now step back and consider broader questions like: Why entities with these labels and responsibilities emerged at this point in time? What accounts for the different emphases of the units in each jurisdiction? Why have some central agencies not seemed threatened or taken on the responsibility for implementation advising and oversight? Here I venture several different broad speculations in response to these questions. [3]

- *Governance challenges, results, and responsible government.* At the outset of this chapter it was observed that the emergence of this handful of implementation units across jurisdictions was not stimulated by any recent manifesto from the scholarly literature (if anything, it appears to be a triumph of circumstance with a tapping into a general concept, well-established for several decades). And, it seems that relatively little attention has been paid to the literature in designing and carrying out the mandate of the units. A better explanation may emerge from the complexity of governance challenges and the expectation that governments need to identify commitments and demonstrate results. In parliamentary systems first ministers are answerable for the progress of the government in implementing its agenda, even if the responsibility for implementation for specific initiatives rests with ministers, departments, and the associated service delivery agencies. In the face of such complexity, first ministers must demonstrate that their governments are making progress on commitments, and react as required if things go wrong. This pressure only increases with demonstrable failures or implementation gaps, particularly so when first ministers were caught unawares. Implementation units can be seen as entirely pragmatic response to contemporary governance pressures.
- *The demonstration effect.* It may be true that the staff of implementation units have not tapped into the implementation literature (and this may be because the literature does not attempt to speak to central institutional designers and agents), there can be no doubt that they have emulated other governments. In designing the PMDU, Prime Minister Blair emulated the approach taken in previous central initiatives associated with public sector reform in the UK, and, subsequently, both Australia and Queensland quickly adopted variants on the theme, even if not as potent and directive as the British model. The point is that all governments in the OECD countries are under similar

governance pressures from Opposition parties and citizens; the emergence of an approach that promises to symbolically and substantively deal with some of those pressures will get examined more closely, and particularly so given the close ties between Australian and British officials.

- *Governance traditions matter*. The PMDU seems more robust and aggressive than the CUI and IU in Australia. One explanation seems interesting, and this involves the 'style' of handling public service reform. Modern British prime ministers have developed a tradition of creating strong central units that tap into a mix of internal and external expertise to design and implement major corporate initiatives (consider the Rayner scrutinies, the Financial Management Initiative, and Next Steps). The PMDU reflects this tradition. Creating such a significant central capability would be far less likely in Australia or Canada, for that matter.

- *Implementation and budget offices*. Earlier we noted that results discourse would explain why first ministers might be anxious to demonstrate symbolically and in real terms how their governments have progressed on key commitments. First ministers and their central governments have strong incentives to get out in front of external auditors and the public before problems with implementation and delivery arise. However, this does not explain the disinterest of budget offices and treasury board agencies, which creates the need and room for implementation units. One answer is that these offices are far more focused on meeting financial targets and working with the principles of accrual accounting, to the exclusion of program management – in other words, programs that 'under-perform' by not getting enough services out the door to target audiences mean that the programs are within tolerances and do not pressure budgets. An implementation frame leads to different, more managerial questions; concern emerges if deliverables or milestones are not met.

- *Fragmented service delivery and fighting guerrillas/knaves*. Another perspective casts the emergence of implementation units as a response to a failure to effect change in the culture and performance of the organisations actually delivering public services, particularly in the context of significantly fragmented service delivery systems. This perspective is consistent with the second hypothesis, that there are recalcitrant or hard-to-change service delivery bureaucracies, but is more elaborate because it points the finger towards ministers and core departments (see David Richards and Martin Smith, 2005). One way to see this argument is that implementation units are devices employed by first ministers to bolster or force ministers and departments more closely monitor and manage the performance of delivery agents, whether departments, agencies, or third-party providers at other levels of government or in the non-profit or for profit sectors – or to use a phrase from Canada, to 'make the managers manage'. Aidan Vining suggested that we depict the predictable resistance of service providers as 'guerrilla warfare' which requires a coordinated, strategic response and the cache of first ministers to make a dent in the problem. In this view, first ministers establish implementation units as ways to stiffen the resolve and create incentives for ministers and top officials to more closely manage service delivery capabilities. In the case of the UK, the Prime Minister is clearly attempting to circumvent ministers and department on priority issues.

The explanatory power and worth of these suggestions is clearly conditioned by the very small number of cases at hand, but they are intriguing nonetheless. At the very least, the three exploratory cases put some interesting questions on the table, and constitute prisms through which we can view larger forces at play.

Functional equivalents and the seeds of destruction

This chapter has been informed by a small, but interesting, set of cases for exploring the role and the evolution of implementation units. There is variation in jurisdictional complexity, ranging from sub-national jurisdictions (Queensland), to a unitary national system (the United Kingdom), and to a federal system (Commonwealth of Australia).

At the level of nation-states, it appears that implementation units have emerged mainly in parliamentary systems, although this is a very small sample from which to draw any firm conclusions. It is well understood that first ministers in many parliamentary countries have sought to exert further increase control over government priorities and managing the public service as a whole even as the challenge of doing so seems to steadily grow more daunting (Savoie, 1999; Weller, 2003; Burch and Holliday, 2004). This suggests that jurisdictions with 'strong' centre traditions are more disposed to such experimentation (Peters, 2003; Lindquist, 2000), in contrast to the more autonomous agency traditions and weaker central institutions often associated with Western European governments.

A comparative methodological perspective leads one to acknowledge that the small number of cases explored in this collection implies that most parliamentary national and sub-national jurisdictions have *not* established policy implementation units. This brute fact is even more interesting because there is likely considerable awareness in different cabinet offices around the world of the delivery and implementation units in the UK and Australia, since both governance systems are often considered exemplars of reform. Many first ministers and political or bureaucratic advisors have undoubtedly examined implementation units in the UK and Australia and decided not to emulate or adapt the concept in their jurisdictions. [4]

There are several reasons why an implementation unit may not be perceived as desirable or needed. First, such oversight can be seen as the responsibility of a budget office or management board, responsible for overseeing the budget and the management of the government and its programs. Second, the normal guidance given to ministers and their deputy ministers by first ministers, as well as the performance review and accountability process could be seen as sufficient for ensuring that a government's priority initiatives are on track and implemented. Finally, having an implementation unit working out of the cabinet office, it could be argued, might be inconsistent with its mission as a coordinating agency and muddy the conventions of ministerial accountability.

Whether or not one agrees with these reasons, it points to the fact that creating policy implementation units are not the only way to improve implementation analysis and monitoring from the centre. There are other ways that this can be done, including the strengthening of the monitoring and challenge capabilities of finance departments, budget offices, and management boards. Moreover, the secretariats to cabinet committees could insist on higher-quality implementation analysis in the upstream of decision-making. This suggests that ministers and senior officials in some jurisdictions may recognise the latest incarnation of the implementation challenge, but find other institutional and process solutions for grappling with them (but we must recognise that many jurisdictions may simply have gaps in this regard). It is either the existence or the possible emergence of functional alternatives that, in jurisdictions that do have implementation and delivery units, may lead to competition, rivalry, or too much clutter or irritation, and the prospect of a first ministers either dissolving them or absorbing them into other central agencies.

Lessons for designing Policy Implementation Units

The three case studies of recently created implementation units, as well as the more theoretical discussions, have practical implications for those who wish to design similar processes or capabilities. They suggest the following:

- *First minister support is critical.* It is obvious that to create implementation units (or the functional equivalent in monitoring capabilities) requires the interest and authority of the first minister, and locating them so that they carry the authority of the position. However, it is equally important that first ministers tap into the advice and reports of implementation units; otherwise their credibility will likely diminish quickly.
- *Create focused capabilities.* The progenitors of implementation units thought carefully about their mandate and limited the scope of their activities with respect to the number of initiatives and how long the monitoring takes place. In part, this is sensible gardening of the ecology of central capabilities, but it can be seen as a shrewd strategy for overstretching resources, building credibility for assembling data and reporting, and avoiding overlap and conflict with other central actors.

- *Systematic reporting.* Although the units may rely heavily on departments and delivery entities for data, following through with regular reporting on progress on key initiatives is bound to increase awareness and focus on implementation in the system. At the very least it creates rhetorical awareness of implementation issues and, if there is gamesmanship in reporting by delivery agencies and departments, then the responsibility for poor performance will rest on those departments and agencies, even if it will undoubtedly constitute a test for the entire government.
- *Possible role expansion.* While implementation units may be precarious, there is a scenario that could see them take up more responsibility consistent with current mandates in the longer term. The upstream vetting, setting and monitoring the achievement of milestones, and reporting all constitute 'transactions' that can increase the knowledge of a central agency unit. After a handling a few cycles, implementation units should build considerable expertise on different strategies for developing indicators and clearing the path for initiatives. This is a medium term strategy, which could lead to a deeper role for such units, consistent with their mandate and capacities.
- *Enhanced role, more capacity.* The case studies suggest that, if implementation units are expected to more deeply evaluate and aggressively negotiate the nature of implementation regimes for specific priority initiatives, then they should have ways to supplement generalist expertise in the units. The UK PMDU provides a good example of how this can be accomplished.

The lessons outlined above presume an interest in creating implementation units, but they could also apply to functional equivalents. Similar capabilities, processes, and reporting could be created or enhanced in other parts of cabinet offices, budget offices, or treasury or management board entities.

Conclusion: Prospects and implications

This chapter has contrasted and analysed the findings of three detailed case studies of implementation and delivery units associated with the cabinet offices of the United Kingdom, Commonwealth of Australia, and Queensland. It demonstrated that these units were multi-faceted and similar in many ways, and two benefited from cross-fertilisition of ideas and practices across jurisdictions, but were nevertheless distinctive in key ways. The chapter sought to explain their emergence and observed patterns, and, to the extent these seemingly precarious capabilities have survived to date, identified lessons on design for building similar capabilities committed to improving implementation analysis and oversight, and elaborating those in place.

There is certainly more research to be done. Beyond monitoring the fortunes of cabinet implementation units, there is a need to carefully explore whether and how functional equivalents in other governance systems handle implementation analysis and monitoring. Another fertile area to explore would be detailed case studies on the effect of particular efforts by implementation units to influence and monitor policy departments and delivery agencies; some interesting work on the UK experience has been reported (Kelman, 2005), but this should also be contrasted with experience from other jurisdictions. Finally, the advent of cabinet implementation units should be understood alongside the emergence of gateway reviews in the UK and the adoption of this approach to learning and oversight in Australia at the Commonwealth and state levels.

What are the prospects for implementation units? Earlier it was suggested that there was great potential for competition and possibility of absorption, but it bears noting that the same could be said for many central secretariats and adhocracies not directly connected to the transactions associated with managing a cabinet system. What is remarkable is the extent to which these units have survived and taken root, albeit in circumscribed ways, and not been attacked. However, their first real test will be to see if they survive once the experienced first ministers who created them step down; if they survive that test, perhaps with changes in roles and repertoires, it would show that successor first ministers (who might have been ministers monitored through those units by the previous first minister!) see their value as another instrument for managing government mandates and ministerial colleagues, and that there are some real political and control imperatives calling for this distinct functional capability. Moreover, the jury is still out in other jurisdictions; they might emerge elsewhere as new governments take power or new issues associated with implementation emerge. On the other hand, the experiment with distinct implementation units could melt away, joining a long list of efforts to more systematically improve the decision-making of governments, and we would be left with the time-honoured question of how to inject good implementation analysis into policy decision-making.

If one were to speculate about sources of competition for implementation units, or places where the units might be transferred to, there are two strong possibilities: the divisions in cabinet offices responsible for general planning and managing of government mandates, and budget offices and management boards. As noted earlier, implementation units can be seen as a critique of existing central agencies, particularly since first ministers and governments are under great pressure to deliver on promises and demonstrate performance, and the critique came from a powerful quarter. This critique suggests that it is not enough for cabinet offices to keep a checklist of whether government commitments are met on schedule nor for budget offices to keep track of financial flows associated with these priorities – there needs to be more thought and effort expended in the upstream and downstream to ensuring that initiatives get the attention they deserve.

It is hard to imagine that this pressure will lessen in the years to come. However, while it might seem natural for cabinet offices and budget offices to take on more responsibility for implementation analysis and monitoring, like any organisation they may resist taking on tasks that threaten to complicate their mission or do not play to the strengths and competencies of staff (Wilson 1989). Cabinet offices may see a conflict between their responsibility for policy advising and managing the decision-making system, and budget offices may want to focus on financial perspectives as opposed to management questions. Even if required to absorb implementation units (or in jurisdictions with functional equivalents), there may be strong incentives to create distinctive units for this purpose. An open question would be whether the implementation units could gain or maintain credibility without the direct support of the first minister; presumably this would require linking the function to key decision-making processes (that is, cabinet decision-making, budget approvals, regular review of programs, and so forth); otherwise, they could quickly lose their effectiveness and, at best, become symbolic nods towards the desire and principles of 'good implementation' thinking and practice.

Finally, it is worth reminding ourselves that the genesis of these units was not inspired nor informed by the modern policy implementation literature, although undoubtedly the recourse to the notion of implementation and alertness to some issues attached to the concept hearkened back to the insights generated during the 1960s and 1970s. There was little evidence from the case studies that the recent progenitors of the implementation and design units surveyed the most recent implementation literature nor did they contact the current gurus in the field. Indeed, one wonders, if asked, what lessons or advice would have been proffered. Arguably, there would have been a blind spot or disinterest based on the modern literature on implementation, which has devoted considerable attention to managing networks and identifying strategies for mutual adjustment and cooperation, insights of considerable sophistication and importance. Early on, the literature could be characterised as against, in principle, the idea of developing strategies for fostering top-down change, let alone advising and monitoring across the sweep of a government's mandate. Political and bureaucratic leaders regularly innovate without reference to any scholarly work, of course, but there has been a missed opportunity to distil from the literature good advice for central authorities about how better to advise on, coordinate, and monitor multiple initiatives, as well as strategies for adjusting those not working. Perhaps the call for improved implementation by first ministers may lead scholars in the field to consider this vantage point and provide an opportunity for recent implementation insight to be coupled with policy advising.

ENDNOTES

[1] See Hill and Hupe (2002) for an excellent description of the genesis of this literature, including precursors to the work of Pressman and Wildavsky.

[2] This chapter contextualizes and sets out a conceptual framework for the three case studies, and interprets them. The case studies will be published as a special issue in the *Journal of Comparative Policy Analysis*.

[3] Many of these ideas arose from discussants, observers, and paper-givers at the Second International Comparative Policy Analysis Forum at Simon Fraser University in Vancouver, BC, on October 3, 2005.

[4] For example, while testifying at Canada's Commission of Inquiry into the Sponsorship Program and Advertising Activities hearings earlier this year, the Clerk of the Privy Council and Secretary to Cabinet indicated his office had considered but rejected the notion of an implementation unit, arguing that the Treasury Board cabinet committee and its Secretariat had this responsibility (Canada, 2004). This despite several other recent and high-profile examples of where far better implementation analysis and monitoring was surely warranted (e.g. the gun registry fiasco, the Office of the Privacy Commissioner, etc.).

Appendix A: Annex: A Guide for Drafting Case Study Papers

The goal of this collection of papers is to describe and analyse the emergence and roles of implementation and delivery units in the UK, Australia and Europe, to understand how they differ from each other, and how they evolved and fared. Their arrival undoubtedly reflected broader developments in the management and evolution of central institutions in each jurisdiction, so some background on this would be useful.

I hope each of the case study papers might address the points identified below, but let me hasten to add that each author or team of authors should feel free to develop their analysis and narrative in the way that makes most sense to them – in other words, do not let the checklist get in the way of a good story! Here are the areas that would be useful to cover:

- What was the rationale for establishing these units? Did they reflect the specific interests of first ministers or other leaders? Did particular failures or scandals lead to their creation, or what there a more general critique in the air? Was their emergence partially as a critique of the inability of other central agencies to make these kinds of assessments?
- What is the location of implementation and delivery units in the immediate organisational ecology of the core executive? Did this evolve over time? Why?
- What kind of leaders and staff were chosen to fill these units? What was the size of these units? Did the type of leader change over time?
- What is the specific role of the units in policy development, agenda management, and oversight processes by first ministers and their governments? Does the label 'implementation unit' really reflect their role? Are they working the upstream of developing policy initiatives, or do they operated more fully in the downstream with the actual implementation of initiatives, or both? Or are they monitoring the progress of other entities – such as departments, ministries or agencies – as they seek to implement a policy initiative? Are they reserved for only dealing with certain kinds of policy initiatives?
- How do these units carry out their mandates in complicated, shifting institutional environments with a multitude of delivery agents but also a good number of other core executive agencies and units? Can you point to instances where these units successfully carried out their roles? Are there instances where they were marginal or ineffective? Has their effectiveness evolved over time?
- Are there functional equivalents or competitors to implementation units, such as central processes or other units and central agencies that provide

implementation thinking in the upstream of policy development and then monitor progress?

- Has 'lesson-drawing' taken place across jurisdictions (Rose, 1993), when the units were created or as they took up their mandates?
- What does the future appear to hold in store for these units? Is the existence of these units precarious, at the whim of first ministers and certain governments? Or do they appear have promise of becoming institutionalised? If so, where?

References

Bardach, Eugene 1997, *The Implementation Game: What Happens After a Bill Becomes Law,* MIT Press, Cambridge.

Barrett, Susan M. 2004, 'Implementation Studies: Time for a Revival? Personal Reflections on 20 Years of Implementation Studies', *Public Administration,* v.82, No.2, pp.249-62.

Berman, Paul 1978, 'Macro- and Micro-Implementation', *Public Policy,* v.26 (Spring), pp.165-79.

Bridgman, Peter and Glyn Davis 2000, *The Australian Policy Handbook,* Allen Unwin, Sydney.

Burch, Martin and Ian Holliday 2004, 'The Blair Government and the Core Executive', *Government and Opposition,* v.39, no.1, pp.1-21.

Canada 2004, *Commission of Inquiry into the Sponsorship Program and Advertising Activities,* 'Public Testimony', September 27, 2004, Volume 12 (English Transcripts) p.1857 at web site http://www.gomery.ca/en/transcripts/

Canada 2004, *Policy Development and Implementation in Complex Files,* National Homelessness Initiative and Canada School of Public Service, Ottawa.

Desveaux, James, Evert Lindquist, and Glen Toner 1994, 'Organising for Policy Innovation in Public Bureaucracy: AIDS, Energy, and Environmental Policy in Canada', *Canadian Journal of Political Science,* vol. 27, no. 3 (September), pp. 493-538.

Exworth, Mark and Martin Powell 2004, 'Big Windows and Little Windows: Implementation in the 'Congested State'', *Public Administration,* v.82, no.2, pp.263-81.

Goggin, Malcolm, et al. 1990, *Implementation Theory and Practice: Toward a Third Generation,* Scott, Foresman, Little, Brown, Glenview, Illinois.

Hill, Michael, and Peter Hupe 2002, *Implementing Public Policy,* Sage, London.

Hogwood, B.W. and L. Gunn 1984, *Policy Analysis for the Real World,* Oxford University Press, Oxford.

Howlett, Michael and M. Ramesh 2003, *Studying Public Policy: Policy Cycle and Policy Subsystems*, 2nd Edition, Oxford University Press, Toronto.

Howlett, Michael 1991, 'Policy Instruments, Policy Styles, and Policy Implementation: National Approaches to Theories of Instrument Choice', *Policy Studies Journal*, v.19, no.2, pp.1-21.

Kelman, Steven 2005, 'Central Government and Frontline Performance Improvement: The Case of 'Targets in the United Kingdom', a paper presented to the Annual Research Meetings of Association for Public Policy Analysis and Management, November 5, 2005, Washington, DC.

Kickert, Walter J.M., Klijn, Eric Hans, Koppenjan, Joop F.M. 1997, *Managing Complex Networks: Strategies for the Public Sector*, Sage Publications Ltd.

Lerner, Daniel, and Harold D. Lasswell (eds.) 1951, *The Policy Sciences: Recent Developments in Scope and Method,* Stanford University Press, Stanford.

Linders, S.H., and B. Guy Peter 1990, 'Research perspectives on the design of public policy: Implementation, formulation, and design' in D.J. Palumbo and D.J. Calista (eds.), *Implementation and the Policy Process: Opening Up the Black Box,* Greenwood Press, New York.

Lindquist, Evert A. 1996, 'On the Cutting Edge: Program Review, Government Restructuring, and the Treasury Board of Canada' in Gene Swimmer (ed.), *How Ottawa Spends 1996-97: Life Under the Knife,* Carleton University Press, Ottawa, pp.226-241.

Lindquist, Evert A. 2002, 'Culture, Control or Capacity: Meeting Contemporary Horizontal Challenges in Public Sector Management' in Meredith Edwards and John Langford (ed.), *New Players, Partners and Processes: A Public Sector Without Boundaries?* National Institute on Governance, University of Canberra, and Centre for Public Sector Studies, University of Victoria, Canberra and Victoria, p.153-75.

Lindquist, Evert A. 2004, 'Strategy, Capacity and Horizontal Governance: Lessons from Australia and Canada', *Optimum Online: The Journal of Public Sector Management*, v.34, no.3 (December) at http://www.optimumonline.ca/

Lindquist, Evert A. 2000, 'Reconceiving the Center: Leadership, Strategic Review and Coherence in Public Sector Reform' in OECD, *Government of the Future*, OECD, Paris, pp.149-183.

Mazmanian, Daniel A. , and Paul A. Sabatier 1983, *Implementation and Public Policy,* Scott, Foresman, Glenview, Illinois.

Meyer, John W. and Brian Rowan 1977, 'Institutionalized Organizations: Formal Structure as Myth and Ceremony', *American Journal of Sociology*, v.83, pp.340-63.

O'Toole, Jr., Laurence J. 2004, 'The Theory-Practice Issue in Policy Implementation Research', *Public Administration*, v.82, no.2, pp.309-29.

Pal, Leslie A. 2001, *Beyond Policy Analysis: Public Issue Management in Turbulent Times*, 2nd Edition, Nelson, Toronto.

Peters, B. Guy 2003, 'Administrative traditions and the Anglo-American democracies' in John Halligan (ed.), *Civil Service Systems in Anglo-American Countries,* Edward Elgar, Cheltenham.

Potter, Evan H. 2000, 'Treasury Board as Management Board: The Re-Invention of a Central Agency', in Leslie A. Pal (ed.), *How Ottawa Spends 2000-01: Past Imperfect, Future Tense,* Oxford University Press, Toronto, pp.95-129.

Pressman, Jeffrey, and Aaron Wildavsky 1973, *Implementation: How Great Expectations in Washington Are Dashed in Oakland,* University of California Press, Berkeley.

Richards, David and Martin Smith 2005, 'Central Control and Policy Implementation in the UK: A Case Study of the Prime Minister's Delivery Unit', a paper presented to the Second Annual International Comparative Policy Analysis Workshop, Vancouver, October 3, 2005.

Rose, Richard 1993, *Lesson-Drawing in Public Policy: A Guide to Learning Across Time and Space,* Chatham House, Chatham, New Jersey.

Savoie, Donald J. 1999, *Governing From the Centre: The Concentration of Power in Canadian Politics,* University of Toronto Press, Toronto.

Schofield, Jill and Charlotte Suasman 2004, 'Symposium on Implementing Public Policy: Learning from Theory and Practice: Introduction', *Public Administration*, v.82, no.2, pp.235-48.

Shergold, Peter 2003, 'A Foundation of Ruined Hopes? Delivering Government Policy', Address to Public Service Commission SES Breakfast Briefing (15 October 2003).

Tiernan, Anne 2005, 'Working With the Stock We Have: The Evolving Role of Queensland's Implementation Unit', a paper presented to the Second Annual International Comparative Policy Analysis Workshop, Vancouver, October 3, 2005.

Wanna, John 2005, 'From Afterthought to Afterburner: Australia's Cabinet Implementation Unit', a paper presented to the Second Annual International Comparative Policy Analysis Workshop, Vancouver, October 3, 2005.

Weller, Patrick 2003, 'Cabinet Government: An elusive ideal?', *Public Administration*, v.81, no.4, pp.701-22.

Williams, Walter 1982, et al, *Studying Implementation: Methodological and Administrative Issues,* Chatham House, Chatham, New Jersey.

Wilson, James Q. 1989, *Bureaucracy,* Free Press, New York.

www.ingramcontent.com/pod-product-compliance
Lightning Source LLC
Chambersburg PA
CBHW061243270326
41928CB00041B/3396